HIDDEN®
Florida Keys
& Everglades

"The guide provides a thorough rundown of the various sights and activities in the Everglades and throughout the Keys."
—*Atlanta Journal Constitution*

"*Hidden Florida Keys and Everglades* covers a lot of ground, with chapters on almost any subject the traveler can think of."
—*San Diego Union-Tribune*

"The new edition of this guidebook returns to favorite haunts and reveals scores of new discoveries."
—*Fort Lauderdale Sun-Sentinel*

"This guide will lead the way to little pockets of natural wilderness that have resisted encroachment by civilization."
—*Nashville Tennessean*

"Lets you discover Florida's greatest treasures."
—*Chevy Outdoors*

HIDDEN®
Florida Keys
& Everglades

Including Key Largo and Key West

Candace Leslie and Ann Boese

NINTH EDITION

Ulysses Press®
BERKELEY, CALIFORNIA

Published by:
ULYSSES PRESS
P.O. Box 3440
Berkeley, CA 94703
www.ulyssespress.com

ISSN 1524-5918
ISBN 1-56975-508-6

Printed in Canada by Transcontinental Printing

20 19 18 17 16 15

MANAGING EDITOR: Claire Chun
COPY EDITOR: Lily Chou
EDITORIAL ASSOCIATES: Leona Benten, Kathryn Brooks,
     Dominic Luxford
TYPESETTERS: Lisa Kester, Matt Orendorff
CARTOGRAPHY: Pease Press
COVER DESIGN: Leslie Henriques
INDEXER: Sayre Van Young
COVER PHOTOGRAPHY: Mark Downey/Gettyimages.com

Distributed by Publishers Group West

Write to us!

If in your travels you discover a spot that captures the spirit of the Florida Keys and Everglades, or if you live in the region and have a favorite place to share, or if you just feel like expressing your views, write to us and we'll pass your note along to the author.

We can't guarantee that the author will add your personal find to the next edition, but if the writer does use the suggestion, we'll acknowledge you in the credits and send you a free copy of the new edition.

ULYSSES PRESS
P.O. Box 3440
Berkeley, CA 94703
E-mail: ulysses@ulyssespress.com

What's Hidden?

At different points throughout this book, you'll find special listings marked with this symbol:

◄ HIDDEN

This means that you have come upon a place off the beaten tourist track, a spot that will carry you a step closer to the local people and natural environment of the Florida Keys and Everglades.

The goal of this guide is to lead you beyond the realm of everyday tourist facilities. While we include traditional sightseeing listings and popular attractions, we also offer alternative sights and adventure activities. Instead of filling this guide with reviews of standard hotels and chain restaurants, we concentrate on one-of-a-kind places and locally owned establishments.

Our authors seek out locales that are popular with residents but usually overlooked by visitors. Some are more hidden than others (and are marked accordingly), but all the listings in this book are intended to help you discover the true nature of the Florida Keys and Everglades and put you on the path of adventure.

Contents

Maps

OUTDOOR ADVENTURE SYMBOLS

The following symbols accompany national, state and regional park listings, as well as beach descriptions throughout the text.

▲	Camping			Windsurfing
	Hiking			Canoeing or Kayaking
	Biking			Boating
	Swimming			Boat Ramps
	Snorkeling or Scuba Diving			Fishing

ONE

Keys & Everglades Dreaming

At the southern tip of Florida lie two of the nation's, and possibly the world's, most spectacular natural treasures. Everglades National Park and the Florida Keys—with its living coral reef—are among the most awe-inspiring places on earth.

Extremely fragile, rich with biodiversity and home to numerous endangered species, they are distinctive yet interconnected ecosystems. In the last century, both places suffered the ravages of human encroachment. Now, with the dawn of a new millennium, these magical water-dependent zones are beginning to receive the official respect and protection that they deserve.

The Florida Keys National Marine Sanctuary, the Tortugas Ecological Reserve, the Everglades Restoration Project and legislation to improve Keys water quality—these and other positive efforts are finally coming together to create a brighter future for this complex region, which includes wetlands, estuaries, bays, reefs, mangrove islands and open water. (However, the possibility of oil drilling off the Gulf of Mexico still poses a major environmental threat.)

All told, the efforts to save the Everglades and the living coral reef (the only one in North America) are colossal, and with each passing year visitors will be able to share in the benefits. The predicted increases in the population and the health of a wide range of animals and plants—including panthers, storks, migratory birds, fish, sponges and corals—will most certainly enhance the experience of all who travel here.

Already, over six million people spend approximately $400 million a year visiting the Everglades-related parks and preserves alone. More than four million people visit the Florida Keys and Florida Bay, primarily to engage in water-related activities, such as fishing, diving, boating and wildlife watching. In fact, the Keys are the most popular destination for scuba divers in the world.

Even artsy, upscale Key West depends on the health of the broad blue Atlantic Ocean and the clear-green Gulf of Mexico. Pristine beaches, clean water, great fishing and a vibrant coral reef are unquestionably essential to this resort island's future success.

As tourist destinations, both the Keys and the Everglades were late on the bandwagon, partly because of their distance from the rest of the nation and partly because nature kept them inaccessible for so long. Today, of course, this has changed. In fact, visitors can see more of both worlds than ever before. Hiking trails, kayaks, charter boats, ferries and seaplanes penetrate even some of the most remote regions.

To truly grasp a sense of South Florida's geography and history, you should explore both the 'glades and the Keys as much as possible. While the 'glades themselves are vast and the waters surrounding the Florida Keys even larger, the roads connecting the land masses are not particularly long. Literally, a person could rent a car in Naples, drive east across the Everglades to Homestead, head south down the Keys archipelago, and reach Key West in the same day.

Obviously, I'm not recommending this time frame—visitors who plan to see both areas should plan on at least a week, although either the 'glades or Key West could be experienced in a few days.

The Everglades, a great, broad and shallow, life-giving river, long kept its secrets to itself in the dark reaches of cypress swamp and deep, watery grasses. In fact, much of the vast wetlands is still inaccessible, and some of the more remote hammocks and islets remain unexplored. But not all. Today the traveler can easily enter portions of this subtle, curious, jungly world, due to the skillfully designed roads and paths provided by the planners and developers of the Everglades National Park. The rich biodiversity of the park is accessible: you can venture through once-impenetrable hardwood hammocks, walk safely among alligators, count endangered wood storks on a tree branch, discover brilliant snails on fragile plant stems, stoop down and observe clear, quiet water ceaselessly flowing through tall saw grass, watch waterfowl winging their way home, silhouetted against a brilliant sunset sky.

Animals and plants from both temperate and tropical zones inhabit this crossover environment. For those searching for hidden destinations, the Everglades is a treasure trove. Even a short walk will introduce you to a host of secrets and likely inspire you to probe ever more deeply. Whether on foot or paddling a canoe, you can follow any of a host of well-designed trails that beckon you into the heart and soul of the subtropics. The longer you stay and the deeper you explore, the greater will be your rewards.

The same can be said of a journey to the Keys, which appear like a sprinkling of afterthought on the tip of the Florida map. In reality, they are a chain of lush subtropical islands built on ancient coral reefs, floating like an emerald necklace that marks the meeting of the Atlantic Ocean and the Gulf of Mexico. Their history resounds with tales of pirate treasure and fortunes gleaned from ships tossed to bits on the still-living reefs that lie a few miles to the east out in the ocean. Long accessible only by boat, today 36 jewels of this necklace are joined by the great Overseas Highway. Fishing craft have replaced the pirate ships; scuba divers and snorkelers now explore the reefs where ships once met their dooms. Artists, adventurers, opportunists and other free spirits call these isles home.

To the south and east of the Keys lies the Atlantic Ocean, usually as calm as a lake, held in check by the coral reef. On the other side, broad, shallow Florida Bay bounds the Upper Keys, opening into the Gulf of Mexico as the islands curve out beyond the tip of the state. Except in stormy weather, these waters to the north and west of the islands also lap the shore with a gentle touch. This lack of wave action means there are very few sandy beaches in the Keys, but water on both sides of the islands rivals the Caribbean in its clarity and its brilliant greens and blues.

Just driving down the Keys can be a thrill. There's something exciting about being able to view the sea on all sides from a bridge seven miles long, about find-

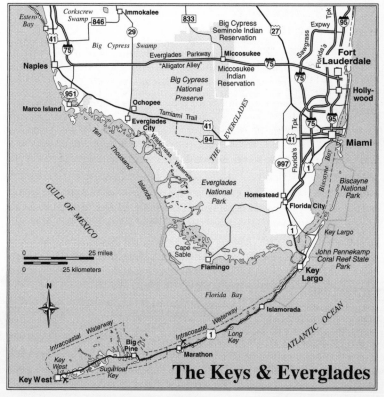

The Keys & Everglades

Text continued on page 6.

Three-day Weekend

Key West and Beyond

While it would take many visits to get to know every nook and cranny of this beautiful and unusual region, you can sample its highlights in a matter of days. The following itinerary begins in Key West and takes you up through Marathon, and provides specific suggestions for visiting historic sights, savoring local cuisine and pursuing outdoor adventures.

Make lodging arrangements in both Key West and Marathon. While you'll need a car to travel Route 1, a rented bike will get you around Key West. Take the **Old Town Trolley Tour** (page 155) at the onset of your weekend for orientation and basic history.

Day 1
- If you haven't already done so, make kayaking reservations for Day 2 with **Mosquito Coast** (page 201). Bike to Bahama Village for breakfast at **Blue Heaven** (page 180). Petronia Street shops open around 10 a.m.; browse nearby **Besame Mucho** (page 186) en route to the **Lighthouse Museum** (page 157) or the **Ernest Hemingway Home and Museum** (page 157).

- Continue down Whitehead Street to the Southernmost Point, then follow the Atlantic shoreline to White Street Pier for a view of **West Martello Tower** (page 163) and the indigenous beach. Head up White Street for lunch at **Mo's** (page 178), followed by a visit to **Lucky Street Gallery** (page 186) and other nearby art galleries.

- Bike toward the Gulf of Mexico to the **Historic Seaport District** (page 163). Beginning at Land's End, at the foot of Margaret Street, walk the bike around the **Key West Bight** (page 163), filled with shops, bars and restaurants.

- This evening take in the **Sunset Celebration at Mallory Square** (page 160), followed by dining al fresco at El Meson de Pepe, also on Mallory Square. Catch an 8 p.m. performance next door at the **Waterfront Playhouse** (page 189). Late-nighters might take in a drag show at **La Te Da** (page 198).

Day 2
- Up early, pick up a cup of joe and bagels from **The Coffee & Tea House of Key West** (page 196); then head over to **Mosquito**

Coast (page 201) for a kayaking adventure. Your guided tour includes transportation to Sugarloaf Key.

- Stroll Old Town this afternoon, with possible stops at the **Oldest House Museum** (page 159), **Mel Fisher Maritime Heritage Society Museum** (page 160), or the U.S.S. *Maine* exhibit at the **U.S. Custom House** (page 156). Enjoy cocktails at sunset at the Pier House Resort's **Havana Docks Bar** (page 187).

- After dinner, take a guided walk under the stars with **Key West Ghost Tours** (page 162). Tours leave nightly from La Concha hotel at 8 p.m.

Day 3
- Check out early and head north on Route 1, stopping for breakfast at **Sugarloaf Lodge** (page 138). Continue to Big Pine Key, turning onto Key Deer Boulevard at MM 30.5 to reach **National Key Deer Refuge** (page 135), Hike at the Blue Hole and Jack C. Watson Nature Trail.

- Proceed north on Route 1, perhaps stopping at **Bahia Honda State Park** (page 141), which boasts one of the country's best beaches, or riding the tram out to **Pigeon Key** (page 131), where Henry Flagler's railroad workers were stationed.

- Cross the Seven Mile Bridge into Marathon and check in to your hotel. This afternoon visit **Crane Point Hammock** (page 118) and the **Museum of Natural History of the Florida Keys** (page 118).

- Try dinner at **Banana Cabana Restaurant** (page 127), overlooking the pool; and maybe take in a blues band at the **Hurricane Bar** (page 129).

ing tropical trees that grow nowhere else in the country, about visiting a house built in the Bahamas and delivered to Key West on a sailing ship. But with the thrill also comes a subtle slowing down, as if the farther out to sea you go, the less the clock matters. Keys folks are proud of this casual, laid-back lifestyle that is impossible to ignore. The best thing you can do is enter into its relaxing spirit by discarding your watch and letting the sun and sea rule your days and the moon and stars your nights. And, remember, surprises are here for the finding. If you look beyond the billboards, down side streets, over on the neighboring out-islands or under the sea, you'll be rewarded with plenty of hidden sights.

There are over 800 islands in the Keys large enough to appear on government charts, though many other tiny mangrove islets exist. About 30 of the Keys are inhabited.

This book is designed to help you explore these very differing regions of South Florida. It takes you to countless popular spots and offers advice on how best to enjoy them. It leads you into some off-the-beaten-path locales, places you learn about by talking with folks at the neighborhood fish market or with someone who has lived in the area all his life. It acquaints you with the area's history, its natural habitats and its residents, both human and animal. It recommends sights that should not be missed. It suggests places to eat, to lodge, to play, to camp, always with consideration for varying interests, budgets and tastes.

The traveling part of this book begins with the Everglades, presenting in Chapter Two the main visitor accesses to this wild natural region as explored via the three entrances to the national park. Included in this chapter, too, are nearby destinations, both natural and manmade. Chapter Three heads down the Florida Keys, "the islands you can drive to," through Key Largo, Islamorada and Marathon, all the way to Big Pine and the Lower Keys. History and hype merge in Chapter Four, a guide to Key West, famous party town, arts center and ethnic village, whose romantic past and charm still color its life.

Where you go and what you choose to see is up to you—these areas include enough sights and activities to appeal to a very broad range of interests. This is verified by the numbers of retired people who return annually or settle down here, by the families who arrive each summer as soon as school is out, by the folks who come in their boats and tie up for a stay, as well as by the fanciers of the fast lane who come to live it up in Key West. For lovers of birds and wildlife and quiet, breathtaking beauty, there are few places as rewarding as the Everglades. For those who fish and dive or simply love the sea, the Keys offer all you could wish for.

These are southern Florida's two great gems. May they hold for you all kinds of hidden, and even not-so-hidden, rewards.

As land masses go, all of Florida is a mere child, having emerged from the sea as recently as 20 to 30 million years ago. For eons its bedrock base lay beneath the warm waters of

The Story of the Keys and Everglades

GEOLOGY

the southern sea. Slowly it collected sediment, building limestone deposits that would eventually rise above the surface. As distant glaciers froze and melted, the seas rose and fell, forming and reforming the shores of Florida, depositing silt and bits of sea life.

The Everglades actually begin at Lake Okeechobee, and to learn their geology, one must look to this shallow lake whose rocky foundation lies only a few feet above sea level. Beneath the lake and extending down into the northern part of the Everglades, the rock is a limestone composed of alternating layers of hardened sea bottom and of freshwater peats and muds. Farther south, it becomes a more porous limestone known as oolite. The surface of this spongy layer often becomes full of holes that have been receptacles for decaying vegetation, fresh water, sand and shells.

Beneath these relatively "young" limestone formations lies the oldest rock in southern Florida, the impervious *Tamiami* formation. Like a giant underground cistern, it collects and holds the rainwater that falls on the spongy Everglades limestones and on Big Cypress Swamp. Nearby cities such as Miami and Palm Beach, as well as the Florida Keys, depend on this life-giving reservoir for their survival. The force and power of this giant aquifer also keep the seawater at bay. Scientists believe that without the Everglades, this reservoir would become salt, and southern Florida as we know it would be no more.

Though it is hardly discernable to the traveler, altitude also plays an important role in the structure of South Florida. From Lake Okeechobee southward, the surface rock slopes like an ever-so-slightly tilting tray to the tip of the state, dropping about a foot every dozen miles. It is down along this crucial slope that the freshwater Everglades "river," as wide as 50 miles and only a few inches deep, flows through saw grass from the rain-fed lake to the sea. Here and there, scattered limestone outcroppings form the "high-altitude" regions of the Everglades, occasionally attaining a barely noticeable few feet. Through the ages these little hillocks have gathered humus and eventually vegetation, including hardwood trees, to become water-surrounded islands known as hammocks.

To the south of the Everglades, the limestone bed continues under the shallow waters of Florida Bay, where the centuries have covered it with an overlay of fine mudlike marl. To the west are the Ten Thousand Islands, an ever-changing archipelago of mangrove islets seated on the tops of old sunken sand dunes of the Gulf of Mexico.

The Florida Keys, like the Everglades, lie on a thick layer of limestone. The rock is covered by an ancient coral reef. In the lower islands, the porous Miami oolite, with its rich vegetation, appears once again. Low-lying islands with slight variations in elevation, the Keys boast a high point of 18 feet, on Windley Key. For the most part, however, they are very flat.

To the east of the Florida Keys lies the only living coral reef in the continental United States. It is located between four and seven miles offshore, running parallel to the Keys from Key Largo to the Dry Tortugas. This living marine marvel, rising as high as a few feet below the surface of the water and descending to dark depths near the Gulf Stream, protects the Keys from the waves of the pounding Atlantic surf and hence from the development of sand beaches, a great surprise to many first-time visitors.

HISTORY   **THE EVERGLADES STORY**   Although it took millions of years for the Everglades to evolve, and American Indians probably wandered into some of the mysterious interiors for a century or two, the real history of the unique region belongs mainly to the 20th century. The story of the Everglades is a microcosm of the global story of the interdependence and tensions between humans and nature, full of despair and promise, of lessons ignored and lessons learned, of life sources and of life itself hanging by a tenuous thread.

Some of the early Indians who roamed coastal portions of the Everglades left a few artifacts and their discarded shells in scattered mounds, but little is known about exactly how they fared in the mosquito-infested, watery environment. Nor is there much evidence that European explorers felt attracted to the marshy tip of Florida, so lacking in solid land and so hostile to travelers. To the casual observer as well as to the ambitious developer, the Everglades long seemed no more than a swamp to be drained and put to better use than nature obviously had in mind. Even as early as 1848, Army and Navy officers chasing Seminole Indians through the muck and swamps returned home stating that the land should be drained for cattle raising and for growing rice, sugar cane, fruits and vegetables. In 1865, a reporter sent to check out post–Civil War conditions in southern Florida commented on the need to get the water out of Lake Okeechobee and the Everglades.

Draining seemed a logical idea at the time and was attempted in little fits and starts as early as the 1880s. But the Everglades were not to be conquered easily. Early attempts were challenged by opponents of taxes and, hence, by lack of money. And whatever progress was made, the task always proved to be much more challenging than originally assumed. In 1905, the state's first comprehensive drainage law was passed, intending to construct a system of canals that would "reclaim" swamp and flood lands. Florida governor Napoleon Bonaparte Broward, convinced that if enough of the Everglades was drained, the state could grow sufficient sugar to supply the whole country, threw government efforts into the project. By 1909, a canal connecting Lake Okeechobee to Miami was completed, smaller waterways were constructed and drainage for farmland was underway in earnest.

The Everglades is the largest mangrove ecosystem in the Western hemisphere.

But even this early in the game, occasional critics warned that crucial studies had not been done, that water tables might be threatened, that not enough money was available to fulfill the dreams. But for many years the promises outweighed the criticisms. Southern Florida land sales boomed. Farming got underway. Then World War I put a damper on most of the enterprises. In the 1920s, a couple of devastating hurricanes, several serious fires in the peat-rich regions and, finally, the collapse of the Florida land boom brought a temporary end to state efforts to conquer the mighty Everglades.

At the end of the decade, the Army Corps of Engineers constructed Hoover Dike around Lake Okeechobee, hoping to end the threat of flooding. But again, in 1947, a hurricane caused floods to wipe out farm and grazing lands, proving once again that manmade canals and dikes could not always hold the waters in check. By then, some people began to realize that, though millions of dollars had been spent for drainage and flood control, effective reclamation of the wetlands had still not been achieved. And new problems were appearing as well. Salt began seeping into freshwater sources as water tables were lowered.

Fires in the peatlike soils created clouds of smoke that could make eyes water as far north as Tallahassee. Thin layers of soil in land that had been successfully drained and farmed began to disappear. Dry summers pointed out the need for irrigation as well as drainage. A water management district was established in hopes of solving some of the problems.

At about the same time as these immediately practical problems were being examined, concerns of a new kind began to be heard. What was all this tampering with nature doing to wildlife, to plant life, to life in general? "Pollution" entered the vocabulary of the concerned, chief of whom was Marjorie Stoneman Douglas, who published her immediate classic, *The Everglades: River of Grass*, in 1947. The good news was that in the same year President Harry Truman dedicated 2000 square miles of the southernmost Everglades as a national park. Here, at last, was an area that could not be touched.

But as fine as the establishment of that important park was, the problems were not over. All the water feeding into the region was, by then, controlled by artificial means. The complex food chain of the Everglades that had always been dependent on natural cycles of rain and drought was now at the mercy of those who manned the pipes and dikes to meet the demands of Florida's evergrowing human population. Two major causeway-style highways, remarkable feats of wetland engineering, now cut across the once-pristine, free-flowing river of grass. Fertilizers and insecticides, so important to farmers but so deadly to many creatures of the wild, also threatened to further upset the fragile balance of nature.

As the problems arose, so did the champions of the preservation of the delicately balanced environment of the Everglades. Sometimes they lost their battles. Sometimes they won, as when they prevented the draining of Big Cypress Swamp, upon which the Everglades is dependent for much of its life, for a mammoth airport. After energetic and skillful protest, the region was turned into a national preserve in the 1970s. But even the park status could not save the Everglades from its most daunting problem: a lack of fresh water. The Central and Southern Florida Project, which was authorized in 1948 to provide flood protection and fresh water to south Florida, had achieved its purpose at a tremendous cost to the Everglades ecosystem. With the project's canals, dikes and other water-control methods cutting off its natural flow of freshwater, the 'glades were dying. The abundant wildlife that once took visitors' breath away had faded. Wading bird populations alone had been reduced by about 95 percent.

In 1996, Congress took action with the Everglades Restoration Project, which invests $7.8 billion into restoring the Everglades' freshwater ecology by freeing up the natural flow of fresh water to the area. Basically, this involves "undoing" a large percentage of the water control systems set up earlier in the last century. The goal is to restore the wetland functions so that they mimic pre-drainage conditions. Experts say this will lead to dramatic environmental benefits, including significant increases in animal populations, the return of large nesting "rookeries" of wading birds to Everglades National Park, the recovery of a number of endangered species, the improved health of seagrasses and other submerged aquatic vegetation, and increased freshwater flows to bays and estuaries. This last item will produce positive effects on Florida Bay and the waters off the Florida Keys.

The restoration will take an estimated 20 years to implement, and the additional $400,000 required to operate, maintain and monitor the plan will be split between the federal government and the state of Florida. A tax imposed upon Florida's sugar industry—a primary polluter of the Everglades—is being funneled directly into the restoration funding.

Despite inhabiting Florida for centuries, the Seminole tribe was not officially recognized by the U.S. government until 1957.

The notion of the Everglades returning to a mirror image of the place Marjorie Stoneman Douglas wrote about over 50 years ago is absolutely thrilling. If all goes as planned, creating a clean river of grass flowing freely from Lake Okeechobee to Florida Bay, visitors to the beautiful Everglades region should find themselves increasingly in the presence of storks, alligators, panthers and other wildlife—including the legendary flocks of birds so vast that their presence once darkened the skies.

AMERICAN INDIANS When the first Spanish explorers approached the Florida shores in the 16th century, a number of native tribes had long resided throughout the peninsula and on its surrounding islands. The southernmost regions were dominated by the Tequestas and the Calusas, who thrived on the abundance provided by the sea and the rich coastal lands. Though the two tribes may have merged from time to time, probably in the Cape Sable region at the tip of the mainland, they were essentially separated by the Everglades. The Tequestas roamed the region from present-day Pompano Beach southward; the Calusas dominated the westward regions from the tip of the peninsula as far north as Tampa Bay and roamed portions of the Florida Keys.

The chickee hut was invented by Seminoles in the 1800s, when they needed simple shelter while on the run from U.S. troops.

The Tequestas were thought to number only about 800 at the beginning of the historical period. They were great fishermen, usually living near the mouths of streams and enhancing their seafood diet with such varied fare as palmetto berries, sea grapes, palm nuts, prickly pears and venison and turtle meat. They made a flour from the starchy arrowroot plant known as coontie. The Calusas, whose number may have been triple that of the Tequestas, lived principally off the conch, clams, oysters and other shellfish abundant in the Ten Thousand Islands region on the western edge of the Everglades. Though they were not agricultural, some of the early natives often lived in villages and developed a high social structure, thanks to the bounties of nature within their reach. They used wood for ceremonial and practical implements, such as masks, bowls and boats. They made spears and bows and arrows; they designed tools and ornaments from bone and shell.

Like the other early Florida tribes, the Tequestas and Calusas eventually disappeared with the coming of Western civilization and its accompanying diseases and conquering spirit. Some of the void was filled, though, by other natives, Creek Indians who slowly moved into the Spanish Florida territory and down the peninsula from what are now the southern states. They were neither welcomed nor beloved by the European and American settlers. They came to be called "Seminoles," a name perhaps corrupted from the Spanish word *cimarrón*, meaning "wild" or from the Creek words *ishti semoli*, meaning "wildmen" or "outlanders" or "separatists."

By the time Spain finally relinquished Florida to the United States in 1821, one war had already been fought against the Seminoles in an attempt to rid the land of Indians for good. But the Indian "problem" did not go away, so Andrew Jackson, the territory's first governor, declared a second Seminole War in 1835, hoping to quickly remove the remaining native inhabitants to Indian territory west of the Mississippi. The Seminoles proved to be a formidable enemy; the war lasted almost seven years and exacted a great price in dollars and lives. Patrols pushed the Seminoles deeper and deeper into the Everglades; bounties were offered for the capture of live Indians—$500 for a man, $250 for a woman, $100 for a child. Finally, after seven years of fighting, the backbone of resistance was broken. Following the death of their great leader, Osceola, most of the surviving Seminoles allowed themselves to be "escorted" out of Florida.

But not all of the Indians left. Several hundred disappeared into the Everglades and Big Cypress Swamp, where they spent the remainder of the century living a nomadic life in the wet, lonely region. Like their prehistoric cousins, they lived off the land and sea. They built adaptable stilt houses, called "chickees," safe above the ever rising and falling waters. They developed unrivaled skills of survival in the difficult environment. Their secluded life continued until the building of the Tamiami Trail in the 1920s, when the outside world began to delve into the region.

Not until 1957 did the Seminoles finally resume official relations with the United States, a century-and-a-quarter after their self-imposed independence. Today their descendants, numbering about 2000, live in two separate groups on reservations. Fifteen hundred Seminoles, the Muskogee-speakers, live near Alligator Alley (Route 84) midway between Fort Lauderdale and Naples. A smaller tribe, the Hichiti-speaking Miccosukees, live in a series of little villages along the Tamiami Trail (Route 41) on the northern edge of Everglades National Park, still carrying out remnants of the Everglades lifestyle. Once considered enemies of settlers, these descendants of the Creeks are now accepted as a vital part of southern Florida's rich tapestry.

EARLY KEYS SETTLEMENT   Though they are neighbors, the Everglades and the Keys have very different histories. It helps to remember that in the early days of exploration, the former appeared as an impenetrable swampland, and the latter a collection of isolated islands accessible only by boat.

Spanish explorers first sighted the Keys early in the 16th century as they searched for rumored gold and eternal youth. One contemporary chronicler of explorer Ponce de León, observing the chain of islands on the horizon, said they appeared as men who were suffering; hence they were given the name *Los Mártires* or "the martyrs." No one knows exactly when the first European set foot on one of the Keys, but as exploration and shipping increased, the islands became prominent on nautical maps. The nearby treacherous coral reefs claimed many actual seafaring "martyrs" from the time of early recorded history. The chain was eventually called "keys," also attributed to the Spanish, from *cayos*, meaning "small islands."

In 1763, the Spanish ceded Florida to the British in a trade for the port of Havana. The treaty was unclear as to the status of the Keys. An agent of the king of Spain claimed that the islands, rich in fish, turtles and mahogany for shipbuilding, were part of Cuba, fearing that the English might build fortresses and dominate the shipping lanes. The British also realized the treaty was ambiguous, but declared that the Keys should be occupied and defended as part of Florida. The British claim was never officially contested. Ironically, the British gave the islands back to Spain in 1783, to keep them out of the hands of the United States, but in 1821 all of Florida, including the necklace of islands, officially became American territory.

Though most of the Florida Keys remained remote and inaccessible until well into the 20th century, their history glitters with romantic tales of pirates, fortunes gleaned from unfortunate shipwrecks, brief heydays for several island cities, struggling pioneer farmers and occasional military occupation. It also holds its share of tragedy resulting from settlers' encounters with hostile Indians, yellow fever–bearing mosquitoes, dangerous hurricanes and unpredictable seas.

PROTECTION AND PROSPERITY By the time of the territorial period, Key West was already recognized as a place with assets. Its proximity to the Florida reef made it a perfect center for the sometimes legitimate, sometimes dubious business of marine salvage. Its deep channels with protected anchorage made it a perfect location for a recoaling station for steamers and a strategic site for a naval base. In 1821, John Simonton bought the island for $2000 from its original Spanish land-grant owner, and the first permanent residents moved in. But by then, pirates had long been reaping great harvests from unfortunate ships in the Gulf of Mexico and West Indies. Pirate history being a colorful blending of fact and myth, in the Keys it rings with names and tales of Black Caesar, Jean Laffite, Blackbeard and other nefarious characters who frightened seafarers and buried as yet unearthed treasures throughout the islands.

In 1822, Lieutenant Matthew C. Perry was ordered to take possession of Key West for the United States and to go after the pirates. By the end of the year, 21 American ships cruised the waters in search of pirates, engaging in occasional confrontations. After one fight in which an American lieutenant was killed, a naval base was established at Key West and the fleet enlarged.

But an even more formidable enemy than pirates was yellow fever. In July of 1823 it took the lives of 68 men, causing the Navy to declare the base unfit from July to October. By 1826, the main operations were moved to Pensacola, leaving only coal and supply depots at Key West. However, the region was still considered to be important militarily, a "Gibraltar of the Gulf." In 1845 the War Department announced the building of fortifications at Key West and in the Dry Tortugas; these would become Fort Zachary Taylor and Fort Jefferson. Lighthouses had already been sending their beacons from these strategic points for several decades.

Dr. Samuel H. Mudd was interned at Fort Jefferson for four years because he had unknowingly set the broken leg of Lincoln's assassin, John Wilkes Booth.

Meanwhile, Key West was on its way to its brief heyday as the wealthiest city in Florida. The chief industry was wrecking and salvage. Many 19th-century entrepreneurs were English Bahamians who brought the distinctive speech and architectural styles that would one day become known as "conch," named for the serviceable mollusk that resided in the surrounding waters. Bahamians also profited from the lucrative harvesting of fish and, along with Greek immigrants, of high-quality sponges. Cuban migrants arrived with their culture and cigar-making skills. The salt manufacturing business also achieved high success in the years before the Civil War.

Prosperity was thriving farther up the Keys as well. At the 1836 Constitutional Convention, when Florida became a state, Dade County was established to take in the vast area from Lake Okeechobee to Bahia Honda Key. The inauspicious island of Indian Key was named county seat. Located halfway between Miami and Key West, it was the prime location for wreckers and salvagers, some of whom were purported to be working outside the law, even perhaps luring ships to their dooms on the treacherous reefs. Like Key West, Indian Key boomed.

But it all came to a tragic halt when, on an August morning in 1840, Indians piloting 17 canoes raided the island, looted and burned crucial stores and buildings and killed several prominent citizens. Four years later, Miami became the county seat, though it would be some time before it reached the former prominence of Indian Key. The final death knell for the wrecking business was the placement of a string of lighthouses to warn sea captains of the dangers of the treacherous reefs.

CIVIL WAR   During the Civil War, though much of Key West's population was loyal to the South, both the city and Fort Jefferson in the Dry Tortugas remained in Union hands. As early as November 1860, a captain of the United States Army of Engineers urged reinforcements so that these two strategic areas of defense would not be lost in case of secession. As the war began, the commanding officer at Key West, determined not to let unfinished Fort Taylor fall into secessionist hands, stealthily led his small force of 44 through a sleeping city to the fort in the dark of night. They set up a defense that the Confederates were never able to capture. Neither of the forts saw any serious action for the duration of the war, though individual blockade runners are thought to have darted about in the waters off the Keys.

The tropical ambience of the Keys has been captured in films such as *Speed 2*, *The Spanish Prisoner* and *True Lies*.

Though Fort Taylor and Fort Jefferson became obsolete with the invention of the rifled cannon, the former was noted for the construction of a 7000-gallon-a-day seawater distilling plant and the latter as a dreary wartime and postwar prison.

Life apparently went on in the Keys with less distress than in the northern regions of the state. Just after the Civil War, a New York newspaperman was sent to southern Florida to check on postwar conditions. He observed that Key West, Florida's wealthiest town, had grown during the conflict. He said that he had to remind himself that it was an American city, so rich was it in tropical plants and foreign tongues. Later in 1865 observers noted that people living on the Keys had a passion for liquor and wrecking, but they also recorded many citizens engaged in fishing, sponging, turtling and harvesting oranges, lemons, limes, coconuts and grapes.

THE CUBA CONNECTION   Just 90 miles from Key West, across the Florida Strait, lies Havana. By the end of Cuba's Ten Years War in 1878—which marked a tragically unsuccessful attempt by Cuba to overthrow Spanish rule—nearly 10,000 Cubans emigrated to Key West.

Most worked in cigar factories, manufacturing handrolled Cuban-tobacco cigars. At the height of production, nearly 130 Key West factories turned out about 100 million clear Havana cigars annually.

Most factory workers contributed a portion of their salaries to support the independence movement in Cuba. They formed more than 80 patriot clubs between 1869 and 1898—and in 1884, they established the secret Cuban Convention, an umbrella group dedicated to freeing their homeland.

Eventually, the cigar industry moved north to Tampa. Key West was plagued by labor strikes, hurricanes and fire—most notably the Fire of 1886, which carbonized many of the wooden factories—while cheap land and financial inducements from Tampa's leaders proved to be irresistible.

THE SPANISH-AMERICAN WAR Key West and other southern Florida coastal cities took on great importance during the struggle for Cuban independence from Spain. American sympathy for Cuban patriots was inflamed by the publication of a Spanish letter disparaging President William McKinley and by the mysterious sinking of the U.S. battleship *Maine* in Havana harbor on February 15, 1898. The United States demanded that Spain withdraw from Cuba, and, on April 24, Spain declared war. Volunteers, both American and Cuban, signed up to join in the fighting.

The War Department first assumed that Key West would be the principal base for American forces, so civilian, Army and Navy activity increased in the busy city. But Key West lacked sufficient storage space, and its harbor needed improvements such as deepened channels for larger ships; Tampa became the main center of military activity. However, the Navy yard at Key West proved important to the invasion of Cuba. Only 90 miles from Havana, the harbor bustled with freight and passenger boats, newspaper dispatch craft, hospital services, Navy coaling and repair work and Spanish prisoner reception. Forts Taylor and Jefferson were reactivated. Newly installed condensers at the distilling plant were designed to increase freshwater supplies.

The war ended on August 12, but the Army and Navy stayed on to complete important projects in Key West. Improved facilities, beefed-up defenses and deeper channels contributed to both base and harbor.

HENRY FLAGLER'S RAILROAD   By 1896, dreamer, entrepreneur and tycoon Henry Flagler had extended his Florida East Coast Railroad to Miami. In the first years of the new century, homesteaders began settling into the regions surrounding the ever-creeping rails. A town, appropriately named Homestead, sprang up where the railroad stopped in 1904. But Flagler's dream kept steaming forward. In 1905, work began on his remarkable "railroad that went to the sea," an incredible line that traversed islands, spanned inlets and ascended bridges, one of them almost seven miles long, down through the Keys and over the ocean to Key West. On January 22, 1912, the first train rolled into town. Flagler believed that Key West would become a terminal from which passengers and freight would set out across the sea to the south and west. In reality, it became just the end of the line.

Though tourists came to the Keys in impressive numbers and the economy picked up, the glory days were not to last. Key West's great boom began to bust with the beginning of World War I. Tourism was halted. The armed forces were eventually reduced to a garrison. Cigar makers began moving to Tampa. Blight and storm wiped out the sponge beds. Florida's pre-Depression land boom had little effect on the islands, but the ensuing Depression years almost destroyed them. Key West's population declined; debts rose. The government declared a state of emergency.

But the railroad had revealed the potential of the Keys as a tourist attraction. The Federal Emergency Relief Administration of the New Deal undertook to rehabilitate the city. Citizens rallied, many learning to make crafts and novelties from local products or organizing fetes and pageants for tourists. Artists on relief decorated walls and buildings with distinctive murals and other works. The influx of thousands of visitors promised great rewards. But the success was again short-lived.

On Labor Day 1935, one of the severest hurricanes on record destroyed the overseas railroad. Winds raged between 200 and 250 miles per hour, 75 miles per hour faster than the strongest winds of Hurricane Andrew in 1992. The barometer dropped lower than it had ever registered anywhere before. Near Islamorada, the storm overturned rescue cars with over 400 passengers on board. A work camp full of war veterans at Tea Table Bridge was destroyed. Whole families disappeared into the sea. Many people predicted this terrible tragedy would mark the end of prosperity for the Keys and moved away. But some long-term residents stayed, determined to rebuild from the rubble of the Depression and storm.

MODERN TIMES   When it was discovered that Henry Flagler's railroad had been built on very sound footings, a new dream emerged. Bridges and trestles, undamaged by the storm, became the underpinnings for what would become the Overseas Highway. Old track was recycled as new guard rails for bridges. Flagler's vision of a route across the sea would still be realized, only now the thoroughfare would carry automobiles instead of trains. The first wheels rolled across its new pavement in 1938. Tourists began returning.

Once again, however, the vision of thousands of annual visitors flocking to the tropical islands was dashed, this time with the coming of World War II. But the war did bring the Navy and more improvements to the Keys. A submarine base was built at Key West. A water main, like a new lifeline, began carrying fresh water into the Keys from the mainland. Population again began to grow.

President Harry Truman fell in love with Key West and established his "Little White House" there for regular visits.

After the war, artists and writers again began lauding the inspirational ambience of Key West, following such luminaries as Ernest Hemingway, Tennessee Williams and Elizabeth Bishop. Tourists began returning in earnest, attracted by sunsets, seafood, colorful history, beautiful seas and general good times. Gays found the town a comfortable place to establish residency. Outlaws and others living on the fringe were drawn to its tolerance.

The 1962 Cuban missile crisis briefly marred the Keys' positive image, but even that brought a little more military prosperity before most of the Navy finally left Key West for good. In 1980, the Mariel Boat Lift, bringing refugees of assorted backgrounds from Cuba, thrust Key West again into the public eye. In recent years, Cubans escaping Castro's rule have braved the Florida Strait in homemade rafts or are smuggled in more sea-worthy vessels. Rafters arrive, often on the the Keys' beaches, after days at sea. Despite the dangers, hundreds of Cubans reach these shores annually—and untold numbers do not succeed.

Today, the once-isolated Florida Keys are a tourist and retirement haven, popular with divers and sport fishermen and folks who love the climate and beauty of the place, and who thrive on its relaxed ambience. Though boasting a genuinely slowed-down lifestyle far from big-city hassle and northeastern work ethics, the Keys are no longer free from the influence of the outside world. Drugs and their attendant dynamics, particularly in a region of open southern seas and myriad uninhabited islands, are, and will probably long be, a challenge to law enforcement both on land and in the surrounding waters. Crime happens, as it will, in towns where a comfortable climate makes it easy to live in the streets. And some folks wonder just when the next hurricane will come.

But the mainstay of the Florida Keys is a booming, cheerful tourism. From the retired couple that settles in for the winter with their small RV to the former president of the United States, George Bush, who battles bonefish with his longtime Keys' friends, the visitors come year-round. They fish, they scuba dive, they sightsee, they eat seafood, they party, they relax, and some of them stay for good. The Overseas Highway is dotted here and there with clusters of chain eateries and motels that make it look like any-strip-U.S.A. But no matter what kind of resorts are built and how many hamburger places go up, the very nature and location of the Florida Keys will keep them as distinctive from their mainland neighbor as when the Spanish first spotted them across the water.

FLORA   One would need a whole book, or maybe several, to deal fairly with the flora of the Everglades and Keys. Fortunately, both the national park and the state parks, as well as bookstores, provide generous amounts of information to those who are captivated by the plants they discover in these botanically rich environments. The brief entries below can only provide a tantalizing mention of a few of the particular plants that one notices at first glance.

Though many plants are distinctive to the Everglades, one dominates above all others—the finely toothed, one- to two-foot bladed sedge commonly known as "saw grass." It is saw grass that makes so much of the Everglades appear as a broad prairie, concealing the shallow freshwater river that runs through it.

But though the saw grass dominates, the Everglades are rich in tropical and subtropical plant life, some found nowhere else on earth. Throughout the vast region, limestone ridges called hammocks rise like little islands in the river of grass, allowing trees to establish themselves above the water line and nourishing a wide variety of flora. Here grow the gumbo-limbo trees, royal palms, wild coffee, mastic, strangler fig, rare paurotis palms and huge mahogany trees. Air plants, including more than a dozen types of bromeliads, thrive among the trees of the hardwood hammocks. So do more than 20 species of wild orchids, some quite rare, and numerous species of exotic ferns and assorted vines.

It is the dwarf cypress, draped with ghostlike Spanish moss, that contributes to the mysterious aura of the Everglades. Despite their stunted size, some of these wispy trees are over a century old. They lose their leaves in the winter, making them appear dead, but they are the hardy survivors of the wetlands. The Everglades also contain forests of tall slash pines that are dependent on the natural, lightning-caused fires to keep their floors clear of undergrowth that might inhibit the young trees.

The gumbo-limbo tree is also known as the "tourist tree" because its peeling red bark resembles the skin of sunburned visitors.

Periodically, hurricanes change the habitat in the Everglades. High winds shear off the leafy treetops, exposing the forest floor, which had been shaded from the blazing Florida sun. Low-lying plants such as orchids and ferns are slowly adapting to the sun, while fallen trees are regenerating from their remaining planted roots. This is an interesting time in the Everglades, a time of transition for much of its tropical life.

Along the coastal regions of the Everglades and throughout the Keys reside some of Florida's true natives, the mangroves, or "walking trees." Best known is the red mangrove, with its arched reddish roots sprawling out like spider's legs where fresh and salt water meet. A little farther inland the black mangrove sends up its masses of tiny pneumatophores for breathing through the still brackish water. Behind them, the white mangrove and buttonwood thrive on hammocks with other tropical trees.

Mangroves reproduce in an unusual manner. Seeds sprout before they leave the tree to drop into the soft wet bottom or float on the tides to suitable locations where they catch hold and become the beginnings of new islands. Mangroves are useful as well as interesting, stabilizing fragile shorelines, catching the brunt of stormy waves, filtering water, serving as rookeries and shelter for birds and wildlife and supporting diverse marine life with their nutritious falling leaves.

The winds of Hurricane Andrew did the most damage to tall trees. The storm affected all of the large hammock trees, knocked down 20 to 40 percent of the slash pines and leveled 70,000 acres of mangrove forests. However, many of the fallen mangroves will survive, fed by the few roots that remain in the ground.

Green in all but very dry winter months, saw grass is one of the oldest plant species on earth.

Plant life in the Keys, though much has succumbed to ever-growing development, has much in common with that of the Everglades. In the surviving natural regions grow gumbo-limbo trees, lignum vitae, West Indian mahogany, wild lime and tamarind, Jamaica dogwood and other tropical residents of the hardwood hammocks. Mangroves also abound, creating new keys and enlarging old ones. In the transition zones just above the mangroves can be found the evergreen sea grape, the toxic poisonwood tree, mahoe and cat claw. The slash pine forests of Big Pine Key gave the island its name.

Many of the plants and trees of the Everglades and Keys arrived from the West Indies and beyond, transported on the waves and currents of the sea. Other exotics were brought in by well-meaning (one assumes) settlers and residents. Most notorious of these transplants is the Australian pine (not a true pine) that, though lovely, especially when the wind sings through its branches, has crowded out many native plants and upset natural ecosystems. Many scientists are worried that Hurricane Andrew's winds brought in more exotic seedlings that will further overtake the native plants. Tropical fruits, as well as the vast but succulent vegetable farms, have also sometimes flourished at the expense of nature's balance, since they require chemical fertilizers and insecticides for their survival and our dining tables.

FAUNA

An abundance of wildlife resides in the unique subtropical environment of the Everglades. Some species here face extinction, the South Florida wetlands being their only remaining protected home. High on the endangered list is the Florida panther, a rare, seldom seen gray cougar whose number has been reduced to an estimated several dozen, due to the continued loss of habitat. Threatened, too, is the gentle manatee—the harmless, bulky "sea cow"—victim of motorboat propellers and abandoned fishing tackle. Though alligators are the most familiar and easily observed residents of the Everglades, their cousin, the crocodile, struggles for survival in a dwindling habitat (see "Alligators and Crocodiles" in Chapter

Two). Facing uncertain futures, too, are the loggerhead and green sea turtles.

But many residents of the region thrive in healthy numbers. Winter's dry season, when they gather at shrinking water holes, is the best time to see them. Exceedingly common, especially around the campgrounds, are the opossum and the raccoon, a paler, smaller creature than his northern cousin. Bobcats appear with some regularity and can sometimes be heard howling on spring and summer nights. White-tailed deer roam freely. The nine-banded armadillo, a native of the Southwest and Central America, has found Florida, including the western Everglades, to be a comfortable home.

Many semiaquatic mammals thrive in the watery environment of the Everglades. Chief among these are the elusive river otter, the endangered Everglades mink, the protected round-tailed muskrat and the marsh rabbit, whose short-eared head is occasionally spied as he pops up on his hind legs on a raised piece of ground to survey his territory.

As one discovers with so much of this subtropical region, it is the visitor who takes plenty of time to explore and examine things closely who reaps the rewards. This certainly applies to those in search of wildlife, for a whole world of miniature creatures resides among the hammocks and prairies. Speedy little lizards of many varieties, colorful grasshoppers and the multi-hued *Liguus* tree snail, as different from one another as snowflakes, are only a sampling of the tiny animals who reside in this distinctive environment. The apple snail is another important resident, being the sole food of the Everglades kite. Photographers find the yellow-and-black zebra butterfly a photogenic delight.

Protected natural areas of the Keys are home to many of the creatures that also reside in the Everglades, but the Keys also claim some species unique to these isolated islands. It is believed that some are the genetically changed descendants of creatures who crossed the once low dry land that is now Florida Bay. When the water rose for the last time, they were isolated forever and slowly changed, adapting to their new environment.

Most famous is the tiny Key deer, a miniature subspecies of the mainland white-tailed deer. Residing mainly on Big Pine Key, where they are protected, they are also thinly scattered over more than a dozen other smaller islands. Distinctive, too, are the Lower

Keys cotton rat, the Cudjoe Key rice rat, the Vaca Key raccoon, resident of the red mangrove hammocks, and the Key Largo wood rat and cotton mouse who, like the deer, are smaller than their mainland cousins. The endangered Schaus swallowtail butterfly appears occasionally on Key Largo.

Among the reptiles distinctive to the Keys are the mud turtle, the mangrove terrapin and the Florida Keys mole slink, a unique lizard. The Florida Keys ribbon snake, the Big Pine Key ringneck and several distinctive rat snakes also make their homes only on certain islands. A small family of alligators reside in the fresh-water pool on Big Pine Key.

Some of the region's most interesting animals reside in the sea. Chief among these are the bottle-nosed dolphin (see "Days of the Dolphins" in Chapter Three) and many species of shark, one of the oldest creatures on earth. Manatees, once abundant in the Keys, are still spotted occasionally. Thirty mollusks, including the two-color crown conch, are among the endemic invertebrates of the Keys. The great reef that lies beneath the waters of the Atlantic Ocean, parallel to the Keys, is also made up of innumerable animals. For divers and snorkelers and passengers of glass-bottom boats, the reef presents a whole distinctive world of wildlife (see "Kingdoms Under the Sea" in Chapter Three).

BIRDS   More than 300 species of birds, natives of both the temperate and tropical zones, take up either temporary or permanent residence in the Everglades/Keys region each year. If, as we are sometimes told, 90 percent of the birds in the region are gone, entering the Everglades must have once been an incredible experience, for even the remaining ten percent that soar through the air, perch in the trees and stalk the shallow waters guarantee rewards for even the most casual birdwatcher. In cooler months, one can observe a wide variety without leaving paved paths and roads. Even the uncommon and beautiful roseate spoonbill can sometimes be seen near Flamingo Lodge on the southern tip of the Everglades or among the mangrove shallows beside Route 1 on Key Largo.

In winter, the prime season for birdwatching, endangered wood storks gather in trees along the Everglades park road and in Big Cypress to fish in the muddy shallows. With binoculars, visitors occasionally observe nesting bald eagles on little islands in Florida

Bay and in the Lower Keys. White pelicans ride the winter waves in congenial groups near the Everglades shore.

Peregrine falcons may be spotted along the coasts in spring and fall on their long migrations between the Arctic and South America. Snail kites still nest in the park, and the Cape Sable seaside sparrow makes its exclusive home in the marshes of Big Cypress and the Everglades. And, of course, sea gulls and their assorted relatives, as well as brown pelicans, are part of the coastal scenery year-round.

The most visually exotic birds of the region are those that wade in the shallow waters, standing like beautiful sculptures for hours or stalking their prey with nary a ripple. Most impressive are the great white egrets and the great blue herons, elegant three-to four-foot-tall fishermen. Other easy-to-identify waders include the little blue heron, Louisiana heron, limpkin and the rarer reddish egret. White ibis are common and easy to identify as they bob their bills in and out of the shallows like needles on sewing machines. Magnificent frigate birds nest on the Marquesas Keys in early winter.

Easy to view, too, are many of the water birds, such as purple gallinules, grebes, bitterns, moorhens and marsh hawks. As if they know they are expected to be there, anhingas slice through the water for fish, then hang themselves out to dry in the trees along Anhinga Trail in the Everglades. Cormorants, too, are expert underwater fishermen, darting through the water in great haste and disappearing below the surface for remarkably long periods. On Bush Key, east of Fort Jefferson in the Dry Tortugas, nesting sooty

FOR THE BIRDS

Though the bird population in the Everglades/Keys region is impressive indeed, it hardly rivals the flocks that caused John James Audubon to feel so astonished, a century-and-a-half ago, that he and his party "could for a while scarcely believe our eyes." Later visitors who crossed the state following the opening of the Tamiami Trail still recall having to wash their cars at the end of the trip, so thick were the birds overhead. Sadly, a big decrease in bird population came about when trendsetters convinced ladies that it was high fashion to wear bird feathers on their bonnets. Flamingos and great white herons and snowy egrets were slaughtered mercilessly; even pelicans and least terns could not escape.

terns from the Caribbean Sea and West Africa are joined by brown noddies and other exotic species in one of the nation's great wildlife spectacles.

Birds of prey include the endangered eagles and snail kites, as well as the swallow-tailed kite and several varieties of hawks, falcons and vultures. Ospreys are especially accommodating to birdwatchers, often building their bulky nests and raising their families on the tops of power poles beside busy Route 1 in the Keys.

Migratory birds, including numerous songbirds, make regularly scheduled visits to the Keys and Everglades. For example, indigo buntings, bobolinks and redstarts appear in the spring. Wintering raptors move in around October. Red-breasted mergansers drop in for their winter stay around November. Prairie warblers, cardinals and common yellowthroats reside in the hardwood hammocks year-round.

Most parks and wildlife refuges provide complete bird lists detailing which species one can expect to observe in a particular region each season of the year. A good bird book is a handy tool for anyone visiting this unique region where one can spot so many species seldom found anywhere else in the country.

NATURAL HABITATS

The Everglades and the Florida Keys contain a variety of habitats, some shared and some distinctive to each region. In this flat, lowlying world, very slight differences in elevation, even an inch or two, can create a dramatic contrast between one area and another. Infinitesimal changes, such as water salinity, can cause striking differences in local microclimates. In this region, human-designed changes—particularly those affecting water supplies—have had devastating effects on the homes and habits of resident wildlife.

The casual visitor to this portion of South Florida can easily learn to recognize a variety of basic habitats:

Pinelands are located on slightly elevated limestone outcroppings of the Everglades and on Big Pine Key and nearby islands. These slash pine forests are dependent on occasional fires to keep them clear of competing undergrowth.

Saw Grass Prairies, dominating the Everglades, consist of hundreds of thousands of acres of grasslike sedge and many other grasses through which the freshwater "river of grass" flows almost imperceptibly from Lake Okeechobee and other northern water sources to the sea.

Hardwood Hammocks, rising to as much as three feet, are islands in the "river of grass" on which thrive jungly collections of mahogany, strangler figs, gumbo-limbo, various palms and other trees. This is also where animals find refuge in high-water times.

The princess of the hardwood hammocks may well be the harmless, showy golden orb weaver, a large female spider whose huge, spectacular webs are so strong that the silk was once used for cross hairs in guns and surveyor's instruments.

Heads, soggy leafy mounds that grow clumps of trees, are often named for their individual dominant tree, such as "coco heads" or "cypress heads."

Dwarf Cypress Forests are collections of small, hardy, moss-draped deciduous trees. These open areas of stunted, scattered bald cypress develop where marl and muds build up in solution holes, dissolved cavities in the limestone bed.

Coastal Prairies, appearing like deserts near the sea, are lowlands featuring salt-tolerant plants such as yucca, agave and varieties of cactus.

Mangrove Estuaries are found on the western edge of the Everglades, the Ten Thousand Islands, in Florida Bay and on many of the Florida Keys. These estuaries are ever-enlarging collections of salt-tolerant trees that serve as barriers against high seas, residences for microscopic life crucial to the food chain, and rookeries and homes for wildlife.

Freshwater Sloughs, slow-moving, marshy freshwater rivers, serve as reservoirs that are crucial to the region's animals and plants during the dry seasons.

Transition Zones, located between the tidal wetlands and hammocks, are dryland regions that, like the coastal prairies, grow only salt-tolerant vegetation. Beside cacti and unusual shrubs, the area is host to joewood, silver palm and various orchids and bromeliads.

Rockland Zones, found on a number of islands, are harsh coastal areas lying between the mangroves and the transition zones and home to buttonwood and saltwort and a few other hardy survivors.

Underwater habitats are an important part of South Florida. These include the following:

Marine Estuaries, crucial spawning grounds for many types of marine life, harbor abundant varieties of wildlife and, in the Everglades, can be best experienced by canoe.

Florida Bay, the shallow waters between the tip of the mainland and the Keys, contains about one-third of the national park,
including many refuges for nesting and shore
birds; manatees, dolphins, turtles, sharks and fish
ply the waters.

> The Keys, long a warm
> haven for winter-weary
> northerners, are
> becoming more and
> more a year-round
> destination.

Sea Grass Beds, highly productive areas of turtle,
manatee and Cuban shoal grasses, serve as nursery and
feeding grounds for numerous species of fish and invertebrates.

Mud Flats, lining the mangrove hammocks and rocky
shores of many islands on both the ocean and bay sides, are
flooded at high tide and exposed at low, attracting many shore
and wading birds to dine on their supplies of worms, mollusks
and fish.

Coral Reefs, considered one of the most complex of all ecosystems, are "underwater gardens" made up of soft animals with
hard, stony skeletons. As they die, their skeletal remains become
a three-dimensional habitat for thousands of animals and plants
ranging from microscopic to gigantic (see "Kingdoms Under the
Sea" in Chapter Three).

When to Go

SEASONS

The subtropical Everglades and Florida Keys are warm,
aquatic lands with a climate much like the islands of the
Caribbean. Winter low temperatures in South Florida average around 60°F with average highs in the upper 70s. Summer
average high temperatures reach near 90°, with average lows in
the comfortable mid-70s.

There are basically two seasons in this region of far South
Florida—winter and summer, or "dry" and "wet." While the Keys,
thanks to cooling ocean breezes, are reasonably comfortable
year-round, the Everglades are chiefly a winter destination. Winter,
which is the dry season, brings droughts of varying degrees to the
Everglades. Mosquito populations drop to their lowest, and
birds and wildlife gather at watering holes, to the delight of park
rangers and visitors alike. Cold fronts from the north can bring
occasional frosts to the Everglades, but generally the weather is
mild and comfortable.

In the summer, the rains come, completing the annual cycle
of drought and flood so necessary to Everglades survival. Great
storm clouds gather to drench the land in spectacular afternoon

electrical storms that replenish the region and bring welcome relief from hot, humid, steamy days. Biting insects thrive, keeping all but the most hardy visitor from exploring the interior Everglades in summer.

Hurricanes, though they can be devastating, need not keep one away during the fall. Usually developing in September, hurricanes have also been known to occur much later. (Ironically, the worst storm in decades, Hurricane Andrew, which struck in 1992, occurred in August.) Unlike many other weather phenomena, hurricanes come with plenty of warning, allowing visitors either to batten down or depart for inland locations.

In the Keys, winter is usually balmy and dry. Key West has never seen a frost. Though the Keys can get hot on summer afternoons, sea breezes keep the region tolerably comfortable for visitors. Welcome summer rains also cool things off from time to time. Downpours begin and end quickly, with little warning, seldom stopping daily activity.

CALENDAR OF EVENTS

Islamorada The **Cheeca Lodge Annual Presidential Sailfish Tournament** is a fishing competition with an emphasis on the billfish-tagging program. It includes dinner and an awards banquet and is dedicated to preserving the environment of the Florida Keys. **JANUARY**
Key West The **Key West Literary Seminar** celebrates the island's famous role as residence to American literary luminaries with a four-day event featuring a different theme each year. The **Annual Key West Craft Show** is a two-day street fair featuring craftspeople from all over the country. A three-month feast of events celebrating the island's rich heritage, **Old Island Days** features house and garden tours, concerts, plays, flower shows, sidewalk art festivals and other happenings from January to March.

Everglades Thousands gather in Everglades City for the **Everglades Seafood Festival** featuring arts and crafts booths, country music entertainment and, of course, lots of tasty seafood. **FEBRUARY**

Key Largo The **Annual Key Largo Home & Garden Tours** visit local homes (old and new) and gardens featuring native flora. **MARCH**
Marathon The **Original Marathon Seafood Festival** celebrates the wondrous variety of seafood cuisine. There are live bands and

children's rides along with savory samples of oysters, shrimps, lobsters and crab legs.

Key West   Shell blowers participate in the **Conch Shell Blowing Contest**.

APRIL   **Marathon and Key West**   Runners set out for a "marathon" dash over the sea in the annual **Seven Mile Bridge Run**, with fun and frivolity following in Key West at the Conch Republic Independence Celebration.

Key West   The **Conch Republic Independence Celebration** includes such tongue-in-cheek events as raising conch colors at Fort Zachary Taylor State Historic Site, electing the royal family, crafts show and food fest, pedicab races and loads and loads of parties.

MAY   **Marathon**   Under the dark of the moon, anglers from all walks of life compete in the **Annual Marathon International Tarpon Tournament**.

Lower Keys and Key West   The annual **Key West Fishing Tournament** is an eight-month-long event with nine divisions and is held throughout the Lower Keys.

JUNE   **Key West**   Get in touch with the Keys' Latin heritage at the **Cuban American Heritage Festival**, complete with a fishing tournament, silent auction and conga line. **PrideFest** showcases the depth and diversity of talent in the gay community—tea dances, plays, films, performance art and musical events.

JULY   **Lower Keys**   Divers glide among the coral heads at Looe Key National Marine Sanctuary while listening to an underwater broadcast of classical, semiclassical and contemporary music at the **Underwater Music Festival** benefitting marine preservation.

Key West   Storytelling, arm-wrestling, fishing tournaments and look-alike contests highlight the week-long **Hemingway Days**, honoring the memory and the works of the island's most famous literary figure. Learn a thing or two about wine while feasting on countless dishes from around the world at the **Key West Food & Wine Festival**.

AUGUST   **Key West**   The **Key West Lobsterfest** celebrates the crustacean with a street fair, live music and a lobster cook-off.

Marathon Stalking the elusive bonefish in his shallow-water **SEPTEMBER**
haunts draws anglers to the **Marathon International Bonefish
Tournament**.

Key West **WomenFest,** one of the largest lesbian events in the
world, draws more than 10,000 women to an activity-packed week
of tea dances, wine-tasting dinners, book signings and more.

Islamorada Complimentary boat rides whisk visitors back 150   **OCTOBER**
years during the **Indian Key Festival** for tours of the little island
townsite destroyed by Indians in 1840. A large group of women
showcase their flyfishing techniques at the **Women's World
Invitational Fly Championship**.

Key West Acclaimed for color, creativity and more than just a
touch of satire, the ten-day-long **Fantasy Fest** is Key West's answer to
Rio's Carnaval and New Orleans' Mardi Gras.

Key Largo Harry Harris Park hosts the **Island Jubilee,** which   **NOVEMBER**
features arts and crafts, live entertainment, cardboard boat races
and a barbecue competition.

Key West The **Pirates in Paradise Festival** brings ten days of
swashbuckling fun with nautical excursions, pirate-raid re-en-
actments and a film festival.

Everglades South Florida ethnic groups join together at the   **DECEMBER**
Miccosukee Indian Village for the **Annual Indian Arts Festival**.

Key Largo Mariners trim their boats with holiday decorations
for the **Key Largo Christmas Boat Parade** along Blackwater Sound.

Islamorada Everyday fishermen team up with film stars, sports
figures and famous fishing guides during the **Islamorada Redbone
Fishing Tournament** (held in both April and December) for a
weekend of redfish and bonefish angling and social events benefitting the Cystic Fibrosis Foundation.

Lower Keys Local and national artists exhibit their talents at
the **Annual Island Art Fair** on Big Pine Key.

Each chapter of this book lists the chambers of commerce   **Before You Go**
and/or visitors centers that provide tourist and travel information. You can obtain materials on the **Everglades**   **VISITORS
National Park** by writing: Information, Everglades National Park,   **CENTERS**
40001 State Road 9336, Homestead, FL 33034; 305-242-7700;
www.nps.gov/ever.

If you require information on the **Florida Keys**, you can call 800-352-5397; www.fla-keys.com.

For a free copy of the *Florida Vacation Guide*, contact **Visit Florida**. ~ 888-735-2872; www.visitflorida.org.

PACKING   Unless you plan to spend your time in South Florida dining in ultra-deluxe restaurants, you'll need much less in your suitcase than you might think. For most trips, all you'll have to pack in the way of clothing are some shorts, lightweight shirts or tops, cool slacks or skirts, a hat for protection from the sun, a pair of quality sunglasses, a couple of bathing suits and coverups, and something *very casual* for any special event that might call for dressing up.

The rest of your luggage space can be devoted to a few essentials that should not be forgotten (unless you prefer to shop on arrival). These include good sunscreens and some insect repellent, especially if you are traveling in the summer or heading into the Everglades, even in winter. If stinging jellyfish are a concern, take along a small container of a papain-type meat tenderizer. It won't keep them away, but it will ease the pain should you fall victim.

In summer especially, be sure to take along an umbrella or light raincoat for the sudden showers that can pop out of nowhere. In winter, a sweater or light jacket can be welcome on occasional cool evenings.

Good soft, comfortable, lightweight shoes for sightseeing are a must. Despite its tropical gentleness, South Florida terrain doesn't treat bare feet well except on rare sandy shores or beside a pool. Sturdy sandals will do well unless you are hiking into the Everglades and other wilderness areas. For these forays, you may need lightweight boots or canvas shoes you don't mind wading in. Surf mocs, inexpensive and extremely handy, are another good choice.

Serious scuba divers and snorkelers will probably want to bring their own gear, but it's certainly not essential. Underwater equipment of all sorts is available for rent throughout the Keys. Fishing gear is also often available for rent.

Campers will need basic cooking equipment and can make out fine with only a lightweight sleeping bag or cot and a tent with bug-proof screens and a ground cloth. Because soil is sparse in many campgrounds, stakes that can penetrate rock are a must. A canteen, first-aid kit, insect repellent, flashlight and other routine camping gear should be brought along.

Be sure to take along a camera; South Florida sunsets are sensational. Binoculars and a magnifying glass enhance any exploration of natural areas. If you plan to take night walks any distance from the lodge in the Everglades National Park, you will need a flashlight. And don't, for heaven's sake, forget your copy of *Hidden Florida Keys & Everglades*.

LODGING

Lodgings in South Florida run the gamut from tiny old-fashioned cabins to glistening highrise hotels. Bed and breakfasts are scarce, except in Key West and a few other isolated locations. Chain motels line most main thoroughfares in populous areas, and mom-and-pop enterprises still successfully vie for lodgers in every region. Large hotels with names you'd know anywhere appear in the few centers of size. Schmaltziest of all are the upscale resorts. Here one can drop in almost from the sky and never have to leave the grounds. In fact, you can take in all the sports, dining, nightlife, shopping and entertainment needed to make a vacation complete, although you may miss a fair amount of authentic South Florida.

Other lodgings, such as historic inns that haven't been too spruced up or guest houses where you can eat breakfast with the handful of other visitors, offer plenty of local personality. A few guest houses in Key West cater exclusively to gays. Whatever your preference and budget, you can probably find something to suit your taste with the help of the regional chapters of this book. Remember, rooms are scarce and prices are high in the winter tourist season. Summer rates are often drastically reduced in many places, allowing for a week's, or even a month's stay to be a real bargain. If you'd like some help with lodging reservations, contact the **Florida Hotel Network**. This resource offers bookings throughout the state including the Keys and Everglades. ~ 800-293-2419; www.floridahotels.com, e-mail info@floridahotels.com. Whatever you do, plan ahead and *make reservations*, especially in the prime tourist seasons.

> Be forewarned that a "waterfront" room can mean bay, lake, inlet or even a channel.

Accommodations in this book are organized by region and classified according to price. Rates referred to are for the high season, so if you are looking for low-season bargains, it's good to inquire. *Budget* lodgings generally are less than $80 per night for a standard double and are satisfactory but modest. *Moderately* priced lodgings run from $80 to $120; what they have to offer in the

Text continued on page 36.

Keys and
Everglades Cuisine

With saltwater on three sides of the Everglades and all sides of the Keys, seafood certainly tops the list of South Florida foods. Add to the saltwater fare freshwater delights from the meandering streams, dark ponds and canals of the Everglades and your fish and shellfish menu has expanded beyond all expectations. Grouper, yellowfin tuna, dolphin (mahimahi), shrimp, spiny lobster and stone crab are only a sampling of the fruits of local seas that offer particular specialties in every season. From freshwater sources come largemouth bass, catfish and delicate panfish of all sorts.

Each cook seems to prepare seafood dishes in his own way. Heaping fried or broiled platters of seafood are found almost everywhere, but creative chefs also try out unusual seafood recipes with the fervor of marathon competitors. Each region, too, has its own particular specialties, such as fried alligator tail, soft-shell terrapin and frogs' legs in the Everglades and spicy conch chowder and fritters down through the Keys.

No matter where you live, you may have partaken of South Florida's abundant winter produce. Fat red strawberries, long green beans, prize-winning peppers and tomatoes grow in abundance in the Homestead area. You can often stop at a roadside stand or go into the fields for a pick-your-own sale of whatever is left over from the great quantities shipped across the country. Citrus fruits, from easily peeled tangerines to sweet grapefruit, are abundant in the winter months. Exotic fruits also join the list of South Florida produce, familiar ones such as mangos, avocados and papayas and lesser-known zapotes, lychees and guavas. Coconuts grow in backyards here in the subtropics. Swamp cabbage yields its heart as the chief delicacy in "hearts of palm" salad.

Everywhere you dine, you will have an opportunity to eat Key lime pie. It's a simple dessert—a traditional baked pastry pie shell filled with a creamy tart-sweet yellow filling. But how to prepare this cool delicacy is a hot topic. Purists simply use the juice of the little yellow native limes, a few eggs and some condensed milk. Some say the tradition began when milk had to be canned before the days of refrigeration in the Keys. The limes "cook" the eggs, which may be whole or just yolks. Whether the pie should include meringue is still a debatable issue, as are green coloring, gelatin and crumb crusts. Many visitors have fun trying to locate the restaurant or bakery that serves up "the best Key lime pie."

Conch chowder also has its experts and its history. Queen conchs were once abundant in the Keys and used in all sorts of dishes. Though conchs are now imported, conch chowder is still wonderful, varying from thin and mild to thick and spicy, each cook possessing a favorite secret recipe. Conch is also prepared raw, marinated, in fritters or "cracked" (pounded, dredged in cracker meal and fried).

American Indian and ethnic foods have also influenced dining throughout the Everglades and Keys. The Miccosukee Indians along the Tamiami Trail serve pumpkin and fry breads and special Indian burgers and tacos. The Keys' Cuban heritage is reflected in such popular dishes as black beans and rice, *picadillo* (a ground beef dish with capers and raisins), *lechón* (roast pork prepared with garlic and citrus fruits) and *plátanos* (fried bananas).

Lately, inventive young chefs have been using local fruits and other tropical ingredients to create a new style of cooking, often called Floribbean. Seafood, chicken, lamb and beef get tropical treatments, and are often grilled, smoked or blackened. Some call it "tropical fusion," while others deem it "new Florida cuisine." Whatever its name, one thing is certain: This brand of cooking is marvelously adventurous. After all, where else can you find Key lime pasta or grilled grouper with mango salsa, plantains and purple potatoes?

way of luxury will depend on where they are located. At *deluxe*-priced accommodations, you can expect to spend between $120 and $200 for a homey bed and breakfast or a double in a hotel or resort. In hotels of this price you'll generally find spacious rooms with a dressing room, a fashionable lobby, a restaurant and often a bar or nightclub. *Ultra-deluxe* facilities begin at $200 for a double and are a region's finest, offering plenty of extras.

If you crave a room facing the sea, ask specifically. If you are trying to save money, lodgings a block or so from the water often offer lower rates than those on the edge of the sea.

DINING

Eating places in South Florida are abundant and fish is often the highlight. Whether catfish from the Everglades or yellowfin tuna from the Atlantic, you can almost always count on its being fresh and well prepared. Each season has its specialties, each region its ethnic influences and its gourmet newcomers.

Within a particular chapter, restaurants are categorized geographically, with each restaurant entry describing the establishment according to price. Restaurants listed offer lunch and dinner unless otherwise noted. Dinner entrées at *budget* restaurants usually cost $10 or less. The ambience is informal, service usually speedy. *Moderate*-priced eateries charge between $10 and $20 for dinner; surroundings are casual but pleasant, the menu offers more variety and the pace is usually slower. *Deluxe* establishments tab their entrées above $20; cuisines may be simple or sophisticated, depending on the location, but the service is more personalized. *Ultra-deluxe* dining rooms, where entrées begin at $30, are often the gourmet places; menus may be large or small, though the ambience is almost always casual.

Some restaurants change hands often and are occasionally closed in low season. Efforts have been made in this book to include places with established reputations for good eating. Breakfast and lunch menus vary less in price from restaurant to restaurant than evening dinners. Even deluxe establishments often offer light breakfasts and lunch specialties that place them in or near the budget range.

TRAVELING WITH CHILDREN

Plenty of family adventures are available in South Florida, from manmade attractions to experiences in the wild. A few guidelines will help in making travel with children a pleasure. Book reservations in advance, making sure that those places accept children. If you need a crib or extra cot, arrange for it ahead of time. A travel agent can be of help here, as well as with most other travel plans.

If you are traveling by air, try to reserve bulkhead seats where there is plenty of room. Take along extras you may need, such as diapers, changes of clothing, snacks and toys or small games. If your child has a favorite stuffed animal or blanket, keep it handy.

When traveling by car, be sure to take along the extras, too. Often a simple picnic or a fast-food place with a playground works best at lunch or suppertime, so children can run and stretch their legs. Restaurant dining can turn into a hassle after long hours in the car; it's better to let them have a romp with a peanut butter sandwich in hand.

> Make sure you have plenty of water and juices to drink; dehydration can be a subtle problem, especially in a sub-tropical climate.

A first-aid kit is a must for any trip. Along with adhesive bandages, antiseptic cream and something to stop itching, include any medicines your pediatrician might recommend to treat allergies, colds, diarrhea or any chronic problems your child may have.

If you plan to spend much time at the beach, take extra care the first few days. Children's skin is usually tenderer than adults', and severe sunburn can happen before you realize it. A hat is a good idea, along with a reliable sunblock. And be sure to keep a constant eye on children who are near any water.

For parents' night out, many hotels provide a dependable list of babysitters. In some areas you may find drop-in child care centers; look in the *Yellow Pages* for these, and make sure you choose ones that are licensed.

Many towns, parks and attractions offer special activities designed just for children. Consult local newspapers and/or phone the numbers in this guide to see what's happening when you're there.

SENIOR TRAVELERS

As millions have discovered, South Florida is an ideal place for older vacationers, many of whom turn into part-time or full-time residents. The climate is mild, the terrain level, and many places offer significant discounts for seniors. Off-season rates make the Florida Keys exceedingly attractive for travelers on limited incomes. Florida residents over 65 can benefit from reduced rates at most state parks, and the Golden Age Passport, which must be applied for in person, allows free admission to national parks and monuments for anyone 62 or older.

The **American Association of Retired Persons** (AARP) offers membership to anyone over 50. AARP's benefits include travel discounts with a number of firms. ~ 601 E Street NW, Washington, DC 20049; 888-687-2277; www.aarp.org.

Elderhostel offers reasonably priced, all-inclusive educational programs in many Florida locations—including Homestead, Key Largo and Key West—throughout the year. ~ 11 Avenue de Lafayette, Boston, MA 02111; 877-426-8056; www.elderhostel.org.

Be extra careful about health matters. Bring along any medications you ordinarily use, together with the prescriptions for obtaining more. Consider carrying a medical record with you—including your medical history and current medical status as well as your doctor's name, phone number and address. Make sure that your insurance covers you away from home.

DISABLED TRAVELERS The state of Florida is striving to make more destinations fully accessible to travelers with disabilities.

Everglades National Park (see Chapter Two) has many facilities, including short trails, that are accessible to travelers with disabilities.

There are several places to find more information, including the **MossRehab ResourceNet.** ~ MossRehab Hospital, 1200 West Tabor Road, Philadelphia, PA 19141; 215-456-9600; www.moss resourcenet.org. The **Society for Accessible Travel & Hospitality** (SATH) is another organization that can provide information. ~ 347 5th Avenue #610, New York, NY 10016; 212-447-7284; www.sath.org. Or try **Flying Wheels Travel**, which specializes in trip packages for the disabled. ~ 143 West Bridge Street, Owatonna, MN 55060; 507-451-5005; www.flyingwheelstravel. com. **Travelin' Talk**, a networking organization, also provides information. ~ P.O. Box 1796, Wheat Ridge, CO 80034; 303-232-2979; www.travelintalk.net. The same people also run **Access-Able Travel Source**, with worldwide information online. ~ 303-232-2979; www.access-able.com.

WOMEN TRAVELING ALONE Traveling solo grants an independence and freedom different from that of traveling with a partner, but single travelers are more vulnerable to crime and should take additional precautions.

It's unwise to hitchhike and probably best to avoid inexpensive accommodations on the outskirts of town; the money saved does not outweigh the risk. Bed and breakfasts, youth hostels and YWCAs are generally your safest bet for lodging, and they also foster an environment ideal for bonding with fellow travelers.

Keep all valuables well-hidden and clutch cameras and purses tightly. Avoid late-night treks or strolls through undesirable parts of town, but if you find yourself in this situation, continue walking with a confident air until you reach a safe haven. A fierce scowl never hurts.

These hints should by no means deter you from seeking out adventure. Wherever you go, stay alert, use your common sense and trust your instincts. If you are hassled or threatened in some way, never be afraid to call for assistance. It's also a good idea to carry change for a phone call and to know a number to call in case of emergency.

For more helpful hints, get a copy of *Safety and Security for Women Who Travel* (Travelers' Tales).

If you are hassled or threatened in some way, never be afraid to scream for assistance. In Key West, the 24-hour **Helpline, Inc.** can provide information and referrals. ~ 305-296-4357, 800-273-4558.

GAY & LESBIAN TRAVELERS

At the tip of Florida floats the island of Key West, a casual, comfortable getaway. Old Town is the center of this gay scene, replete with guesthouses, restaurants, stores and nightspots. (See "Key West Gay Scene" in Chapter Four.)

A great source of Key West information for gay and lesbian travelers is the **Key West Business Guild**, which offers materials on bars, weddings, events, accommodations, as well as a great map and directory. ~ 728 Duval Street, 800-535-7797, 305-294-4603; www.gaykeywestfl.com.

Another of Key West's central clearinghouses for gay and lesbian visitors is the **Gay & Lesbian Community Center**, a friendly relaxed gathering place that hosts a free internet café and offers information, referrals, literature and suggestions of what to do and where to go. ~ 513 Truman Avenue; 305-292-3223; www.glcckeywest.org.

The gay community lent a big hand in reviving Key West's historic district.

For a weekly rundown on the trendiest nightspots in Florida, pick up *Contax Guide* at any gay club; it serves the entire state (and other states, too). ~ 305-757-6333. *Hotspots* covers weekly nightlife and entertainment in Key West, South Beach and Fort Lauderdale. ~ 954-928-1862; www.hotspotsmagazine.com.

TWN (*The Weekly News*) focuses on the South Florida scene (including the Keys). In it you'll find news and features pertaining to the gay community. Can't think of anything to do? They also have a comprehensive events listing. You can pick up a copy at many Key West guesthouses. ~ 901 Northeast 79th Street, Miami; 305-757-6333.

In Key West, **Helpline, Inc.** is a 24-hour crisis and general information line benefitting the Keys area. ~ 305-296-4357, 800-273-4558. For help booking a variety of accommodations, call the **Florida Hotel Network.** ~ 800-293-2419; www.floridahotels.com.

FOREIGN TRAVELERS

Passports and Visas   Most foreign visitors need a passport and tourist visa to enter the United States. Contact your nearest United States Embassy or Consulate well in advance to obtain a visa and to check on any other entry requirements.

Customs Requirements   Foreign travelers are allowed to carry in the following: 200 cigarettes (1 carton), 50 cigars or 2 kilograms (4.4 pounds) of smoking tobacco; one liter of alcohol for personal use only (you must be 21 years of age to bring in alcohol); and US$100 worth of duty-free gifts that can include an additional quantity of 100 cigars. You may bring in any amount of currency, but must fill out a form if you bring in over US$10,000. Carry any prescription drugs in clearly marked containers. (You may have to produce a written prescription or doctor's statement for the custom's officer.) Meat or meat products, seeds, plants, fruits and narcotics are not allowed to be brought into the United States. Contact the **United States Customs and Border Protection** for further information. ~ 1300 Pennsylvania Avenue NW, Washington, DC 20229; 202-927-6724; www.cbp.gov.

Driving   If you plan to rent a car, an international driver's license should be obtained before arriving in the United States. Some car rental agencies require both a foreign license and an international driver's license. Many also require a lessee to be at least 25 years of age; all require a major credit card. Seat belts are mandatory for the driver and all passengers. Children under the age of six or under 60 pounds should be in the back seat in approved child-safety restraints.

Currency   United States money is based on the dollar. Bills come in denominations of $1, $5, $10, $20, $50 and $100. Every dollar is divided into 100 cents. Coins are the penny (1 cent), nickel (5 cents), dime (10 cents) and quarter (25 cents). Half-dollar and dollar coins are rarely used. You may not use foreign currency to purchase goods and services in the United States. Consider buying traveler's checks in dollar amounts. You may also use credit cards affiliated with an American company such as Interbank, Barclay Card and American Express.

Electricity and Electronics   Electric outlets use currents of 110 volts, 60 cycles. To operate appliances made for other electrical systems, you need a transformer or other adapter. Travelers who use laptop computers for telecommunication should be aware that modem configurations for U.S. telephone systems may be different from their European counterparts. Similarly, the U.S. format for videotapes is different from that in Europe; National Park Service visitors centers and other stores that sell souvenir videos often have them available in European format on request.

> Only female mosquitos suck blood (male mosquitos feed on the sugar from flowers and fruits).

Weights and Measures   The United States uses the English system of weights and measures. American units and their metric equivalents are: 1 inch = 2.5 centimeters; 1 foot (12 inches) = 0.3 meter; 1 yard (3 feet) = 0.9 meter; 1 mile (5280 feet) = 1.6 kilometers; 1 ounce = 28 grams; 1 pound (16 ounces) = 0.45 kilogram; 1 quart (liquid) = 0.9 liter.

Outdoor Adventures

CAMPING

South Florida offers a wide variety of camping opportunities, from primitive camping in wilderness areas to recreational vehicle parks that resemble fashionable resorts without the condos. Campgrounds in the Florida Keys are often crowded, with sites very close together. For a listing of all the state parks and recreation areas, with information on making reservations, send for the *Florida State Park Guide*. ~ Department of Environmental Protection, Division of Recreation and Parks, 3900 Commonwealth Boulevard, Mail Station 49, Tallahassee, FL 32399-3000; 850-245-2157; www.dep.state.fl.us/parks.

Everglades National Park will send you information on both developed and wilderness camping within the park. ~ 40001 State Road 9336, Homestead, FL 33034; 305-242-7700; www.nps.gov/ever. **Big Cypress National Preserve** has information on primitive camping opportunities within the preserve. ~ HCR61

Box 110, Ochopee, FL 34141; 239-695-4111; www.nps.gov/bicy.
Permits are required for some of the primitive campsites located
on keys within **Biscayne National Park**. ~ 9700 Southwest 328th
Street, Homestead, FL 33033; 305-230-7275;
www.nps.gov/bisc.

When swimming and boat-
ing, keep your eye on the
weather. When there are
electrical storms and
high winds approach-
ing, it's time to head
for dry land.

The **Florida Association of RV Parks and
Campgrounds** puts out an annual *Florida Camping
Directory* of over 200 private campgrounds and RV
parks in the state. Local chambers of commerce will
also have information on private campgrounds in the
area. ~ 1340 Vickers Drive, Tallahassee, FL 32303; 850-
562-7151; www.floridacamping.com.

An excellent book for visitors planning to camp in the state
is *Florida Parks*, by Gerald Grow (Longleaf Publications).

PERMITS   Backcountry campsites in the **Everglades National Park** are accessible by boat, bicycle or foot. ~ 40001 State Road 9336, Homestead, FL 33034; 305-242-7700; www.nps.gov/ever/visit/back
coun.htm. A free permit, issued on a first-come, first-served basis
no more than 24 hours before the start of your trip, is required
and may be obtained at the visitors centers. Permits for wilderness
exploration in **Big Cypress National Preserve, Biscayne National
Park** and certain state parks may be obtained by contacting the
individual sites, as found in the "Beaches & Parks" sections of
the regional chapters of this book.

BOATING   From paddleboat to cruise ship, just about every imaginable
method of ploughing the waters is available in South Florida. You
can bring your own boat if you wish and travel the Intracoastal
Waterway or laze away the day on a quiet inlet with a fishing pole.
And if you have no boat, you can rent or charter a craft of just
about any size or speed. Each chapter in this book offers suggestions on how to go about finding the vessel of your choice. Most
marinas and other rental agencies will arm you with maps and advice. Boating regulations and safety information may be obtained
from the **Florida Fish and Wildlife Conservation Commission**. ~
Office of Enforcement Planning and Policy, 620 South Meridian
Street, Tallahassee, FL 32399; 850-245-2929; www.state.fl.us/fwc.

Canoeing is a popular sport in the western and southern Everglades and in several areas of the Keys. To obtain the *Florida Rec-*

reational Trails System–Canoe Trails brochure, contact the **Office of Greenways and Trails** or print off trails from their website. ~ 325 John Knox Road, Building 500, Tallahassee, FL 32303; 850-245-2052; www.floridagreenwaysandtrails.com. Individual state and national parks also provide canoe trail information.

Because many interesting destinations are located offshore, tour boats and cruises are also available in numerous regions.

Few places match South Florida for the variety of water sports available. Swimming, scuba diving, snorkeling or just basking on a float are options wherever you can get to the shore. Drownings do occur now and then, but they can be avoided as long as one respects the power of the water, heeds appropriate warnings and uses good sense.

WATER SAFETY

Wherever you swim or dive, never do it alone. Though the surf is seldom high in this region, should the wind whip up incoming waves, keep your face toward them. They can bring unpleasant surprises even to the initiated. If you get caught in a rip current or any tow that makes you feel out of control, don't try to swim against it. Head with it or across it, paralleling the shore. Respect signs warning of undertows.

If you dive or snorkel, practice all the proper techniques and emergency procedures with an expert before starting out. Even professionals consider training updates to be essential for underwater safety. Always display a "Diver Down" flag when in the water, and avoid wearing shiny objects that might attract unwanted sea creatures. Check all equipment prior to any dive, and always dive into the current so it can help you on your return to your boat.

Jellyfish stings are commonly treated with papain-type meat tenderizers. If you go lobstering or crabbing or wading around in murky waters and where shellfish dwell, wear canvas shoes to protect your feet.

Remember, you are a guest in the sea. All rights belong to the creatures who dwell there, including sharks. Though they are rarely seen and seldom attack, they should be respected. A wise swimmer or diver simply heads unobtrusively for the shore or boat. On the other hand, if dolphins are cavorting in your area, don't worry. Dolphins are equipped so as not to run into things, even you, and they may put on quite a show.

Life jackets are a must if you want your boating trip to end happily. This goes for canoes and kayaks as well as larger and faster craft. Don't mix alcohol and water; excessive drinking is involved in over 50 percent of all drownings and boating accidents. Learn boating rules and obey them; collisions resulting from operator error and high speeds are the primary cause of boating injury.

And never, never take your eyes off a child who is near the water, no matter how calm conditions may appear.

Surrounded by so much water in South Florida, the best protection is to know how to swim, and to use your good sense.

WILDER-NESS SAFETY

Certain precautions should be taken whenever leaving the main roads and heading into wilderness regions, especially in the Everglades and Big Cypress. First of all, be sure to let someone know your planned route and schedule before setting out. The biggest problem will likely be biting insects, especially mosquitoes, in all but the coolest winter months. Plenty of insect repellent, long-sleeved shirts, long pants and head covers are the best protection.

Learn to recognize poisonous plants, such as poison ivy, poison-wood and machineel, so they can be avoided. Coral snakes, water moccasins and diamondback and pygmy rattlesnakes do reside in South Florida; by being alert and looking before exploring, you can usually avoid unpleasant encounters. When hiking off the trails, be careful of your footing. Sharp-edged rock, mucky soil and hidden holes can make walking tricky. Check with the individual parks and preserves concerning rules for fires and use of off-road vehicles.

FISHING

No matter what the season of the year, the Everglades and Keys are an angler's paradise. How you approach the sport is up to you. You can dangle a hook from a cane pole into a sluggish slough or chase bonefish off Islamorada or wrestle with a tarpon on the edge of the Gulf Stream. You can even harvest great rewards by casting your line off an abandoned bridge of the Overseas Highway. Of course, the best way to fish—unless you know you are going to eat your bounty—is by using catch-and-release methods. This way, you get the thrill of the catch and the rewarding experience of watching a carefully revived fish return to the wild.

Popular fishing of the Everglades includes both inland waters, where freshwater canals and ponds harbor impressive largemouth bass, black crappie, catfish and bream and other panfish, and the coastal waters of the Gulf of Mexico and Florida Bay. The most sought-after saltwater species here are trout, redfish and snapper. For information on freshwater and saltwater options, contact the **Fish and Wildlife Conservation Commission.** ~ 2574 Seagate Drive, Marathon Building #204, Tallahassee, FL 32301; 850-488-4676. Some areas of the national park are closed to fishing, so it is important to obtain a copy of the regulations from a visitors center or ranger station before dropping a hook.

A good resource is the monthly publication *Florida Sportsman*, found at marinas and bait-and-tackle shops; it features seasonal information and in-depth fishing articles.

Saltwater fishing in the Keys can be roughly divided into three types; reef fishing, offshore fishing (on the oceanside, beyond the reef and out into the Gulf Stream, or westward out on the Tortugas Banks) and inshore and "backcountry" fishing in the Gulf and Florida Bay.

Habitual area fishermen will tell you that there is enough variety in this region to keep you busy and learning for a lifetime, as well as something to catch every day of the year. In the spring, permit, tarpon and bonefish are abundant in the flats, and sharks move into shallow waters to spawn. Spring is also a good time for yellowfin tuna, white marlin, swordfish and snapper. The calm days of summer promise good catches of dolphin (mahimahi). As fall days get cooler, action on the reef for snapper and grouper improves; permit, marlin, tuna, wahoo and the challenging bonefish are some autumn rewards. Kingfish show in big schools in the winter; grouper and mackerel fishing also gets underway then. Barracuda and Atlantic sailfish, along with many other species, can be found all year round.

Numerous crustaceans are also harvested from the coastal waters of Florida. Perhaps the most popular is the spiny lobster, resident of both bay and ocean. Also delectable is the pugnacious blue crab. Stone crabs are harvested for the meat of their tasty claws, which they graciously grow back after being returned to the water. Shrimp are an important commercial fruit of the sea. Be sure to check on the legal seasons and sizes before taking any of these creatures.

If you'd like to try a kind of fishing that is new to you, you will find guide services available just about everywhere boats are rented and bait is sold. Charter fishing is the costliest way to go out to sea; party boats take a crowd but are less expensive and usually great fun. In the ponds and streams of the Everglades region and in the backcountry of Florida Bay, guides can show you the best place to throw your hook or skim a fly. Whatever your pleasure, in saltwater or fresh, a good guide will save you both time and grief and increase the likelihood of a full string or a handsome trophy. For those who wish to go it alone in their own boats, there are a number of public access landings throughout the region.

If you go freshwater fishing, you will need a license, and you will have to get it through the local county tax collector. It's easy to do, though, because most fish camps, bait-and-tackle shops and sporting goods stores act as agents. Just look for signs that say "Fishing License for Sale."

For information on freshwater and saltwater licenses, check at a local marina or with the **Florida Fish and Wildlife Conservation Commission**. ~ Bureau of Licensing and Permitting, 2590 Executive Center Circle, Suite 200, Tallahassee, FL 32301; 850-488-3641; www.state.fl.us/fwc. The **Florida Fish & Wildlife Conservation Commission** nearest the area you are fishing can also provide you with the latest saltwater fishing facts on licenses, closed seasons and bag and size limits. ~ 1275 Northeast 79th Street, Miami, FL 33138, 305-956-2500; or 2796 Overseas Highway, Marathon, FL 33050, 305-289-2320.

There are also fish just to be viewed in the seas of South Florida, especially wherever the living reefs thrive. (See "Kingdoms Under the Sea" in Chapter Three.) Vivid yellows, reds, blues and greens characterize the reef fish, some of which take on almost electric hues. A face mask, with or without a snorkel, will open up an undersea world of incredible beauty and surprises, whether it be along the shore or out among the reefs. In fact, colorful tropical fish may well be some of Florida's loveliest hidden treasures.

TWO

The Everglades

From the air, it seems a vast, mysterious world of land and water at whose edge civilization suddenly stops, a place where no one dwells. From the highway, it appears an endless prairie above which birds fly in winter and clouds build into towering summer storms that flash and crash and deluge the land in torrents. Both impressions are right, but, like the seasonal breezes in this subtropical land, they skim the surface only. For here in the Everglades, perhaps more than anywhere else in the country, the old cliché rings true: there is far more than meets the eye.

In the Everglades, life teems, water flows, creatures struggle for survival in miraculous cycles that have repeated themselves over and over again since prehistoric times. Only today there is one difference. Now the cycles have been altered by humans, who have tamed the waters and channeled the streams and, as a result, now hold the survival of this beautiful, fragile region in their hands.

An understanding and appreciation of the Everglades has come only in recent decades, far too long after the waters that once spilled out of Lake Okeechobee and gently fed this region were diked and rechanneled. For decades, dreamers, developers and farmers were unconcerned about the devastating effects of the changes they so drastically wrought on the natural world of South Florida. To most of them, the Everglades were simply a vast swamp that could be drained and tamed for building and for growing food.

Then, in 1947, Marjorie Stoneman Douglas wrote a book that acclaimed the treasures of this subtropical wilderness, once inhabited by American Indians and home to myriad creatures and plants found nowhere else in the U.S. She also struck at the consciences of those who were doing irreparable damage to a region whose existence contributed to the life of the whole peninsula. "There are no other Everglades in the world," she began *The Everglades: River of Grass*. "They are, they have always been, one of the unique regions of the earth, remote, never wholly known."

In the same year, President Truman dedicated Everglades National Park. The region has also been designated both an International Biosphere Reserve and a World Heritage Site in recognition of its value as a crucial natural wonder of the world. Although the Everglades actually extend far beyond the park's 1.5 million acres, it is in this protected region that visitors can explore the wonders of this world.

Next to human beings, hurricanes are the most powerful force in the Everglades. While only a couple have hit the area in the last 30 years, their devastating winds have had dramatic effects on the landscape. Hurricane Andrew, the most recent to strike (1992), leveled groves of trees, stripped the forest canopies of their leaves and exposed the delicate forest floor to the sun. Slowly the forests have been rebuilding themselves. But the storm has changed certain parts of the Everglades forever.

At first glance, much of the Everglades looks like inviting prairie that visitors could easily hike through on a nice day. But looks are deceiving. Most of this plain is actually a shallow, gently flowing river, hidden beneath the tall saw grass and reeds. Except in the pinelands and hardwood hammocks, there is water everywhere. Luckily for visitors, well-designed roads, trails and boardwalks keep feet dry while allowing travel through remote areas. And for those who want to explore watery pathways, a number of canoe trails offer adventure into spots accessible only by boat. Bicycling along park roads also lets visitors get closer to nature and discover places that might be missed while traveling in a car.

Four visitor areas lie in Everglades National Park, and each shows a different side of the region's rich character. Shark Valley, the northeastern entrance off the Tamiami Trail, offers tours into the saw grass prairie, abundant in birdlife and alligators. The northwest area at Everglades City is a jumping-off place to the Ten Thousand Islands, a mangrove estuary popular with anglers and vacationers. The main visitor area, southwest of Homestead, marks the beginning of a 38-mile park road that meanders through saw grass prairie, hardwood hammock, cypress swamps and lake regions, ending at Flamingo on the edge of Florida Bay. This main road offers access to numerous Everglades habitats via a variety of short and long trails.

Winter is the time to visit the Everglades, the only season when mosquitoes won't eat you alive. In winter you can leave your car, walk the trails, canoe the streams and contemplate the subtle beauty of the place. There are no breathtaking panoramas in this region, where the altitude seldom rises above three feet, but rich rewards await those who take the time to explore. Slumbering alligators lie like half-sunken logs in shallow ponds. Comical anhingas gather on low branches, hanging their wings out to dry after fishing forays. Bird populations are spectacular and diverse, including such easily recognized favorites as roseate spoonbills, osprey, brown pelicans and bald eagles. Subtly colored snails and wild orchids adorn the woods in season. Endangered and rare animals such as the gentle manatee, the Florida panther and the American crocodile, though seldom seen, reside deep within the watery world of the Everglades.

Although well-placed signs explain where to go and what to see, the Everglades are also a region of hidden treasures that will reward all who are willing to quietly search, to wait and watch.

It is almost impossible to visit the Everglades without coming away caring about what happens to this wondrous wet world where life cycles begin and the flow of fresh water keeps the salt of the sea in balance so that life can survive. One cannot forget Douglas's words: "There are no other Everglades in the world."

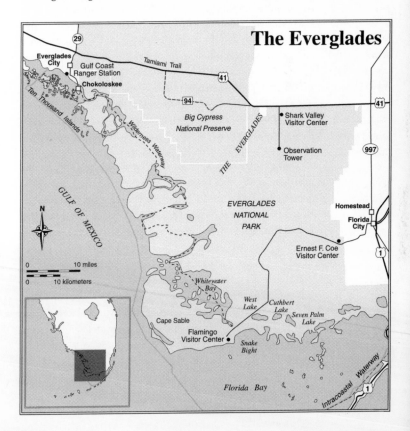

Tamiami Trail Area Heading westward from Miami, Route 41, known as the Tamiami Trail, provides an almost straight shot from the Atlantic to the Gulf Coast. For many years, until the building of the faster, wider parallel Route 84 (Alligator Alley) to the north, this was the only route across southern Florida. Route 4 plunges through the heart of the Everglades, skirting the northern edge of Everglades National Park and cutting through the southern portion of the Big Cypress National Preserve. Though not wildly scenic, it is an intriguing road, traveling through miles and miles of what the American Indians called *pa-hay-okee*, or "grassy water." Sometimes the narrow highway is paralleled by canals, their banks busy with people fishing with cane poles. But mostly the landscape is saw grass prairie, with the great, wide—almost hidden—life-giving river running imperceptibly through it. Drivers are instructed to travel this road with lights on at all times, a safeguard against possible tedium and the strange effect the region seems to have on one's depth perception.

SIGHTS A few entrepreneurs have set up shop along the Tamiami Trail, mostly in the business of airboat rides, which environmentalists frown upon. For the most part, however, the highway, while a masterful engineering feat in its day, is a lonely one, blessedly short on billboards and long on Everglades mystique.

Part of that mystique is conveyed by the region's only human inhabitants, the Miccosukee Indians. Although they trace their ancestry back to centuries before the United States became a nation, they were not recognized as a tribe by the federal government until 1962. About 500 of them now live on a reservation along Route 1. They are descendants of a group which successfully hid in the Everglades during the period when Florida's American Indians were being captured and forcibly sent west. A guided or self-guided tour of the designed-for-tourists **Miccosukee Indian Village** includes a museum, cooking and living chickees (palm-thatched native houses), a nature walk, craft areas and an arena where you can watch alligator shows. Admission. ~ Route 41, about 25 miles west of Florida's Turnpike; 305-223-8380, fax 305-223-1011; www.miccosukee.com. Also in the Indian village, the **Miccosukee Airboat Rides** offer noisy, environmentally questionable trips over the saw grass deeper into the Everglades. It includes a stop at an old hammock-style American Indian camp.

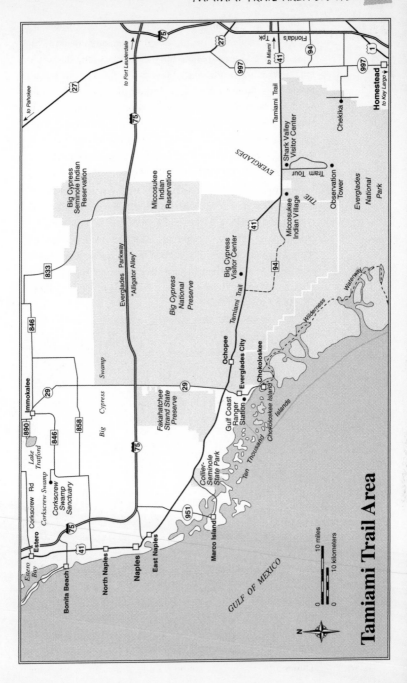

Tamiami Trail Area

The 15-mile, two-hour tram tours offered in the **Shark Valley** section of Everglades National Park acquaint visitors with the heart of the saw grass region. Stops are made along the way to spot birds or alligators, and for lessons on the park's hydrology, geology, vegetation and wildlife. Time is also allowed for climbing the observation tower to the 50-foot-high platform, which provides excellent views of the vast wetlands. Sightseers may also travel the tram road on foot or bicycles, which can be rented there. Admission. ~ Route 41, about 25 miles west of Florida's Turnpike; 305-221-8455, fax 305-221-4372.

Where Route 41 veers northwestward, you can head straight and take a scenic detour on **Route 94**, which meanders deep into cypress and pineland backcountry on its way out toward Pinecrest. This is called the "loop road," but even when it's passable, it can be a tight squeeze. Unless you have a four-wheel-drive vehicle, you would do best to turn back when the road begins to deteriorate (about eight miles in), near an interpretive center. ~ 239-695-1201.

HIDDEN ▶

Back on Route 41, slow down as you come up to the microscopic community of **Ochopee**, or you might miss "the smallest and most photographed post office in North America." You will know it by the American flag, the blue letter box, the sign that reads **Post Office, Ochopee, FL** and all the tour buses disgorging passengers so that they can go into the tiny frame building and get their postcards stamped. Closed Sunday. ~ 239-695-2099.

Soon you will enter **Big Cypress National Preserve**, 729,000 acres of subtropical Florida swampland vital to the preservation of the Everglades. To get an idea of Big Cypress' beauty and importance, stop at the **Big Cypress Visitors Center** and see the excellent audiovisual introduction to this crucial region. ~ Located 38 miles west of Route 997; 239-695-4111, 239-695-1201; www.nps.gov/bicy.

Big Cypress National Preserve exists to protect the watershed as well as the abundant wildlife living in the Everglades.

Serious nature lovers can contact **Dragonfly Expeditions, Inc.** for a six-hour backwater trek through Big Cypress Swamp. Field biologists and naturalist guides lead the watery way through the subtropical landscape, searching for wading birds, otters and alligators. The tour price includes transportation, water gear, guide services and gourmet lunch. ~ 1825 Ponce de Leon Boulevard #369, Coral Gables; 305-774-9019, 888-992-6337; www.dragonflyexpeditions.com.

At the privately owned **Eden of the Everglades** you can board a quiet jungle boat or airboat to observe some of the flora and fauna of the area in a natural setting. The service also operates an Everglades wildlife safari tram ride. Admission. ~ 611 Collier Avenue, Everglades City; 239-695-2800, fax 239-695-4506; www.edenoftheeverglades.com.

Head south on Route 29 to **Everglades City**, the western edge of Everglades National Park. You can stop at the **Everglades City Chamber of Commerce** to procure information about this little town and the neighboring region. ~ 32016 Tamiami Trail East, Everglades City; 239-695-3941, fax 239-695-3941; e-mail info@evergladeschamber.com.

Two thousand years of human habitation in the southwest Everglades are presented at the charming **Museum of the Everglades**. Housed in a restored 1927 laundry building that served Tamiami Trail construction workers, the museum covers Florida Indian and settler history, with an emphasis on Barron Collier's company town. Closed Sunday and Monday. ~ 105 West Broadway, Everglades City; 239-695-0008, fax 239-695-0036; www.colliermuseum.com, e-mail virginiasaalman@colliergov.net.

Continue south to the **Everglades National Park Visitors Center**. Here you can obtain information about the western regions of the park, including the **Ten Thousand Islands** area, the second-largest mangrove forest in the world. This is a popular starting point for the 99-mile wilderness waterway, and canoe or kayak rentals are readily available from a number of vendors. ~ Gulf Coast Ranger Station, Route 29, south of Everglades City; 239-695-3311, fax 239-695-3621; www.nps.gov/ever.

The privately run **Everglades National Park Boat Tours** cover portions of this territory on the Gulf of Mexico, informing visitors how the mangrove islands are formed and acquainting them with the resident wildlife, especially shore and wading birds like the roseate spoonbill. American bald eagles, gentle manatees and playful dolphins often reward the sharp-eyed explorer. Some of the tours take visitors through a dense mangrove swamp. ~ Ranger Station, Everglades City; 239-695-2591, 866-628-7275, fax 239-695-4279.

Nature trips by boat and kayak into the Ten Thousand Islands area are offered by **Chokoloskee Charters.** ~ P.O. Box 824, Chokoloskee Island, FL 34138; 239-695-9107, fax 239-695-9108; www.evergladeskayaks.com, e-mail captwright@chokoloskeecharters.com. **Chokoloskee Island Outfitters** offers nature and fishing trips. ~ P.O Box 460, Chokoloskee Island, FL 34138; phone/fax 239-695-2286; www.cyberangler.com.

HIDDEN ►   **Chokoloskee,** a small island filled with motor homes, cottages and little motels, is a popular spot for visitors wishing to fish the Ten Thousand Islands region. It also has the distinction of being built on a gigantic shell mound created by early Colusa Indians. ~ Route 29, across the causeway south of Everglades City.

At the southern end of Route 29, deep in the Everglades, sits the **Smallwood Store Ole Indian Trading Post and Museum.** Built on stilts above the brackish waters of the Everglades, Smallwood retains the authentic flavor it had when it was constructed in 1906. Placed on the National Register of Historic Places in 1974, this time capsule of Florida pioneer history uses artifacts, displays and exhibits to tell the story of the trading post and the settlers who tamed the Everglades. The gift shop sells cool Florida stuff. Admission. ~ Route 29, Chokoloskee; 239-695-2989, fax 239-695-4454.

After you leave the park's western area, you can travel seven miles north on Route 29 to get to **Fakahatchee Strand State Preserve,** the major drainage slough of the Big Cypress Swamp (see the "Parks" section below). You can walk the boardwalk through the tall, dense, swamp forest of royal palm and bald cypress and admire the many orchidlike air plants that are said to grow only here. From November through February rangers conduct week-

SWAMP STOP

If your trip takes you northwest from Everglades City to Naples (via Route 41) or due north to Immokalee (via Route 29), detour to **Corkscrew Swamp Sanctuary** for an excellent and easy foray into the Everglades. The National Audubon Society saved this 11,000-acre reserve from foresters in the 1950s; it now serves to protect endangered wood storks and other species. A two-and-a-quarter-mile-long loop trail leads through lakes of lettuce fern and a broad variety of Everglades ecosystems. Admission. ~ Sanctuary Road off Route 846; 239-348-9151, fax 239-348-9155.

end "wet" walks into the swamp to see other rare plant life. ~ 239-695-4593, fax 239-695-4947; www.floridastateparks.org.

Collier-Seminole State Park offers a good introduction to the vegetation and wildlife of the western Everglades (see the "Beaches & Parks" section). Besides interpretations of the natural world of rare Florida royal palms, tropical hammocks, cypress swamps, mangroves, salt marshes and pine woods, there is a replica of a blockhouse used in the Second Seminole War and a display of a "walking dredge" used to build the Tamiami Trail. Admission. ~ Route 41, 20 miles northwest of Everglades City; 239-394-3397, fax 239-394-5113.

When an Everglades excursion is planned, the traditional starting point is always Miami. But Naples, on Florida's west coast, is actually much closer—less than 20 miles in some cases—to wilderness areas. And your Everglades education can begin in Naples itself. Founded in 1960, **The Conservancy of Southwest Florida** is dedicated to conserving the area's native ecosystems. Along with programs designed to inform the public, it organizes guided boat trips and nature walks, and welcomes visitors to a wildlife rehabilitation center where injured eagles, owls, hawks and other native wildlife are nursed back to health. Closed Sunday from April to November. Admission. ~ 1450 Merrihue Drive, Naples; 239-262-0304, fax 239-262-0672; www.conservancy.org, e-mail info@conservancy.org.

Somewhat more commercial is the safari-type half- and full-day trip offered by **Everglades Excursions**, which transports you in an air-conditioned "Safari Wagon." An airboat ride and Jungle City boat cruise are part of their narrated nature tour through the saw grass prairies and mangrove wilderness. An Everglades luncheon with alligator nuggets and a visit to the Seminole Indian Village are included. If you've been burning to see a wrestling match where the 'gator takes a fall or to hold one of the scaly babies before its jaws become fearsome, this is your trip. ~ 1010 6th Avenue South, Naples; 239-262-1914, 800-592-0848, fax 239-262-6967; www.everglades-excursions.com.

LODGING

If you prefer to stay close to the western park area, try the **Captain's Table Lodge and Villas**. This large resort offers rooms and suites in its main lodge and one-bedroom villas, some featuring screened decks. There's a large pool and a boat ramp. Boat tours of the Ten Thousand Islands are available nearby. ~ Route 29, Everglades City; 239-695-4211, 800-741-6430, fax 239-695-2633. BUDGET TO MODERATE.

HIDDEN ▶

The **Rod and Gun Lodge,** is an 1864 hunting and fishing club that has been lovingly converted into an inn. You can sit on its airy screened porch or admire the mounted game fish and red cypress paneling of the massive old lobby. Or stay in the 17-room cottages on the grounds, swim in the screened-in pool, play tennis and feast on the large waterfront veranda. Complete docking facilities alongside attract some pretty impressive boats. The lodge is strictly nonsmoking, due to fire hazard. ~ 200 Riverside Drive, Everglades City; 239-695-2101. MODERATE.

Ivey House Bed and Breakfast offers three forms of accommodation on one site. The Ivey House Lodge is a shotgun-style residence built in 1928 with a large living room and library and ten twin- to queen-bedded rooms furnished in Southern pine. You can also rent a two-bedroom cottage with a bath, a kitchen and a screened porch. The Ivey House Inn offers 18 rooms, each with two queen beds and a small refrigerator. There are daily guided canoeing/kayaking and boating excursions; overnight trips are also offered. Complimentary bicycles are available for touring on your own. Non-smoking. The lodge and cottages are closed May through October. ~ 107 Camellia Street, Everglades City; 239-695-3299, fax 239-695-4155; www.iveyhouse.com; e-mail info@iveyhouse.com. BUDGET TO MODERATE.

The **Bank of the Everglades** is located on the site of a former bank (built in 1926), and is now listed on the National Register of Historic Places. Each of the seven guest rooms has a private bath and a full or mini kitchen, and the surrounding premises offer a parlor, library and sunning deck complete with parasol tables. A fresh, full breakfast is served each morning. ~ 201 West Broadway, Everglades City; 239-695-3151, fax 239-695-3335; www.banksoftheeverglades.com, e-mail claudia@banksoftheeverglades.com. MODERATE TO DELUXE.

If you are seeking the amenities of a full-service resort while exploring the western Everglades, try **Port of the Islands** about ten miles northwest of Everglades City. Residing on about 500 acres and surrounded by parklands, the resort offers deluxe-priced hotel rooms and ultra-deluxe-priced efficiencies. You can keep yourself busy with skeet and trapshooting, swimming, dining, spa and health club activities, and nature cruises and guided fishing trips into the Ten Thousand Islands. The freshwater river that flows through the grounds feeds a harbor that has been designated a manatee sanctuary. ~ 25000 Tamiami Trail East/Route 41, Naples; 239-394-3101, 866-348-3509, fax 239-394-4335; www.poiresort.com. DELUXE TO ULTRA-DELUXE.

The **Miccosukee Restaurant** is a typical roadside restaurant with fried-fish fare. But the local American Indians who own and operate this place add their own special dishes to the menu—good things such as pumpkin bread, chili and fry bread, Miccosukee burgers and tacos, and hushpuppies and Everglades-caught catfish. It's the best place to eat while traveling the Tamiami Trail. Breakfast and lunch only. ~ Route 41, Miccosukee Indian Village; 305-894-2374. BUDGET TO MODERATE.

DINING

◄ HIDDEN

Along with steak, chicken and the usual fried and broiled seafood, you can try grilled pompano and such delicacies as 'gator tail and lobster tail at the **Oyster House**. Ships' wheels and other nautical paraphernalia create a very pleasant, informal seaside atmosphere. ~ Route 29, Everglades City; 239-695-2073, fax 239-695-3423; www.oyster houserestaurant.com. MODERATE.

Never get closer than 15 feet to an alligator— they'll look like statues one minute, and move with lightning speed the next.

Based on the sign hanging on the building, you might accidentally call Everglades City's **City Seafood** the "Café Now Open." Actually, this wholesale/retail fish business also offers prepared food and outdoor wooden tables. Open mid-October to late April, it serves fried grouper sandwiches, soft-shell crabs, smoked mullet plates, and steamed blue crabs from nearby waters. Everything is homemade and à la carte, including delicious cole slaw, tartar sauce, mustard and potato salad. Don't miss the fresh-brewed iced tea. Sit along the Barron River, where the fishing boats are tied up and the manatees surface every few minutes. ~ 702 Begonia Street, Everglades City; 239-695-4700; www.city-seafood.com. BUDGET.

The menu at the **Rod and Gun Club**, like so many area eateries, features frogs' legs, stone crab claws and native fish in season, but the ambience is unlike any other in far South Florida. You may dine in the massive, dark, cypress-paneled dining hall of this once-elegant old hunting and fishing lodge or be seated on the large, airy veranda where you can have a splendid view of the yachts and other fine boats that dock a stone's throw away. The selection of seafood, steak and chicken is small but well prepared. ~ 200 River-side Drive, Everglades City; 239-695-2101. DELUXE.

Locals head to **Glades Haven Deli** for sandwiches, subs, burritos, ice cream and memorable Key lime pie. ~ Glades Haven RV Park, 801 South Copeland Avenue, Everglades City; 239-695-2746. BUDGET.

SHOPPING   Along with the usual souvenirs, you will find handcrafted baskets, beaded jewelry and the intricate, colorful patchwork clothing for which the Miccosukee Indian women are famous at the **Miccosukee Indian Village Gift Shop**. ~ Route 41, 25 miles west of Florida's Turnpike; 305-552-8365.

HIDDEN ►   If you've about given up on finding a souvenir of Florida that's truly Floridian and a work of art to boot, stop in at **Big Cypress Gallery**, where Clyde Butcher, photographer extraordinaire, produces and displays amazing black-and-white scenes of Florida, particularly its wetlands. Take home a wall-size limited-edition image, a poster or maybe even a T-shirt you might sooner frame than wear. The gallery's wilderness setting alone is worth the trip (45 miles west of the Turnpike and about 60 miles east of Naples) and mosquitos are not a problem in the summer. Closed Tuesday and Wednesday. ~ 52388 East Tamiami Trail, Ochopee; 239-695-2428; www.clydebutcher.com.

If you are a souvenir hound, stop at **Wooten's** and you'll never have to go anywhere else for those plastic flamingos and alligator heads. ~ Route 41, Ochopee; 239-695-2781.

PICK STOP

On your drive to the main entrance of Everglades National Park, you'll pass an old-fashioned, open-air produce stand known as **Robert Is Here**. Robert has fresh fruit such as mangos, lychees, monstera, tamarind and star fruit, and he has added sweet onions, cabbage, broccoli and cauliflower to the array. He serves up Key lime milkshakes and pies and sells an assortment of jellies and preserves. In addition, you may view his collection of animals, from emus to finches. Closed September through October. ~ 19200 Southwest 344th Street, Homestead; 305-246-1592; www.robertishere.com, e-mail fresh@robertishere.com.

One Everglades City resident explained, "We don't have much **NIGHTLIFE** nightlife here, and we like it that way!" So unless you can be contented with the dark, tropical night and the jungle sounds, you'll usually have to head up to Naples and beyond for bright lights.

Take the opportunity to carouse 24 hours a day at the American Indian–owned **Miccosukee Indian Gaming Casino**, which offers round-the-clock poker, slots, bingo and video games. Part of the Miccosukee Resort, the 67,000-square-foot gambling facility features restaurants, live entertainment and, of course, ATM access. ~ Krome Avenue and Tamiami Trail, 18 miles east of the Miccousukee Indian Village; 305-222-4600, 800-741-4600, fax 305-226-9254; www.miccosukee.com.

"The Glassroom" at the **Oyster House** is great for private parties. The main bar of this father-and-son establishment has sports trophies on the wall, a jukebox and a pool table, all beside an 80-foot observation tower—the highest in the Everglades. There is dancing to live bands on weekends seasonally. Closed June through August. ~ Route 29, Everglades City; 239-695-2073, fax 239-695-3423; www.oysterhouserestaurant.com.

SHARK VALLEY/EVERGLADES NATIONAL PARK 🚶🚴 This **PARKS** public access to the park features a 15-mile loop road that delves deep into the saw grass expanses of the Everglades. Because no private vehicles are allowed in this protected region, you must visit either on foot, by bicycle or via one of the open-sided trams. There's an \$10 per vehicle or \$5 per person (walk-in or bike-in) fee. During the winter (and depending on budget allowances), there are ranger-led bicycle and hiking trips, including the "slough slog" wet hike through the freshwater marsh. Facilities include restrooms, vending machines, a hiking and biking trail, and a nature trail; there are also bicycle rentals and tram rides (305-221-8455). ~ Located off Route 41, 25 miles west of Florida's Turnpike; 305-242-7700, fax 305-242-7711; www.nps.gov/ever, e-mail ever_information@nps.gov.

EVERGLADES CITY/EVERGLADES NATIONAL PARK 🚤 🛶 🚣 This entrance to the park allows access to the vast, ever-changing Ten Thousand Islands, a mangrove archipelago that serves as both a nesting grounds for birds and a nursery for sea life. There's excellent fishing here for snapper, redfish and sea trout. Sportfishing is the region's greatest drawing card, but visitors can also take guided boat tours to observe dolphins, manatees and birds, and to learn of the American Indians who once fished these waters and left their shell middens behind. The 99-mile Wilderness Waterway, popular with experienced canoeists, twists through marine and estuarine areas all the way to Flamingo at the tip of the state. Several area rivers offer shorter canoeing opportunities. Swimming is not recommended, except on certain island locations accessible only by boat. There's a visitors center, restrooms, concession stand, boat tours and canoe rentals. ~ The entrance is located on Route 29 off Route 41 at Everglades City; 239-695-3311, fax 239-695-3621; www.nps.gov/ever.

▲ There are 22 free primitive sites on the Gulf Coast. They are accessible by boat only and require a backcountry permit (fee during winter months).

BIG CYPRESS NATIONAL PRESERVE A 729,000-acre area of subtropical Florida known as Big Cypress Swamp makes up this preserve. Its establishment reflected a serious concern for the state's dwindling wetlands and watersheds, especially those affecting Everglades National Park. Established in 1974, this preserved wilderness area of wet and dry prairies, coastal plains, marshes, mangrove forests, sandy pine woods and mixed hardwood hammocks has few facilities for visitors. There are picnic tables at several roadside parks, restrooms at the visitors center, bike trails and a hiking trail. Anglers hook bass and gar. Off-road and all-terrain vehicles are allowed with a permit (fee). ~ The visitors center is on Route 41 between Shark Valley and Everglades City; 239-695-1204, fax 239-695-3493; www. nps.gov/bicy.

▲ There's primitive camping in the three campgrounds. All have sites that accommodate motor homes; however, there are no hookups or facilities. Monument Lake campground has water and flush toilets; $16 per night. A dump station is located at Dona Drive; free for campers, but $6 for all non-campers.

FAKAHATCHEE STRAND STATE PRESERVE This strand, the drainage slough for the Big Cypress Swamp, is the largest and most interesting of these natural channels cut by the flow of water into the limestone plain. The slough's tall, dense, swamp forest stands out on the horizon in contrast to the open terrain and saw grass plain around it. Its forest of royal palms, bald cypress trees and air plants is said to be unique on earth. Approximately 20 miles long and three to five miles wide, the preserve offers visitors views of some of its rare plant life, including numerous orchids. From November through February, rangers conduct "wet" walks every third Saturday of the month into the swamp to see other unusual and endangered plant life; reservations are required. The only facilities at the preserve are an interpretive trail and a boardwalk leading into the swamp. Canoeing is allowed south of Route 41, in East River only. ~ Route 29, six miles north of Everglades City. The Boardwalk is on Route 41, seven miles west of Route 29; 239-695-4593, fax 239-695-4947.

> Because so much of the terrain in the Everglades is submerged in water, it is wise to stick to the paths provided unless you go exploring with a park ranger.

COLLIER-SEMINOLE STATE PARK The wildlife and vegetation of this park are representative of the Everglades region with tropical hammocks, salt marshes, cypress swamps, mangroves and pine flatwoods. A number of endangered species, such as West Indian manatees, Florida black bears, crocodiles and Florida panthers, are protected, and sometimes spotted, in this rich and diverse region. On display are a "walking dredge" used to build the Tamiami Trail and a replica of a blockhouse from the Second Seminole War. A limited number of visitors each day are allowed to canoe into the park's pristine mangrove swamp wilderness preserve, a 13.5-mile trip. There's saltwater fishing for mangrove snapper, redfish and snook. Facilities include a picnic area, restrooms, a nature trail, hiking trails, canoe rentals, a boat ramp, a concession stand and an interpretive center. Day-use fee, $4. ~ Located about 20 miles northwest of Everglades City on Route 41; 239-394-3397, fax 239-394-5113.

Main Visitor Area

Early settlers came to Homestead to cultivate the rich land that was slowly "reclaimed" from the swampy Everglades. They planted and harvested vegetables and citrus and other tropical fruits suited to the far South Florida climate. Much of the area is still agricultural today, a winter fruit and vegetable basket that feeds people all across the country. The Homestead/Florida City area, which was hit harder by Hurricane Andrew than anywhere else in the state, is also a crossroads of sorts. Miami, to the north, is close enough that some of Homestead's street numbers are continuations of those in the big city, and crime is a problem from time to time. Head southeast and you are on your way to the Florida Keys. Due east is Biscayne National Park, a mostly underwater preserve of sea and reef and islands that are an upper continuation of the Keys but accessible only by boat. To the west is the main section of Everglades National Park where visitors can travel a 38-mile road all the way to Florida Bay and experience the many wonders of this exotic landscape.

SIGHTS

For information on this area, you might begin at the very fine **Tropical Everglades Visitors Association** in Florida City. Here you can obtain information seven days a week about the main public portion of Everglades National Park as well as a number of other places to see and things to do in the Florida City/Homestead and Florida Keys areas. ~ 160 Route 1, Florida City; 305-245-9180, 800-388-9669, fax 305-247-4335; www.tropicaleverglades.com, e-mail tevisitor@cs.com.

Everglades, The Story Behind the Scenery, by Jack de Golia is a beautifully illustrated, reasonably priced book that introduces many of the Everglades' hidden treasures. You can find it in most area bookstores and gift shops.

There is a lot to be seen off the Atlantic coast east of Florida City in **Biscayne National Park**, most of it underwater (see the "Parks" section below). But even if you are not a snorkeler or scuba diver, you can get an excellent view of the nearby coral reef from the **glass-bottom boat** that departs from the Dante Fascell Visitor Center at Convoy Point. Daily trips to the reef, with occasional island cruises in the winter, are offered by **Biscayne National Underwater Park Tours Inc.** Reservations are required. ~ Biscayne National Park Headquarters, end of 328th Street, east of Florida City; 305-230-1100 (tours), 305-230-1144 (park), fax 305-230-1120 (tours); www.nps.gov/bisc, e-mail bisc_information@nps.gov.

Florida City is the hub of the most southern farming area in the continental United States. A drive northward on Krome Avenue or along any side road in the area will take you through vast truck gardens where you may see—and even pick from—great fields of tomatoes, corn, strawberries, okra, peppers and other fruits and vegetables. Large areas are also devoted to avocados, limes, mangos and papayas.

You can get an idea of how the early settlers lived in this fertile, challenging region between the eastern edge of the Everglades

Main Visitor Area

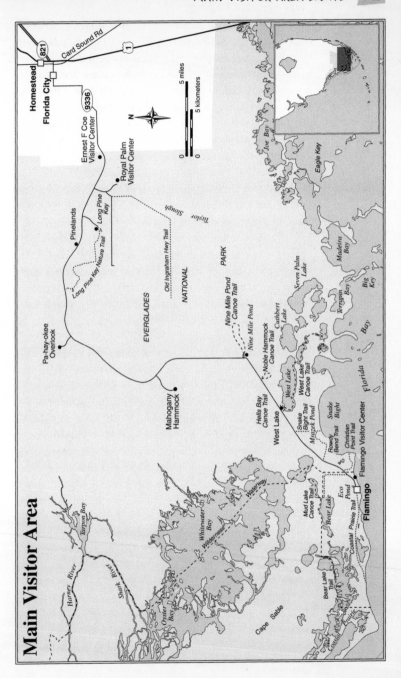

HIDDEN ▶ and the sea by visiting the **Florida Pioneer Museum**. The down-home collection consists mainly of fine old photographs and items from Florida family attics, and is housed in a caboose—a reconstructed railway station and an agent's house left over from the days of Henry Flagler's "railroad that went to the sea." Call for hours. Admission. ~ 826 North Krome Avenue, Florida City; 305-246-9531.

A Syrian brown bear in the Everglades? That's right. There are also bison, a tiger, several binterong, and myriad other exotic species that have been given refuge alongside Florida animals at HIDDEN ▶ the **Everglades Outpost**, a non-profit organization dedicated to wildlife and exotic animal rescue and rehabilitation. This unusual facility began when its founders took up the cause for exotic animals used for commercial purposes such as television advertisements and then abandoned, mistreated or abused. Its mission has expanded to include Florida wildlife conservation, rehabilitation and release, and an education program. Day membership available. ~ 35601 Southwest 192nd Avenue, Florida City; 305-247-8000, fax 305-247-0500; www.peaceday.org; e-mail evergladesrefuge@aol.com.

The **Coral Castle** is a strange place; some claim it's almost mystical. According to legend, this curious limestone mansion was built between 1923 and 1940 because of an unrequited love. Its creator, a Latvian immigrant, claimed to know the secret of the construction of the pyramids. Perhaps he did, for he was able to move multi-ton pieces of local coral rock to the site and construct towers, massive stone furnishings, a nine-ton gate that swings open to the touch, a 5000-pound valentine heart and other strange symbols of devotion to his mysterious lost love. Supposedly, no one has ever figured out the builder's secret, but you can go and give it a try, and marvel at this historic curiosity. Take the 35-minute self-guided audio tour in English, Spanish, French or German. Admission. ~ 28655 Route 1 (South Dixie Highway), Homestead; 305-248-6345, fax 305-248-6344; www.coralcastle.com, e-mail info@coralcastle.com.

North of Homestead, the **Preston B. Bird & Mary Heinlein Fruit & Spice Park** is a 35-acre random grove planted with over 500 exotic and subtropical varieties of fruit, spices and herbs from around the world. Visitors are invited to stop by the gift shop and stroll among the banana, lychee, mango, starfruit and other tropical trees. Admission. ~ 24801 Southwest 187th Avenue, Homestead; 305-247-5727, fax 305-245-3369; www.miamidade.gov, e-mail fsp@miamidade.gov.

EVERGLADES NATIONAL PARK   South of Homestead, the cultivation suddenly stops—and Everglades National Park begins, almost like a boundary of uneasy truce between man and nature. You quickly forget that Miami is just up the road a piece or that tended gardens lie behind you. Before you lies the mysterious world of what some call "the real Florida," the home of the alligator, the panther, the royal palm and the endangered bald eagle.

There are a number of ways to tackle this area of the park. For help in designing your plan, stop at the **Ernest F. Coe Visitor Center**. Here park staff members will provide you with all sorts of helpful information, including weather, trail and insect conditions and listings of the season's varied and informative ranger-guided tours. A fine audiovisual presentation and a wide assortment of books provide good introductions to the area. All visitors centers in the park are wheelchair accessible. ~ 40001 State Road 9336, ten miles southwest of Homestead; 305-242-7700, fax 305-242-7711; www.nps.gov/ever, e-mail ever_information@nps.gov.

> Believe it or not, the Everglades is really a river running 50 miles wide and a few inches deep. A close look into the tall saw grass reveals the area's true nature.

Once you have paid your admission and entered the park, you are on the single park road that will eventually arrive at **Flamingo**, 38 miles away, at the tip of the state on the edge of Florida Bay. This winding, lonely road traverses the heart of the park, meandering among tall pines, through seemingly endless expanses of saw grass prairie and alongside mysterious dark ponds. Off this road lie a number of paths, trails, boardwalks and waterways designed to give the visitor as wide an Everglades experience as possible. Some of the trails require only short strolls of half a mile or less, but they reward with close-up views of a great range of environments and inhabitants.

About two miles into the park (or two miles to the left at the turnoff), watch for signs to the **Royal Palm Visitor Center** on your left. Even if you have already spent a good amount of time at the main center, you should take a stroll down each of the two half-mile trails that begin here. Close together but very different,

Text continued on page 68.

Alligators
and Crocodiles

Stroll the boardwalk of Anhinga Trail, take the loop tour in Shark Valley or explore many of the other paths in the Everglades National Park and you will be certain to see the area's chief resident, the American alligator. Like dark, greenish-black, lifeless logs, they often lie basking motionless on the sunny banks of water holes or glide through ponds and sloughs with only their nostrils and eyes breaking the surface.

Once hunted for the stylish shoes, boots, luggage and pocketbooks produced from their tough hides, or for the slightly chewy, chicken-flavored tail meat, alligators are a now a success story of preservation. Classified as endangered and protected by law for several decades, their once perilously low population has recovered so well that alligators are once again a common sight in the Everglades. They appear in many other parts of Florida as well, occasionally to the distress of nearby human residents. While human encroachment still takes its toll on this ancient creature, the comeback has been so dramatic that the alligator has been reclassified from endangered to threatened.

The American crocodile has not been so fortunate. Only about 500 are believed to remain in Florida, and they are rarely seen. However, the sign along Route 1 on the way to Key Largo warning "Crocodile Crossing" can be believed. Regular drivers of this road claim to have occasionally spotted the reptiles, who make their homes in this marshy region. Lighter in color than alligators, crocodiles possess narrower, more pointed snouts than their cousins. They can also be identified by a long lower fourth tooth that protrudes impressively when the jaw is closed. Occasionally growing to lengths of 12 feet, they are considered to be more aggressive than alligators.

But one should not be misled by the seeming docility of the Everglades alligator. An active predator, the alligator roams freely in search of food and will eat anything from turtles to wading birds to unlucky mammals trespassing on its territory. Females build impressive nests, piling up mud and grass and debris to as high as six or eight feet. Here they lay their eggs, which heat from the sun and decaying mulch will hatch after about nine weeks. The alligator is a good mother, staying nearby so she can care for her young as soon as the eggs hatch. Male alligators can measure up to 14 feet in length, though most adults average between six and ten feet.

Of particular importance is the alligator's role as the "Keeper of the Everglades." Getting ready for the region's annual dry season, the alligator prepares its own water reservoirs by cleaning out large solution holes, dissolved cavities in the limestone bed of the Everglades. As the rains decrease, these "'gator holes" become important oases for all manner of wildlife. Fish, snails, turtles and other freshwater creatures seek refuge in the pools. Here many will survive until the rains return, when they will leave to repopulate the Everglades. Others will serve as food and sustenance for resident mammals and birds, as well as for the accommodating, future-thinking alligator. This role has made the alligator's comeback particularly important to the continuing life cycles of the Everglades.

While alligators are generally not considered dangerous to humans, warnings for avoiding close contact should be taken seriously. Tragic accidents do happen from time to time, particularly when people carelessly trespass on an alligator's territory. These reptiles are known to be especially aggressive during the spring breeding season, and mothers remain protective of their young for quite some time.

But alligators are certainly the chief attraction of the Everglades, and the national park has designed a number of excellent observation points in a variety of habitats. Alligators also reside at **Blue Hole** on Big Pine Key in the lower Florida Keys. ~ Key Deer Boulevard, two and a quarter miles north of Route 1.

Crocodile and alligator ancestry reaches back millions and millions of years. The Everglades is the only habitat in the world where alligators and crocodiles live side by side. Viewing them, one is looking back into another time. Though their surroundings may have changed greatly, these creatures and their habits and habitats have not.

each plunges into a distinctive Everglades environment. Interpretive signs help you notice things you might otherwise miss, such as how the strangler fig got its name or why alligators are so vital to the survival of the region. Ranger-led walks are offered here year-round. Most trails are wheelchair accessible.

That bird standing with outstretched wings is the anhinga. It needs to dry out after diving for fish, since its feathers have no natural oils.

The **Anhinga Trail** (0.5 mile) travels a boardwalk across Taylor Slough, a marshy pool that attracts winter birds and other wildlife that assemble with apparent unconcern for the season's thousands of visitors with cameras and zoom lenses. This is a perfect spot for viewing alligators and numerous water birds, including anhingas. Here, too, you can gaze across broad vistas of saw grass prairie.

Nearby, the **Gumbo-Limbo Trail** (0.5 mile) leads through a jungly tropical hardwood hammock rich in gumbo-limbo, strangler fig, wild coffee, royal palms and other tropical trees as well as numerous orchids and ferns. Air plants and butterflies often add to the beauty of this spot; interpretive signs help visitors get acquainted with the tropical flora that appears again and again throughout the park.

About six miles from the main entrance, the half-mile **Pinelands Trail** is a mile beyond the Long Pine Key campground; it circles through a section of slash pine forest. Here the ground is dry; occasional fires keep undergrowth in check so the pines can thrive without competition. This is a good place to get a look at the rock and solution holes formed in the shallow bed of limestone that lies under South Florida. Or just to picnic beside a quiet lake. For a view of pinelands closer to the park road, stop at the Pinelands sign about a mile farther on.

As you continue down the park road and gaze across the saw grass prairie, you'll notice stands of stunted trees that, during winter, appear dead or dying, since they are hung with moss from ghostlike grey branches. These are bald cypress, which thrive in watery terrain but remain dwarfed due to the peculiar conditions of the Everglades. In spring they put out lovely green needles. Some, though dwarfed, have been growing here for over a century.

About six miles beyond the Pinelands, you come to the **Pa-hay-okee Overlook** (0.25 mile), named for the American Indian word for Everglades, meaning "grassy waters." Walk the short boardwalk and climb the observation tower for a wonderful panorama of the saw grass prairie dotted with collections of ancient dwarf cypress and small island hammocks of hardwoods. This is one of the best overviews in the park; it's a great place for birdwatching.

Park rangers refer to hammocks as the "bedrooms of the Everglades," the places where so many wild creatures, large and small, find dry ground and shade from the tropical sun. About seven miles from Pa-hay-okee, you can explore one of these magnificent "highlands" that thrive just above the waterlines. The half-mile **Mahogany Hammock Trail** enters the cool, dark, jungly environment of a typical hardwood hammock, where there are rare paurotis palms and large mahogany trees, including one said to be the largest mahogany in the United States. Look and listen closely— barred owls, golden orb spiders, colorful Liguus tree snails and many other creatures make their homes in this humid "bedroom."

From Mahogany Hammock the park road heads due south through stands of pine and cypress and across more saw grass prairie. You are now nearing the coast and will begin to see the first mangrove trees, evidence of the mixing of saltwater from Florida Bay with the freshwater that flows from the north. You will pass several canoe-access spots along the road here, including the one at West Lake, about 11 miles from Mahogany Hammock.

Stop at the **West Lake Trail** for a good close-up look at mangroves. You can walk among the three varieties that thrive here along the half-mile boardwalk trail. With practice you will be able to identify them all—the predominant red mangroves with their arched, spidery prop roofs, black mangroves sending up fingerlike breathing tubes called "pneumatophores" from the mud and white mangroves and buttonwood on the higher, dryer shores of the swampy areas. The West Lake shoreline is one of many important spawning grounds for fish and shellfish that in turn attract raccoons and other wildlife who come to feed. You may see a gourmet diner or two if you walk quietly and keep your eyes open.

As you near the end of the park road, you will pass **Mrazek Pond**, another lovely birdwatching spot, especially rewarding during the winter months. Roseate spoonbills, along with many other common and exotic waterfowl, often come to this quiet, glassy pond to feed.

The road ends at the **Flamingo Visitor Center**, where a remote fishing village once stood. Early settlers could reach the area only by boat, and along with fishing, farming, the making of charcoal and all sorts of other activity—legal and not—went on here. (At some point during its existence, enterprising residents of the area that is now the visitor center produced moonshine whiskey and gathered bird plumes for ladies fashionwear.) The town is gone now, replaced by a marina, concessions, a motel and cabins, a campground, a gift shop and a visitor center. At Flamingo you can select from a variety of sightseeing opportunities, such as ranger-guided walks, wilderness canoe trips and hands-on activities. Offerings vary with the seasons; check at the visitor center for a schedule. ~ Located 38 miles from the main entrance; 239-695-2945, fax 239-695-3854; www.nps.gov/ever.

Sightseeing by boat is particularly enjoyable. Most boat tours in this region, including some backcountry explorations, are available year-round. Sunset cruises are a delight, offering views of spectacular skies as well as allowing close-ups of a wide variety of birds winging their way to shore. In winter, pelicans ride the gentle waves, and gulls soar up and around the boat. Some boat trips will take you to **Cape Sable**, the farthest-out point of southwestern Florida, where the Gulf of Mexico laps a broad, sandy beach.

For more birdwatching, especially in winter, take a short stroll from the visitors center to nearby **Eco Pond**. At dusk you may see ibis, egrets and other water birds winging in for the night to nest in nearby trees.

For more information on exploring other regions of the park's main visitor area, see the "Canoeing & Kayaking" section in "Outdoor Adventures."

LODGING   The usual chain motels line Route 1 in Homestead and Florida City. If you're looking for less expensive lodgings, head into the downtown areas where you'll find rows of mom-and-pop motels along Krome Avenue. The **Super 8 Motel** is near several restaurants and offers plain but clean and roomy units. A swimming pool, coconut palms and other tropical plants set this one somewhat apart. ~ 1202 North Krome Avenue, Florida City; 305-245-0311, 800-800-8000, fax 305-247-9136; www.super8.com. BUDGET.

The **Hampton Inn** offers comfortable accommodations within easy reach of both Biscayne and Everglades national parks. The 123-unit facility is clean and modern, and has the obligatory swimming pool. A rarity for chain hotels, there's no charge for the breakfast bar or calls within the continental U.S. ~ 124 East Palm Drive, Florida City; 305-247-8833, 800-426-7866, fax 305-247-6456; www.hamptoninnfloridacity.com, e-mail fcmia@hcifl.com. MODERATE.

To really experience the Everglades, stay at least a couple of nights in the **Flamingo Lodge**. This, the only accommodation in the park, is a plain old motel with window air conditioners and jalousies that can be opened to let in the intriguing watery smells of the 'glades and the shallow bay. Far from city lights and surrounded by jungle sounds, Flamingo Lodge lies in the heart of the Everglades. Flamingo also offers rustic cottages with fully equipped kitchens. Park entrance fee of $10 is not included in the rates. ~ State Route 9336, in the Everglades National Park; 239-695-3101, 800-600-3813, fax 239-695-3921; www.flamingolodge.com, e-mail info-flamingo@xanterra.com. MODERATE TO DELUXE.

DINING

There is only one restaurant in Everglades National Park, but there are a variety of eating places in Homestead. Mexicans make up a substantial portion of this agricultural area's labor force. Thus, Homestead supports several Mexican restaurants, including some that aren't particularly tourist-friendly.

El Toro Taco, however, bustles with a mixed clientele. Tops with dining critics, this is a noisy, happy place. Decorated with terra-cotta tile, fake adobe and huge windows, El Toro Taco

AUTHOR FAVORITE

The super-inexpensive **Everglades Hostel and Tours** was an Old Florida boardinghouse in the 1930s. Ideally located ten miles from both Everglades and Biscayne national parks, the hostel is walking distance from restaurants and a supermarket. Clean and cozy rooms are available as private or communal accommodations, with kitchen privileges. The owners live on the premises, which include cute and funky grounds, a gazebo, a movie room, internet access and a coin laundry. Kayaking, biking, canoeing and camping gear are available for rent. You can go one step further and opt for an intensive Everglades trek via the hostel. Trips range from one to eleven days. Air conditioning is available only during summer. ~ 20 Southwest 2nd Avenue, Florida City; 305-248-1122, 800-372-3874, fax 305-245-7622; www.evergladeshostel.com, e-mail gladeshostel@hotmail.com. BUDGET.

serves up terrific *carne guisada* (an authentic beef-and-potato stew), *mole de pollo*, and *menudo* (tripe soup with lime and onion). Tacos, enchiladas and fajitas should sate the less adventurous. Try the spicy breakfasts. ~ 1 South Krome Avenue, Homestead; 305-245-8182. BUDGET TO MODERATE.

The Mexican fare at the light and airy **Casita Tejas** includes such Tex-Mex favorites as fajitas and chimichangas but also features genuine south-of-the-border dishes like *carne guisada* (spicy stewed beef and potatoes) and shrimp à la Mexicana (grilled shrimp with tomatoes, jalapeños and onions). The setting is fun and cheery, styled with wooden tables and floors and woven blankets. ~ 27 North Krome Avenue, Homestead; 305-248-8224. MODERATE.

Though ultimately rural and a bit rough around the edges, Homestead has developed something of a tearoom culture in recent years. Locals, especially seniors, love lunching at a tearoom and then antiquing in downtown Homestead. The most popular place for tea and lunch is **White Lion Cafe**, folksy, friendly, and cluttered with pewter, baskets and other finds. Diners settle into well-worn wood booths for sandwiches like the "june buggy," with roast beef, horseradish and green olives. At night, there's music by Katie P. Jones on the piano and "Blue Plate Specials." Closed Sunday and Monday. ~ 146 Northwest 7th Street, Homestead; 305-248-1076, fax 305-248-3451. MODERATE TO DELUXE.

Tiffany's Cottage Dining offers more traditional tea fare: lots of crisp, cold salads, soups and quiche. They serve Sunday brunch as well; if you're hungry, order the scrambled egg on country biscuit. For dinner, there's Continental-inspired dishes like seafood ravioli and chicken *cordon bleu*. Tiffany's has lots of pink—pink lace, pink roses of silk, real pink carnations on deeply pink tablecloths. After lunch, everyone wanders into the adjacent boutiques filled with "Enchantables, Country to Victorian." No dinner Sunday through Wednesday. ~ 22 Northeast 15th Street, Homestead; 305-246-0022. MODERATE.

Although it's the only place to dine in Everglades National Park, the **Flamingo Lodge Restaurant** is surprisingly good. The small but satisfactory menu features chicken, seafood and beef dishes. Located on the second floor of a small complex, the multilevel restaurant presents pretty views of Florida Bay. Tropical plants within and the dark night without remind you that while the menu is routine, the setting is quite exotic. Closed mid-April through October. ~ State Route 9336, in Everglades National Park; 239-695-3101, fax 239-695-3921; www.flamingolodge. com, e-mail dine-flamingo@xanterra.com. MODERATE.

Cauley Square has a Miami address, but Homestead claims it, **SHOPPING** too. This restored area of historic homes and buildings encompasses a variety of shops, including a shop selling African and Haitian art, and the Cauley Square Tearoom. ~ 22400 Old Dixie Highway, Miami; 305-258-3543; www.cauleysquareshops.com.

The **Redland Fruit & Spice Park Gift Shop** is located on the grounds of the Preston B. Bird & Mary Heinlein Fruit & Spice Park. Here you can browse among shelves of imported and domestic dried and canned exotic fruits, unusual spices and seeds, and out-of-the-ordinary juices, jellies and jams. There's a good selection of cookbooks and reference books on tropical fruits. Admission to the park. ~ 24801 Southwest 187th Avenue, Homestead; 305-247-5727; www.miami dade.gov, e-mail fsp@miamidade.gov.

> Naturalist and artist John James Audubon noted that during his trip to the Everglades flocks of birds "appeared in such numbers to actually block out the sun for some time."

The **Knaus Berry Farm** is owned and operated by a family of German Baptists who make delicious sticky buns. You can also buy spectacular berries in season here, along with guava, strawberry and other homemade jams to eat on the bakery's mouthwatering breads. Closed May through November. ~ 15980 Southwest 248th Street, five miles northeast of Homestead; 305-247-0668.

While the **Gift Shop at Flamingo Lodge** has lots of the usual Florida souvenirs, they also have some interesting books on the Everglades along with high-quality shirts. Closed mid-April through October. ~ 1 Flamingo Lodge Highway, in Everglades National Park; 239-695-3101.

In Homestead and Florida City, there is an assortment of roadside **NIGHTLIFE** taverns, and some of the motels keep their lounges open and provide occasional entertainment for late-night socializers. But most folks will tell you that the sidewalks roll up early around here.

If you spend any nights in Flamingo, deep in the Everglades, take time to walk outside (providing it's not mosquito time) away from the lights of the lodge and marina. On a moonless night, you'll experience a darkness that is ultimate and hear sounds made nowhere else in the United States as the subtropical jungle creatures begin their night-long serenades.

PARKS   **BISCAYNE NATIONAL PARK** 🏃 ⛵ 🎣 ⚓ 🚤 This 173,500-acre marine park is the largest of its kind in the National Park system, but much of it is hidden from the average traveler since it lies beneath the waters of Biscayne Bay and the Atlantic Ocean. The park includes a narrow remnant of mangrove shoreline, most of the bay's southern reaches, a line of narrow islands of the northern Florida Keys and the northern part of the Florida Keys coral reef tract. Brown pelicans, little blue herons, snowy egrets and a few tropical fish can be seen by even the most casual stroller from the mainland jetty, but to fully appreciate the beauty of this unusual park you should take a glass-bottom boat tour or go snorkeling or scuba diving around the colorful reef. The park may also be explored by canoe. The mangrove-fringed keys allow discovery of such tropical flora as gumbo-limbo trees, strangler fig and devil's potato. Birdlife abounds.

Look for marsh rabbits, river otters and red-bellied turtles on your forays through the Everglades back-country.

This park features excellent saltwater fishing in open waters; fishing, however, is prohibited in harbors. Lobster may be taken east of the islands in season. A Florida State saltwater fishing license is required for most anglers. Swimming is not recommended except on the tiny beaches of Elliott and Sands keys, where care must be taken to avoid sharp coral rock and spiny sea urchins. Picnic areas, restrooms, canoe rentals and boat tours can be found here. ~ Park headquarters are at Convoy Point, nine miles east of Homestead. The rest of the park is accessible by boat; 305-230-7275, fax 305-230-1190; www.nps.gov/bisc, e-mail bisc_information@nps.gov.

▲ Tent camping is allowed on Elliott and Boca Chita keys in about 30 sites, boat access only; $15 per night docking fee or $10 per night for camping only. Prepare for mosquitos and other biting insects.

HOMESTEAD BAYFRONT PARK 🚲 ⛵ 🚤 This is a next-door neighbor to the mainland part of Biscayne National Park (see above). It's a very popular spot enhanced by a small manmade beach, grassy areas and some shade offered by pines and palms. Entrance to the park is through a dense grove of mangroves, allowing a close look at these amazing island-building trees. There's good shore fishing for snapper. Swimming is pleasant and facilities include picnic areas, a playground, restrooms, showers and a marina. Day-use fee, $4 per vehicle. ~ Follow signs at Biscayne National Park (see above); 305-230-3034, fax 305-230-3032.

EVERGLADES NATIONAL PARK With an area of 1.5 million acres, this protected section of Florida's Everglades covers the southwestern end of the state and a vast section of shallow Florida Bay dotted with tiny keys. There is no other park like it in the world. Geologically and climatically unique, the Everglades is a 50-mile-wide subtropical "river of grass" flowing almost imperceptibly from Lake Okeechobee to the sea. To fully appreciate it, one needs to spend time here, for it does not overwhelm with spectacular scenery. Rather, its gently waving grasses dotted with stunted bald cypress, its clear ponds, its hardwood hammocks and pinelands are home to plant and animal life native to both the Caribbean Islands and the temperate United States. Inhabitants such as roseate spoonbills, wood storks, crocodiles and alligators, green sea turtles, southern bald eagles and manatees can be discovered by walking the trails, canoeing the waters and exploring with park rangers. Fishing is excellent in inland waters, especially for largemouth bass, and in coastal waters for snook, snapper, redfish and trout. Swimming is not recommended except on certain island locations accessible only by boat. Winter is the most comfortable time to visit, unless one is well-equipped to do battle with mosquitos. Facilities in Flamingo, the most developed area, include a campground, picnic areas, restrooms, a seasonal restaurant, a motel with cabins, a grocery, a marina, interpretive trails, boat tours and boat rentals, a pool for motel guests and canoe and bike rentals. In Shark Valley there are restrooms, hiking and biking trails, bicycle rentals and tram rides. In Everglades City you will find restrooms, a visitors center, boat tours and canoe rentals. Food is always available at the marina store in Flamingo. Some of the facilities are closed from May 1 to October 31.

There are three main accesses to Everglades National Park. On the northern boundary, Shark Valley (305-221-8776) is a day-use area; the entrance is off Route 41, 35 miles west of downtown Miami. Everglades City (239-695-3311), on the western side, offers access to the Ten Thousand Islands region; the entrance is on Route 29 off Route 41. The main park area (305-

242-7700, fax 305-242-7711; www.nps.gov/ever, e-mail ever_
information@nps.gov) for visitors encompasses the southern tip
of the Florida mainland; the entrance is off Route 9336, ten miles
southwest of Florida City.

▲ There are two main campgrounds inside the park: Long
Pine Key and Flamingo; $14 per night. There are no hookups.
There are five group camping sites at Long Pine Key, four at
Flamingo; $28 per night. From June through August, fees are not
charged. Wilderness camping is allowed, with a permit, in the
main area and Everglades City area; $10 for the permit, $2 per
person per night, November through May. There are also many
privately owned campgrounds throughout the park. For reservations from November to mid-April, call 800-365-2267, up to
five months in advance.

Outdoor Adventures

▼▼▼▼▼▼▼▼▼▼▼▼▼▼

Tarpon, snook, redfish and trout are the four
most popular fish that charter captains will
help you locate in the western Everglades and

SPORT-FISHING

Ten Thousand Islands region. **Rod and Gun Lodge** will take you
on a full- or half-day trip into the Ten Thousand Island backcountry with a private guide. Box lunches can be prepared upon
request at the lodge. ~ Everglades City; 239-695-2101; www.
boat-charters.com/rodgun.htm. About 40 miles south of Naples,
Captain Dave operates **Chokoloskee Island Outfitters**, taking up
to three people out into the Everglades after the elusive snook
and tarpon. ~ Chokoloskee; 239-695-2286.

DIVING

For scuba and snorkeling trips via glass-bottom boat to little-
traveled, beautiful outer reefs and the patch reefs closer to shore,
contact the **Biscayne National Underwater Park, Inc.** Their dives
focus mainly on the reef, including advance-level dives to the
Wall, a vertical cut ledge that drops from 65 to 110 feet and is
decorated with combs of black coral and sponges up to six feet
in diameter. ~ Convoy Point, in the Dante Fascell Visitor Center
building; 305-230-1100; www.nps.gov.bisc.

BOATING

Based in Everglades City, **North American Canoe Tours** offers
three excellent guided boating adventures in addition to renting
canoes, kayaks and bicycles for the day or extended trips. Try the
backcountry paddling adventure with a nature guide. It runs from

9 a.m. to 3 p.m., includes lunch, and explores places like the brackish environments of Half Way Creek, Turner Lake and low mangrove tunnels. Trips can be customized to include hiking. ~ 107 Camelia Street, Everglades City; 239-695-3299; www.everglades adventures.com.

To explore the shoreline of Biscayne National Park by canoe, **CANOEING** contact the **Biscayne National Underwater Park, Inc.** ~ Convoy **& KAYAKING** Point, east of Homestead; 305-230-1100; www.nps.gov/bisc. For kayak and canoe rentals, outfitting and guided trips in the northwestern Everglades, try **North American Canoe Tours**. Closed August through October. ~ Ivey House Bed and Breakfast, 107 Camellia Street, Everglades City; 239-695-3299; www.ivey house.com. You can canoe the streams and ponds of the southern Everglades with **Flamingo Marina**. ~ State Route 9336, Flamingo; 239-695-3101.

Narrated boat tours exploring the mangrove estuary and Florida Bay depart daily from the Flamingo Marina. Call for schedule and ticket information. ~ 239-695-3101.

A limited number of canoes are allowed (and may be rented) each day for exploration of the **Collier-Seminole State Park**. ~ Route 41, 20 miles northwest of Everglades City; 941-394-3397, fax 941-394-5113.

Following are a number of popular canoe trails in Everglades National Park.

Tamiami Trail Area   **Wilderness Waterway** (99 miles) extends through a well-marked mangrove forest in the Ten Thousand Islands region of the national park. The entire trip can take from several days to a week. Backcountry permits are required, and arrangements must be made in advance for pickup and canoe transport.

Main Visitor Area   All Flamingo canoe trails are accessible from the main park road. Check with rangers before you set out, as varying water levels may close portions of some trails in dry seasons. The park provides maps and guides for canoe trails. Many of these trails prohibit motorized vehicles.

Nine Mile Pond Trail (5.2 miles) travels through a shallow saw grass marsh and past islands of mangroves. It is the best summer trail in the park.

Noble Hammock Trail (2-mile loop) was once used by bootleggers, whose old "cutting" markers are still on the trees. This trail meanders across open country and small alligator ponds through buttonwood, red mangrove and saw grass.

Hells Bay Trail (5.5 miles) travels through overgrown passageways of red mangrove and brackish water environments. A backcountry permit is recommended for this trip, even when not camping. There are campsites at the four- and eight-mile points.

West Lake Trail (8 miles) includes a long exposed crossing of the lake as well as a meandering trail through coastal lake country bordered by red and black mangrove and buttonwood trees and through the remains of a once-great living forest destroyed by hurricanes. Alligators and fish are numerous.

Mud Lake Trail (6.8 miles) crosses shallow Mud Lake, which has a prairie, mangrove and buttonwood shoreline, making it good for birdwatching. The trip continues to Coot Bay through what may have once been a Calusa Indian canal and returns via the Buttonwood Canal.

Canoeing is also possible in **Florida Bay**, depending on wind and weather conditions. There is good birding in the shallows; during the dry months, the bay is the only realistic way to reach the beach at Cape Sable. But be sure to check with rangers on tides and weather conditions before setting out. It's a hefty jaunt to the beautiful but isolated sandy beach area, and sudden winds could make the return trip very difficult.

HOUSE-BOATING

To go houseboating in the southernmost Everglades and back country, contact **Flamingo Lodge and Marina,** which has three-pontoons that sleep eight. There's a two-night minimum. Limited availability from mid-April through October. ~ Flamingo; 239-695-3101, 800-600-3813; www.flamingolodge.com.

GOLF

At Homestead, try the **Redland Golf & Country Club**. ~ 24451 Southwest 177th Avenue; 305-247-8503.

BIKING

You can bike the paved roads of the visitor areas in Everglades National Park; the only specific bikeway is the 15-mile loop road at Shark Valley, which is shared with hikers and the sightseeing tram.

Bike Rentals   Bicycles for exploring the **Shark Valley** day-use area of Everglades National Park can be rented at **Shark Valley Tram Tours**. ~ Route 41, about 25 miles west of Florida's Turnpike; 305-221-8455.

There are some intriguing trails into the Everglades suitable for
both novice strollers and serious explorers. All distances for hiking trails are one way unless otherwise noted.

EVERGLADES AREA   Shark Valley Trail (15-mile loop) in Everglades National Park leads hikers and bikers across a saw grass
waterway where they are sure to see alligators and a wide assortment of birds such as snail kites, wood storks and ibis. They may
also observe deer, turtles, snakes and otters. About half way is an
observation tower that offers a good overview of the "river of
grass." Because of a lack of shade and few facilities along this
single-lane, paved walkway, only well-equipped, hardy hikers
should attempt the entire loop. A short nature trail is located
near the entrance to Shark Valley.

Florida National Scenic Trail (South Section) (33 miles) is a
trail that begins at the Big Cypress Visitor Center on Route 41
west of Shark Valley. This wilderness trail, for experienced hikers
only, plunges deep into the Big Cypress Swamp (the trail is usually under water from May to November), which is actually a
vast region of sandy pine islands, mixed hardwood hammocks,
wet and dry prairies and mysterious marshes. Stunted bald cypress stand amid the grasses; wildlife is abundant. Bring your
own drinking water.

Collier-Seminole State Park Hiking Trail (6.5 miles) explores
a section of the northwestern edge of the Florida Everglades. This
low-lying trail winds through pine flatwoods and cypress swamps
where you can observe a variety of plants and wildlife, including
a number of endangered species.

MAIN VISITOR AREA   A number of **short interpretive trails,** a half
mile or less, are accessible in the main section of the Everglades
National Park from the park road (State Road 9336) between
the main entrance and Flamingo. These short walks acquaint visitors with some of the varied flora, fauna and terrain of the huge
park (see "Main Visitor Area" in this chapter).

Longer trails allow hikers to explore the coastal prairie and
delve deeper into the mysteries of the Everglades. As they are sometimes under water, be sure to check at the ranger station or visitors center before starting out. These trails include the following:

Long Pine Key Nature Trail (7 miles), beginning on the road to
Long Pine Key, is a network of interconnecting trails running
through an unusually diverse pineland forest. About 200 types of

plants, including 30 found nowhere else on earth, grow here. Among the mammals you can spot along the trail are possums, white-tailed deer, raccoons and the seldom-seen, endangered Florida panther.

Snake Bight Trail (2 miles) commences about three miles northeast of Flamingo off the park road and heads due south to a boardwalk at Florida Bay. Two miles along, it is joined by **Rowdy Bend Trail** (2.6 miles). The two make a good loop hike through a variety of terrains and flora.

If you spot a small bird with a vibrant blue head, a yellow-green back and a red rump then you've seen the male painted bunting (females are entirely greenish-yellow).

Old Ingraham Highway Trail (11 miles) begins at the Royal Palm Visitor Center and follows an old road through hammocks, saw grass prairie, and pine forest. This flat hike is ideal for birdwatching. Look for deer along the way.

Bear Lake Trail (1.6 miles) begins about three miles north of Flamingo's visitors center at the end of Bear Lake Road. This raised trail was made with fill dirt from the digging of the Homestead Canal and heads due west, skirting a canoe trail and the north shore of Bear Lake. Woodland birds are abundant here.

Christian Point Trail (1.8 miles) begins about one and a half miles northeast of Flamingo, travels across coastal prairie and winds through mangrove thickets to the shore of Florida Bay.

Coastal Prairie Trail (7.5 miles) follows an old road bed leading to Cape Sable. This trail can be quite demanding, depending on ground conditions, as it progresses through open salt marsh and tends to flood. The trail begins at Flamingo and ends at Clubhouse Beach on the edge of Florida Bay.

The sign at the beginning of **Everglades Trail** (24 miles) advises hikers to bring water, sunscreen, a cellphone, first-aid kit and bug repellent—it is, after all, 24 miles of asphalt, and there is not a speck of shade to be found. What you will find is a window on South Dade's farmland, views into the cabbage and corn patches, across tomato fields that bleed into the sunset (mountain biking and horseback riding are also recommended). And you will likely find solitude, as this new-in-1997 trail, which runs alongside a canal on the east side of the Everglades, is slowly discovered. Access points to Everglades Trail include one at Southwest 136th Street west of Krome Avenue, and another at Route 9336, two miles east of the entrance to Everglades National Park.

BISCAYNE NATIONAL PARK   Beginning at Elliott Key harbor in Biscayne National Park, the **East-West Trail** (.5 mile) is a self-guided nature trail that leads through a tropical hardwood hammock of rare vines, flowers and trees. If you're up for a longer hike, the **Spite Highway** (about 7 miles) runs the full length of the island.

Transportation

CAR

From Miami, **Route 41**, the Tamiami Trail, heads due west through the middle of the Everglades, skirting the northern boundary of Everglades National Park. **Route 1** and the almost-parallel **Florida Turnpike** head toward Homestead and Florida City, where **Route 27** branches off into the heart of Everglades National Park. If you prefer the road less traveled, start from Naples and head east along Route 41.

AIR

Many visitors to the Everglades arrive via Miami. **Miami International Airport** (Wilcox Field) is a megaport served by numerous domestic/international carriers, including American Airlines, Continental Airlines, Delta Air Lines, Northwest Airlines, United Airlines and US Airways.

There are even more international carriers: Aerolíneas Argentinas, Aeromexíco, Air Canada, Air France, Air Jamaica, Bahamasair, British Airways, BWIA, Cayman Airways, El Al, Iberia, LAB, Lacsa, Lan Chile, Lufthansa, Mexicana, Varig and Virgin Atlantic.

BUS

Greyhound Bus Lines bring passengers from all over the country to the Miami area. The main Miami terminal is at 4111 Northwest 27th Street. The Homestead terminal is at 5 Northeast 3rd Road. ~ 800-231-2222; www.greyhound.com.

Astro Tours offers shuttles between Miami and New York on Thursday and Saturday. ~ 2909 Northwest 7th Street, Miami; 305-643-6423. **Omnibus La Cubana** has daily service between Miami and Virginia, Philadelphia, New York and New Jersey. ~ 1101 Northwest 22nd Avenue, Miami; 305-541-1700, 800-365-8001, fax 305-643-2165; www.lacubanabus.com.

TRAIN

Amtrak (800-872-7245; www.amtrak.com) will bring you into Miami from the northeastern states on its "Silver Meteor," "Silver Star" or "Palmetto." From the western United States, there are three trains to Miami by way of Chicago and Washington, D.C. The Miami station is at 8303 Northwest 37th Avenue.

CAR RENTALS   Avis Rent A Car (800-331-1212), Budget Rent A Car (800-527-0700), Dollar Rent A Car (800-800-4000), Hertz Rent A Car (800-654-3131) and National Car Rental (800-328-4567) are represented at both the Miami and South Florida airports.

Companies offering free airport pickup in Miami are Alamo Rent A Car (800-327-9633), Enterprise Rent A Car (800-325-8007) and Thrifty Rent A Car (305-871-5050).

AERIAL TOURS   For an aerial view of the Ten Thousands Islands area on the western side of Everglades National Park, consider a flightseeing trip with Wings 10,000 Islands Aero-Tours. Low-level 20- to 90-minute flightseeing tours buzz over 35 miles of the park with views of sawgrass prairies, cypress forests and tiny islands dotting the waters. Closed May through October. Part of the Everglades Chamber of Commerce. ~ Everglades Airport, Route 29, Everglades City; 239-695-3296.

THREE

The Keys

The Florida Keys are a narrow, gently curving chain of sub-tropical islands that mark the meeting of the Atlantic Ocean and the Gulf of Mexico off the tip of Florida. "Key" comes from the Spanish word *cayo*, meaning "small island," though it is said that the earliest explorers designated this particular group *Los Mártires*, for the land appeared to them as a succession of suffering martyrs lying low on the horizon.

Until early in this century, the Keys were accessible only by boat. Isolated bits of jungly land, they attracted only the hardiest of adventurers and those who, for whatever legal or illegal reasons, desired to get away from civilization. The Keys' relatively brief history is dotted with pirates, salvagers, smugglers, struggling farmers and fisherfolk. In contrast, today these islands are easy to get to and represent one of the country's prime travel destinations.

In 1912, developer Henry Flagler, spurred by dreams of carrying sportsmen to luxurious fishing camps and freight to ships sailing from Key West to Cuba and Central America, completed his greatest project, a railroad from Florida City to Key West. The remarkable line crossed three dozen islands over bridges spanning lengths from less than fifty feet to seven miles. The state's worst recorded hurricane destroyed the railroad in 1935, but its sturdy bridges and trestles became the links for the Overseas Highway, which would make these out-to-sea islands accessible to anyone who could drive, hike or bike the hundred-plus miles from the mainland to Key West.

Some of the Keys are so narrow that you can watch the sun rise over the Atlantic and see it set into the Gulf of Mexico just by strolling across the road. To the east of the chain lie the continental United States' only living coral reefs, popular with divers, snorkelers and passengers in glass-bottom boats. Because of these protective reefs, there is little surf, hence few sandy beaches in the Keys, a surprise to most visitors.

Time, folks claim, means little in the Keys. Visitors soon discover that slowing down is both easy and essential, especially if there's a traffic problem on the Overseas Highway (Route 1) or when the weather is too good to pass up, which it is most of the time. The Keys are basically vacation and retirement havens these days, now that wrecked sailing ships no longer yield up their booty on the rocky reefs, now that the sponge beds are gone and the commercial fishing industry has greatly dwindled. Romantics call these Keys "America's Caribbean Islands," "the islands you can drive to" and even "the last resort." Accommodations range from crowded RV and trailer parks to motels with a boat dock for each room to luxurious resorts. Dining runs the gamut from shrimp boils beside a dock to gourmet feasting in sedate restaurants. The basic fare, naturally, is seafood.

Fishing, boating and diving are the main sports of the Keys. Marinas lie on both sides of many of the islands; you can put out a rod for game fish from unused bridges as well as from classy yachts. Each of the centers of population claim to be the best of something, whether it be fishing, diving, relaxing, eating or partying.

Largest of all the islands, Key Largo is the gateway to the Keys and the beginning of the 113-mile journey to Key West. As Route 1 meanders out to sea, it passes through populated areas that could be anywhere in the country, with chain motels and restaurants, little shopping areas and ever-increasing development. But that's where the similarity ends, for this is a water-borne highway, heading into magnificent sunsets, bordered by sea or mangroves or marinas and even bits of surviving junglelike hammocks. Alongside it runs the vital viaduct, a huge pipe carrying water from the mainland. These dependent islands, though surrounded by the sea, once offered little but rainwater for drinking.

Closest Key to John Pennekamp Coral Reef State Park, Key Largo is the premier diving site of the Keys. Less than 20 miles farther along, Islamorada, on Upper Matecumbe Key, is centerpiece of a group known as the "purple isles," thanks to an explorer who probably named them for the violet sea snails that thrived there.

The region is famous for sportfishing and was once the prosperous headquarters for wreckers. The next good-sized center of population is the town of Marathon on Vaca Key. The whole area is a popular winter resort and choice fishing spot.

Crossing the famous Seven Mile Bridge, Route 1 enters the Lower Keys, whose population center is Big Pine Key. The flora and fauna here are different from much of the rest of the Keys. Big Pine is home to the endangered tiny Key deer. One of the Keys' few fine beaches is found on nearby Bahia Honda Key. From here on, the population thins out considerably until Route 1 approaches Key

The Keys

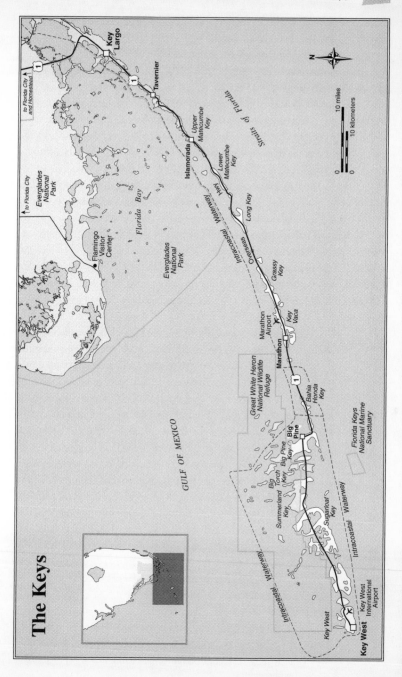

West (presented in detail in Chapter Four), almost the outermost region of the state. Only the Dry Tortugas lie beyond.

One might suspect that the Keys, being such a narrow chain of islands with a single highway running through them, could not provide any "hidden" sites to explore. But they are there for the finding, little pockets of natural wilderness that have so far survived the encroaching civilization, small restaurants away from the highway, quiet lodgings on out-of-the-way islands, bits of history and treasure out to sea. Though winter is the chief tourist season in the Keys, breezes keep the days pleasant and the mosquitoes down most of the year. Rates are considerably lower in the summer.

So, if you are planning a trip to the Keys, get ready to slow down, to relax, to veer away from the fast-food chains along Route 1, to enjoy some sunsets, do a little fishing and find out what hidden pleasures the Keys have in store.

Note: Mile Markers, often called mile posts, can be seen each mile along Route 1 in the Keys. These small green signs with white numbers appear on the right shoulder of the road, beginning with Mile Marker (MM) 126 just south of Florida City and ending at MM 0 in Key West. If you ask for directions in the Keys, you'll likely get a Mile Marker number. We use them throughout this chapter.

Key Largo

Key Largo is the first of the Keys you will reach along the Great Overseas Highway, Route 1, when you head south from Florida City. Motels, resorts and campgrounds abound through much of this, the largest of the Keys. Both the island and its main town are called "Key Largo," a name made famous by the spellbinding 1948 film about crime and a hurricane. You'll still hear a lot about the movie today, and a few local spots claim to have been featured briefly.

The island's main thoroughfare, with its "any-strip-U.S.A." fast-food ambience, tends to disappoint some visitors who had expected a more subtle tropical-island feeling. But there's also the overwhelming assortment of dive shops, which point to something that makes Key Largo unique indeed: just a few miles offshore lies the country's only living coral reef outside Hawaii. The jewel of Key Largo is the John Pennekamp Coral Reef State Park, the only underwater state park in the continental United States. Here are facilities to introduce even the most confirmed landlubber to the sea kingdom and its living treasures.

Key Largo has a few other interesting sights, a couple of historic spots, plenty of shopping and eating opportunities and a wide variety of accommodations. Many visitors, especially city dwellers from Miami and environs, make Key Largo their sole Keys destination.

To get there, you can travel the busy, narrow Route 1, with its "crocodile crossing" warnings, or go via the slower Card Sound Road. The latter features a high toll bridge that affords good views of the mangrove swamps and a real feel for the early Keys, when fishermen lived in functional shacks and chain eateries were still to come.

Soon after arriving on the Key, you'll reach the hiking/biking path that begins at Mile Marker 106 and parallels Route 1 for about 20 miles. It ties in with a short nature trail, passes the John Pennekamp Coral Reef State Park, follows an old road to a county park and leads to some historic sites.

For lots of good information on the Key Largo area, stop at the **Florida Keys Visitor Center** in the Key Largo Chamber of Com-

SIGHTS

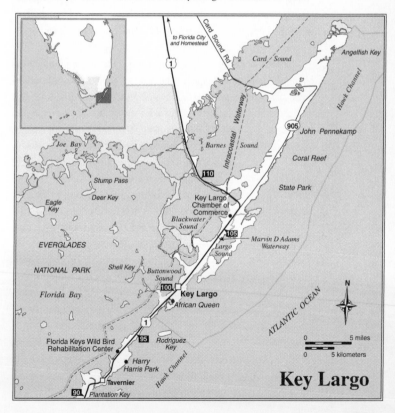

Key Largo

merce. ~ MM 106, Key Largo; 305-451-1414, 800-822-1088, fax 305-451-4726; www.keylargochamber.org, e-mail info@keylargo chamber.org.

Island Smoke Shop is where Cuban master cigar rollers ply their craft, and the air is redolent as a result. A visit to the "humi-dor," the back room where the air is kept a constant 70°, refreshes the weary and keeps expensive stogies—each one lying in state in its own little sarcophagus—in peak condition. "El Original" is the shop's house brand; its creator, Santiago Cabana, frequently demonstrates the art of rolling. ~ In the Pink Plaza, MM 103.4, Key Largo; 305-453-4014, 800-680-9701, fax 305-453-0448; www.islandsmokeshop.com, e-mail info@islandsmokeshop.com.

Slow down as you approach the short bridge that crosses the **Marvin D. Adams Waterway**, a manmade cut that creates a chan-nel all the way across a narrow section of Key Largo. The banks on either side of the cut are the one place you can really get a good look at the geological makeup of the Upper Keys. There are fine examples of petrified staghorn coral, coral heads and other pieces of the ancient coral reef on which the islands are built. ~ MM 103.

Whether or not you're a snorkeler or scuba diver, **John Penne-kamp Coral Reef State Park** offers many ways to enjoy this under-water treasure (see the "Beaches & Parks" section below). An excellent visitors center features a giant reconstruction of a living patch reef in a circular aquarium and other exhibits of the under-sea world, mangrove swamps and hardwood hammocks. Admis-sion. ~ Route 1, MM 102.5, Key Largo; 305-451-6300, fax 305-853-3555. The concession area offers daily glass-bottom boat tours, as well as scuba and snorkeling tours, are offered daily. ~ 305-451-1621, fax 305-451-1427; www.floridastateparks.com.

HIDDEN ►   Hidden under the Atlantic waters, the **Christ of the Deep** statue is a favorite destination of divers in the state park. This nine-foot-high bronze statue, located in the Key Largo National Ma-rine Sanctuary, was created by an Italian sculptor and given to the Underwater Society of America by the Florida Board of His-toric Memorials. A duplicate of *Christ of the Abysses* in the Med-iterranean Sea near Genoa, its uplifted arms are designed to be a welcome to "all who lived for the sea and who, in the name of the sea they so dearly loved, found their eternal peace."

Glass-bottom boat cruises to the reef are also available on the **Key Largo Princess**, which sails to Molasses Reef in the National

Marine Sanctuary. Choose from daily public cruises as well as seasonal sunset cruises with underwater lights. ~ MM 100, Holiday Inn gift shop, Key Largo; 305-451-4655, fax 305-453-9553.

Atlantic bottle-nosed dolphins can often be spotted swimming and cavorting in Key Largo area waters, especially on the bay side. For a closer experience with these delightful and intelligent sea mammals, make an appointment to visit family-run **Dolphins Plus,** one of several places in the Keys where you can   ◄ *HIDDEN* actually swim with dolphins (although you must be at least seven years old to swim). Basically a research center, Dolphins Plus studies how dolphins relate to human beings. They are also researching the dolphin's role in "zoo-therapy" with disabled individuals. Admission. ~ MM 99, Key Largo; 305-451-1993, 866-860-7946, fax 305-451-3710; www.dolphinsplus.com, e-mail info@dolphinsplus.com.

The little town of **Tavernier** boasts a bit of history that local   ◄ *HIDDEN* folks are hanging onto as best they can. Along with the Old Methodist Church on Route 1, a few **old frame houses** with big shutters for protection against hurricanes remain, mementos of the farming days before pizza parlors and gas stations. You can see them if you wander the few side streets and peer into the dense grove of tropical trees. ~ Around MM 92.

Watch for an unobtrusive entrance just south of Key Largo on the bay side. **Florida Keys Wild Bird Rehabilitation Center** is   ◄ *HIDDEN* a nonprofit organization—it started with one caring woman and continues to grow with the help of dedicated donors and a handful of volunteers—that cares for injured and ailing avians. Stop by and get close up and personal with healthy wild birds that you would usually see only from very far away. You'll find it somewhat heartrending when you realize that much of the damage is done by human negligence and environmental irresponsibility,

BOGIE'S BOAT

If you want a very small bit of nostalgia, you can usually see the original *African Queen* (the little boat in which Humphrey Bogart and Katharine Hepburn battled the jungle and found romance) on display at the Holiday Inn docks. If the ship's gone for the day, you can have a look at the prop for the *Thayer IV*, the boat seen in the Hepburn film *On Golden Pond.* ~ MM 100, Key Largo.

but heartwarming at the same time to find that there are still many people who care deeply. ~ MM 93.6, Key Largo; 305-852-4486, 888-826-3811, fax 305-852-3186; www.fkwbc.org, e-mail info@fkwbc.org.

For Everglades airboat rides and sightseeing tours, contact **Everglades Airboat Tours**. Three trips depart daily. Call for reservations and directions. ~ Key Largo; 305-852-5339, 305-221-9888; www.everglades-airboat-tours.com.

LODGING

Accommodations are numerous in the Keys, from small motels to condominiums to chain hotels to luxurious resorts. Almost all offer something special, from a dock for snorkeling to extensive dive and fishing charters. Lodging information may be obtained from the **Key West Chamber of Commerce**. ~ Mallory Square, 402 Wall Street, Key West; 305-294-2587, 800-352-5397, fax 305-294-7806; www.keywestchamber.org, e-mail info@keywest chamber.org.

Calling itself the "PADI gold palm resort," **Kelly's On the Bay & the Aqua-Nuts Dive Resort** offers Caribbean-style charm where diving enthusiasts can almost roll out of bed and into the water. Right on the bay, on the sunset side of Key Largo, Kelly's has 34 comfortably furnished rooms and efficiencies, a dive center, a pool, two 42-foot dive boats and both PADI and NAUI scuba courses. Kayaks and bicycles are provided free of charge to guests. Weekend breakfast is included. Holidays require a three-day stay minimum. ~ MM 104.2, Key Largo; 305-451-1622, 800-226-0415, fax 305-451-4623; www.aqua-nuts.com, e-mail info@aqua-nuts.com. MODERATE.

The **Marriott Key Largo Bay Beach Resort** impresses with its rambling four-story sun-washed buildings, embellished with white

---

PARADISE ON A BUDGET

Tropical trees, dense foliage, ibis in the yard and a nice little bayside beach reinforce the claim at **Largo Lodge** that "paradise can be reasonable." For the reasonable price you get one of six very nice, roomy apartments with a kitchen, a living room and a big screened porch. The place is beautifully maintained and the owner is delightful. Adults only. ~ MM 101.740, Key Largo; 305-451-0424, 800-468-4378; www.largolodge.com, e-mail info@largolodge.com. MODERATE.

wrought iron and coral rock pillars, and looking across a great sweep of shimmering bay. Along the bay is more fantasy design, including a suspension bridge and numerous peak-roofed gazebos, a swimming pool and a manmade beach with attendant lounge chairs. Only 40 of the 153 rooms do not command a bay view; most rooms feature plush surroundings that include white-washed oak and vibrant tropical patterns, as well as spacious balconies. Amenities include a restaurant, café, tiki bar, tennis court, day spa, dive shop and exercise room. ~ MM 103.8, Key Largo; 305-453-0000, 866-849-3753, fax 305-453-0093; www. marriottkeylargo.com, e-mail reservations@marriottkeylargo. com. ULTRA-DELUXE.

Jules' Undersea Lodge is so hidden that you can't even see it   ◄ *HIDDEN* when you get there because it's 22 feet below the surface of a trop- ical lagoon. You don't have to be an advanced scuba diver to get into your air-conditioned quarters (there are two rooms for guests and an entertainment room); the staff will give you lessons. The reward is a unique underwater experience—with fish swimming by your 42-inch windows, no noise except the comforting reminder of the air support system and the knowledge that you are stay- ing in the only underwater hotel in the world. Dinner included in the rate. ~ 51 Shoreland Drive, near MM 103.2, Key Largo; 305-451-2353, fax 305-451-4789; www.jul.com, e-mail info@ jul.com. ULTRA-DELUXE.

Marina del Mar Resort is one of those places with everything —lodging, marina, restaurant and nightclub, tennis courts, fitness center, pool and diving services. On the oceanside of the island, it is convenient to the popular nearby diving waters. The one- to three-bedroom suites are spacious and airy with tile floors; there are also studios with full kitchens. Continental breakfast included. ~ MM 100, Key Largo; 305-451-4107, 800-451-3483, fax 305-451- 1891; www.marinadelmarkeylargo.com, e-mail salesdirectory@ holidayinnkeylargo.com. DELUXE TO ULTRA-DELUXE.

The **Sunset Cove Motel** is really a complex of small, old-time, plain but neat rooms and apartments. This modest spot has a real old Keys feel. It's set among life-sized carved panthers and pelicans and enhanced with wonderful, relaxing Jamaican swings in the shade of thatched chickees huts. Guests may catch sight of a manatee (if you're lucky!), watch the pelicans and use their paddleboats, canoes, kayaks and sailboat. ~ MM 99.5, Key

Largo; 305-451-0705, 877-451-0705, fax 305-451-5609; www.
sunsetcovebeachresort.com. MODERATE TO DELUXE.

The gardens at bayfront **Kona Kai Resort and Gallery** are
filled with fruit trees—jackfruit, breadfruit and Key lime—and
there are stands of great old gumbo-limbos. Four low-slung
buildings with tin roofs are tucked among the flora, their 11
suites tiled in pale ceramic and furnished with rattan and tropically patterned fabrics. The feeling is very villagelike. A tennis
court, heated pool and jacuzzi, fishing pier with dockage, a perfect little white-sand beach—everything is here. The lobby dou-
bles as an art gallery. ~ MM 97.8, Key Largo; 305-852-7200,
800-365-7829, fax 305-852-4629; www.konakairesort.com,
e-mail konakai@aol.com. ULTRA-DELUXE.

Select from motel rooms with refrigerators and microwaves,
efficiencies, or fully equipped cottages at the modest and clean
Bay Harbor Lodge. Shaded by palms, poincianas and frangipani,
this lodging offers a small, swimmable sandy beach on Florida
Bay, a heated pool, and free use of the dock and its kayaks and
paddleboats. Pets are welcome. ~ MM 97.8, Key Largo; phone/
fax 305-852-5695, 800-385-0986; www.bayharborkeylargo.
com. MODERATE.

Here is a resort that reminds one of what the Keys used to
look like. The **Sheraton Beach Resort Key Largo,** obscured as it
is in hardwood hammock, offers a glimpse of a natural habitat.
Footpaths wend along the property, and signs point to wild papaya plants and a mahogany tree—surely one of the few remaining in the Upper Keys. The 200 balconied rooms are far
from woodsy, offering luxuries such as marble vanities with theater lighting, cushy carpets and coffee makers. Fourth-floor
rooms, with views of the bay instead of the forest, are most coveted. Another plus: twin swimming pools—one for families, the
other for adults. ~ MM 97, Key Largo; 305-852-5553, 800-539-
5274, fax 305-436-6045; www.keylargoresort.com, e-mail
info@keylargoresort.com. MODERATE TO ULTRA-DELUXE.

At the **Stone Ledge Hotel** you'll have access to a nice dock, a
small bayside beach, a shady yard and a pleasant motel room, efficiency or studio apartment in the long, low cream-colored stucco
building. Typical of many of the area's mom-and-pop motels, this
one is quite pleasant. Ask for a unit away from the highway. ~
95320 Overseas Highway, Key Largo; 305-852-8114. MODERATE.

DINING

The innovative seafood dishes at **Sundowner's** won't disappoint. It's a casual but classy place, with friendly waitstaff. The glass-walled dining room faces the bay for splendid sunset gazing. There are steak, pasta and chicken dishes, but best are the nightly fish specials such as crabmeat-stuffed yellowtail with béarnaise sauce, fresh Florida lobster tail and grilled or blackened mahimahi. ~ MM 103.9, Key Largo; 305-451-4502, fax 305-453-9661. DELUXE.

Within Marriott's Key Largo Bay Beach Resort, **Gus' Grille** appears as a large, airy space with natural woods and coral-rock walls. Window walls overlook Florida Bay for a spectacular show each evening as the setting sun turns the waters crimson and gold. The food is as gorgeously presented as the view, but, alas, lacks character. Outdoors, by the pool, you can sip a piña colada while watching the dive boats come and go. They serve breakfast, lunch and dinner. ~ MM 103.8, Key Largo; 305-453-0029, fax 305-453-0093; www.marriottkeylargo.com. MODERATE TO DELUXE.

Lauren Bacall and Humphrey Bogart, the stars of the 1948 movie *Key Largo*, apparently never set foot on the island for the filming.

If it swims in the ocean or dwells on the sea floor, **The Fish House** serves it up and serves it up well. Part restaurant, part smokehouse and part fish market, this long-time eatery has been a favorite of both locals and visitors thanks to an extensive menu of all things from the sea. Only the freshest daily catch is used and can be prepared any way you like: Jamaican jerked, baked, broiled, fried, blackened, pan-sautéed or *Matecumbe* style. A copious raw bar, a luscious Key lime pie and an ultra-casual ambiance are only part of the secret to this eatery's success. ~ MM 102.4, Key Largo; 305-451-4665, 888-451-4665, fax 305-451-1727; www.fishhouse.com, e-mail info@fishhouse.com. MODERATE TO DELUXE.

At the traffic light at MM 99.5, turn toward the ocean and follow side streets until you come to **Calypso's Seafood Grille**. This open-air terracotta patio is the domain of Chef Cad, a wiry, witty, chain-smoking vegetarian who knows not only how to cook great food but how to create it. He buys his seafood every morning from Key Largo Fisheries, located just across the marina, then turns it into dishes like wet black dolphin chargrilled and topped with seared pepperoncinis and feta cheese. Pitchers of sangria are loaded with fresh fruit and dusted with grated cinnamon. His yel-

◄ HIDDEN

lowtail Grand Marnier is crispy, light and buttery. Closed Tuesday. ~ 1 Seagate Boulevard, Key Largo; 305-451-0600. MODERATE.

The fresh fish at **Makoto** is far from Keys-standard: It's served raw and wrapped in seaweed, with rice and cucumber and various other accompaniments. Makoto is surprisingly good. Located in a yellow-awninged building with a glass wall facing the ocean, it's adorned with Japanese prints and paper lanterns. Choose from sushi and sashimi combos, tempura, teriyaki, sukiyaki or interesting appetizers such as soft-shell crab with teriyaki sauce. The chefs also cook steak "Benihana-style." Closed Wednesday. ~ MM 101.6, Key Largo; 305-451-7083. BUDGET TO MODERATE.

Hidden within a small grove of large coconut palms is the lilac canopy that leads to **Snook's Bayside Restaurant & Grand Tiki Bar**. This is an intimate spot for casual dining on seafood, black Angus beef, veal and chicken inside or out on the patio, complemented by a fine wine selection. There's live music four days a week. A waterfront all-you-can-eat brunch buffet rounds out the week on Sunday. ~ MM 99.9, Key Largo; 305-453-3799, fax 305-453-3793; www.snooks.com. MODERATE.

Cafe Largo serves good Italian food—all the traditional pasta, chicken and veal dishes plus excellent daily specials using yellowtail and dolphin, stone crabs, lobster and other local seafood. The Mediterranean setting is indoors and typical of family-style Italian places. Dinner only. ~ 305-451-4885. On the same property, connected by a walkway, is the **Bayside Grill**. Diners enjoy steak and seafood dishes in the glass-enclosed dining room situated on the waterfront. ~ MM 99.5, Key Largo; 305-451-3380, fax 305-451-4467. MODERATE TO DELUXE.

If you want a little down-home mainland food, stop at **Mrs. Mac's Kitchen**. This shack-style eatery has about the best chili east of Texas and pita bread concoctions almost too fat to bite

AUTHOR FAVORITE

For an exotic treat, I curl up on the big, satin cushions in the tatami room at **Sushi Nami** and wait for fresh delights from this sushi bar. They also offer traditional fare such as teriyaki, tempura, soba noodles and sashimi. The mounted fish on the walls help me remember I'm in the Keys. No lunch on the weekend. ~ MM 99.5, Key Largo; 305-453-9798, fax 305-451-9650. MODERATE.

down on. The chefs cook up huge breakfasts, broil delicious steaks and feature different theme specials (Italian, meat, fresh local seafood, etc.) for dinner every night. The place is small, with more varieties of beers than seats, so it's noisy and fun. Closed Sunday. ~ MM 99.4, Key Largo; 305-451-3722, fax 305-451-0516. BUDGET TO MODERATE.

Ballyhoo's Historic Seafood Grille has a menu that relies heavily on seafood, with steak thrown in for good measure. The atmosphere is updated Keys: burnt-edged tables and wicker chairs, with some of the old wall-unit air conditioners grumbling and a view of the highway through the windows. ~ MM 98, Key Largo; 305-852-0822, fax 305-453-9661. BUDGET TO MODERATE.

Slow down for children and pets as you pass through Mandalay trailer park to reach the historic **Mandalay Restaurant, Marina and Tiki Bar**. This place is so "old Florida Keys"—from the driftwood to the frayed ropes—it could double as a '70s movie set. Nestled on busy Rock Harbor, Mandalay attracts an eclectic mix that includes locals, fishermen, attorneys, writers and adventurous tourists. This arrangement of shack-like structures offers seating at the funky inside bar or at picnic tables on the deck over the water. Featuring seafood straight off the boat, favorite entrées include grouper stuffed with crab meat, seafood alfredo, and Florida lobster. An excellent Key lime pie is made on the premises. Don't be surprised if the place is packed: folks will tolerate the tight quarters for the food, which is served until 10 p.m., and nightly entertainment. ~ MM 97.5, 80 East 2nd Street, Key Largo; 305-852-5450, fax 305-852-6395; www.the mandalay.com. MODERATE TO DELUXE.

◄ *HIDDEN*

Most of the patrons at **Snappers Waterfront Saloon and Raw Bar** wear shorts and T-shirts. Dressing for dinner means throwing on a pair of Docksiders. One of the few oceanside dining spots in Key Largo, the restaurant's outdoor tables let you smell the salt air, count the boats and watch the wide scrim of the blue sky and the Atlantic. Seafood stars on the menu; fish platters are oversized and fresh. Don't miss the smoked fish dip and for dessert, the Key lime pie. ~ MM 94.5, Key Largo; 305-852-5956, fax 305-852-1111; www.thefloridakeys.com/snappers, e-mail snapperd@bellsouth.net. MODERATE TO DELUXE.

Old Tavernier Restaurant grew so popular it had to relocate to a bigger spot just to accommodate the nightly mobs. Now, between the spacious dining room and outdoor veranda along a mangrove canal, there's plenty of room to enjoy what Old Tavernier does best: huge portions of sauce-drenched pastas that arrive bubbling at your table. Nightly specials often depart from pasta with such dishes as rack of lamb, grilled veal chops and fresh fish. Dinner only. ~ MM 90.3, Tavernier; 305-852-6012, fax 305-852-1999. MODERATE TO DELUXE.

SHOPPING   Key Largo is the main spot for Upper Keys shoppers, so there are shopping centers, groceries and all the functional kinds of stores you might need, as well as tacky souvenir and T-shirt shops.

There are dive shops all along the highway of Key Largo. One of the premier popular full-service shops is the dockside **Captain Slate's Atlantis Dive Center**. You'll find masks, fins, weight belts, tanks, wet suits and so on for sale and for rent, as well as T-shirts and swimwear. If you want an underwater wedding or would like to meet some dolphins at sea, Atlantis will arrange that, along with their standard assortment of reef trips. ~ 51 Garden Cove, off MM 106.5, Key Largo; 305-451-1325, fax 305-451-9240; www.pennekamp.com/atlantis, e-mail capslate@safari.net.

For items ranging from jewels to junk, check out the **Key Largo Flea Market**. Vendors hock everything from fishing equipment and nautical decorations to pet items, books and food. Open weekends only. ~ 103530 Overseas Highway, Key Largo; 305-451-0677.

The **Pink Plaza** is one-stop shopping, Keys style. Among the noteworthy shops is **Moore Books** (305-451-1468), which features a selection of local authors among their new and used books. The **Island Smoke Shop** (305-453-4014, 800-680-9701; www.islandsmokeshop.com) features cigars rolled by Cuban masters. ~ MM 103.4, Key Largo.

TROPICS TO GO

If you're eager to take a little bit of the Keys back home with you, Tom of **Tom's Caribbean Tropicals** will oblige. He captures and sells all species of colorful tropical sea life to grace fish tanks anywhere in the country. Call ahead for directions to his facility. ~ 305-852-7810; www.divertom.com.

A well-known underwater photographer offers all the necessary equipment—for sale or for rent—for capturing your diving and snorkeling adventures on still or video film at **Stephen Frink Photographic**. He will also process your slides. Closed Sunday. ~ MM 102.5, Key Largo; 305-451-3737; www.stephenfrink.com.

Too bad **T-Shirt City/Sandal Factory** has such a tacky exterior—neon yellow and blue bubble awnings and giant logos shouting toward the highway—because the merchandise inside is reminiscent of that found in a tropical boutique. The sandal selection for men, women and children is terrific, and so are the prices. You'll find the latest platform sandals in leather, wood and foam, deck shoes and quality flip-flops, with brands by Mia, Birkenstock and Sebago. There are tasteful T-shirts, linen walking shorts, tropically patterned dresses and shirts, and great straw hats. ~ MM 102, Key Largo; 305-453-9644, fax 305-453-9604.

The Book Nook has a large variety of books about the area and Florida in general, as well as maps and charts for divers. They also keep a good selection of classics as well as plenty of recent bestsellers, magazines and newspapers (including a large selection by local mystery and thriller writers), to keep you busy when you've had too much sun, and "island" music to relax to. ~ MM 100, Waldorf Plaza, Key Largo; 305-451-1468, fax 305-451-9349.

Divers Direct sells just about anything you might need to play in or near the water. In addition to dive equipment and snorkeling gear, you'll find a selection of beach apparel, accessories and swimsuits. ~ MM 99.9, Key Largo; 305-451-0118; www.shop diversdirect.com.

If you left it at home, you'll probably find it at **Anthony's Ladies Apparel**. They carry a large selection of swimsets, tropical-inspired sportswear, casual dresses, sandals and more. ~ MM 98, Key Largo; 305-852-4515.

The two floors of merchandise that make up **Shellworld** are divided between home furnishings, sportswear, and shells and souvenirs. Especially notable is the latter section, which consists of several hundred different types of shells—more than 100,000 individual shells in all. Here, you'll find 15-cent commons, 24-inch giant clam shells (at $4000 apiece) and a caboodle of everything in between. ~ MM 97.5, Key Largo; 305-852-8245.

Text continued on page 100.

Florida Keys Overseas Heritage Trail

When Henry Flagler completed his Florida East Coast Oversea Railroad in 1912 he probably didn't think his construction marvel would give rise to a highway, let alone a biking and hiking trail. But nearly a century later, that's precisely what's happening.

The **Florida Keys Overseas Heritage Trail** is a paved recreational path that follows along Flagler's 21 remaining railroad bridges and the Florida Department of Transportation right-of-way. The trail includes interpretive trailheads designating attractions—cultural, archeological, historical, scenic, environmental and recreational—and other public areas on and off Route 1. Work started on the trail in 2002.

Eventually, the trail will span the Keys from MM 106.5 to MM 0, with crossways between bayside and ocean side. Today, about 40 miles of the trail between Key Largo and Key West are maintained, and this number will grow steadily until the project's completion.

Right now the best way to use the trail is in segments: a half-day of casual biking through the Middle Keys or a backpacking hike in the Key Largo area. It is not safe to cross most bridges by foot or bike at this time.

Here are descriptions of accessible trail segments, according to Mile Marker area.

KEY LARGO (MM 106 TO MM 92)   A 14-mile bike path runs the length of Key Largo, an area dense with hardwood hammocks. Side trips along this segment include John Pennekamp Coral Reef State Park, Key Largo Hammocks and Harry Harris Park.

ISLAMORADA (MM 92 TO MM 75)   The Old Highway parallels Route 1 south of Tavernier Creek. About ten miles of bike path ends at the highway bridges. Founders Park and Windley Key Fossil Reef Geological State Park are trailhead locations.

LONG KEY (MM 75 TO MM 62)   About one mile of path connects the City of Layton to Long Key State Park and the Long Key Historic Fishing Bridge.

MARATHON (MM 62 TO MM 40)   This area includes Grassy Key, the City of Key Colony Beach and the City of Marathon. The 11-mile bike path runs from Grassy Key past Curry Hammock State Park to the Seven Mile Bridge at the southwest entrance to the city.

The four-mile stretch along Grassy Key (MM 54.5 to MM 58.5, bayside) is eight feet wide, landscaped, and protected by bollards and a split-rail fence.

The Florida Keys Overseas Heritage Trail segment ends at the north end of Seven Mile Bridge, where hikers and bikers can proceed safely along an old bridge to Pigeon Key, a historic landmark and railroad museum. The Seven Mile Bridge has a narrow shoulder and should only be attempted by experienced bicyclists.

SOUTHERN KEYS (MM 40 TO MM 10)   There's a one-mile trail segment in Big Pine, and a new trail at MM 15 links Lower Sugarloaf to Big Coppitt, with access over five Saddlebunch historic bridges.

KEY WEST (MM 10 TO MM 0)   In a way, Key West is one big maze of bike paths. This is definitely the place to walk or rent a comfortable bicycle to get you around.

If you'd like additional information on this trail-in-progress, please contact the **Florida Parks Service**. ~ 3 La Croix Court, Key Largo, FL 33037; 305-451-3005, fax 305-853-3553; www.floridastateparks.org.

Cover to Cover Books, the only bookstore/coffee house combination in the Keys, is flooded with classical music and the smells of mocha java and almond joy cafés being made. The two sisters who run it will help you find the right read, from books on Florida and the Keys to gardening and archaeology; children's books and games are a specialty. ~ 91272 Overseas Highway, MM 91, Tavernier; 305-853-2464; www.covertocoverbks.com.

NIGHTLIFE Some of the larger hotels and resorts in the area have nightly or weekend entertainment.

If you're willing to experience a raunchy sort of bikers' beach bar in exchange for some possible nostalgia, stop at the **Caribbean Club.** It is claimed that some parts of the movie *Key Largo* were filmed here, and it just may be true. Even if it's not, the sunsets from the deck are terrific. The joint is open from 7 a.m. to 4 a.m. and offers live rock, blues and reggae bands Friday and Saturday nights. ~ MM 104, Key Largo; 305-451-4466.

The twin coral rock and glass gazebos called **Breezers' Tiki Bar** are great for baywatching, especially at sunset, when the canvas shades are drawn up, the tradewinds blow through, and the waitresses serve pricey pastel drinks that match the floor tiles. In season there's live music Tuesday through Thursday, off season on Friday and Saturday. Located at the Marriott Key Largo Bay Beach Resort, MM 103.5, Key Largo; 305-453-0000.

The motto of the Conch Republic: "We seceded where others failed." Look for the flag at Snappers.

Coconuts is a waterfront spot with live entertainment every night ranging from Top-40 to reggae. Inside, the huge dancefloor has a classy light show; outside, you can enjoy a drink (happy hour is weekdays, 4 to 7 p.m.) on the canopied deck overlooking a canal with boats. Ladies' night on Wednesday. ~ MM 100 at Marina del Mar, Key Largo; 305-453-9794; www.coconutsrestaurant.com.

At **Snook's Bayside Restaurant and Grand Tiki Bar,** the natives gather by car or by boat to watch the sunset and enjoy a friendly drink. There is dining seating indoors and out, with live entertainment every Thursday, Friday, Saturday and Sunday evening on the patio. ~ MM 99.9, Key Largo; 305-453-3799; www.snooks.com.

Snappers is a restaurant with a great bar alongside a crowded, eventful marina. And every April, Snappers stages a reenactment of the Keys' 1982 secession from the United States (a ceremonial secession, in protest of border patrol roadblocks in Florida City, it was followed by a week-long party and a request for U.S. foreign aid). During the reenactment, a miniature bridge to the mainland gets blown up while everyone raises their margaritas to the Conch Republic. In season there's nightly live entertainment; the rest of the year on Thursday, Friday and Saturday nights, and Sunday-morning jazz. ~ MM 94.5, Key Largo; 305-852-5956; www.thefloridakeys.com/snappers.

JOHN PENNEKAMP CORAL REEF STATE PARK

BEACHES & PARKS

This remarkable place is the first underwater state park in the United States. Together with the adjacent **Florida Keys National Marine Sanctuary** (305-852-7717, fax 305-853-0877), the park encompasses an area of about 178 nautical square miles, most of which lies out in the Atlantic Ocean north and east of Key Largo. Most visitors come to see the coral formations, seagrass beds and spectacular marine life of the reefs, either by scuba diving, snorkeling or taking a glass-bottom boat tour. Fishing is another popular activity. It's allowed in the mangroves (for mangrove snapper, trout, sheepshead and snook) and in the Atlantic (for gamefish such as kingfish, mackerel and yellowtail). Tropical fish, however, are protected. There are also two small manmade swimming beaches with a replica of a sunken ship offshore. The land section of the park acquaints visitors with mangrove swamps, numerous shore birds and a tropical hardwood hammock with many varieties of indigenous plant life. An excellent visitors center, featuring a replication of a patch reef complete with marine life in a 30,000-gallon aquarium, allows even those who prefer staying on dry land to experience a bit of the underwater world. Other facilities include picnic areas, restrooms, a bathhouse, showers, nature trails, an observation tower, a snack bar, a gift shop, a dive shop, a marina and docks. Day-use fee, $5 per car, plus a $.50 Monroe County surcharge per person. ~ Entrance at MM 102.5 on Route 1 in Key Largo. Much of the park is accessible only by boat; 305-451-1202, 800-326-3521, fax 305-853-3555.

▲ There are 47 sites, all with electricity and water, at the state park; $31.49 per night.

Private RV and tent campgrounds are nearby. **Key Largo Kampground and Marina** has 38 tent sites and 60 RV sites; $30 to $33 per night for tent sites, $52 to $63 per night for RV sites. Boat dock also available seasonally. ~ MM 101.5, Key Largo; 305-451-1431, 800-526-7688, fax 305-451-8083; www.key largokampground.com.

HARRY HARRIS PARK This county park is one of the few public parks in the area for spending a day beside the ocean. It is spacious, with broad grassy areas and scattered trees. The beach isn't much, but the water is clear and full of fish. Fishing off the pier is not allowed. You can only fish off a boat. Swimming in the tidal pool here is good for kids. Facilities include picnic areas, restrooms, playgrounds, a basketball court, a baseball field and chickee huts. Day-use fee on weekends and holidays, $5 per person. ~ Take Burton Drive at MM 92.5 in Tavernier; it's about a quarter of a mile to the park; 305-852-7161, fax 305-852-7117.

Islamorada Area

Islamorada (*eye-lah-mor-ah-dah*) was named by Spanish explorers and means "island home" or "purple isles," perhaps for the way the land appeared on the horizon, perhaps for the abundant violet snail shells or the brilliant flowering plants found there when the islands were wild.

The Islamorada area begins at Plantation Key and Anne's Beach (MM 90) and runs through Long Key (below MM 73.5). The community of Islamorada, on Upper Matecumbe Key, is its center of population. The area's brief ventures have included shipbuilding, tropical fruit and vegetable farming, turtling, sponging and the immensely prosperous business of salvaging shipwrecks. Fishing has always been especially fine in this area (Islamorada proclaims itself the sportfishing capital of the world), and today tourism is the chief enterprise here.

The town is a collection of businesses that provide local folk with essentials while inviting visitors to "stay here," "eat here," "party here" and "buy here." Holiday Isle, a gigantic resort and entertainment complex, dominates Windley Key with the latest in youthful party hype.

SIGHTS

Laid down about 125,000 years ago, Windley Key is highest in a chain of limestone islands. In the early 1900s, Henry Flagler

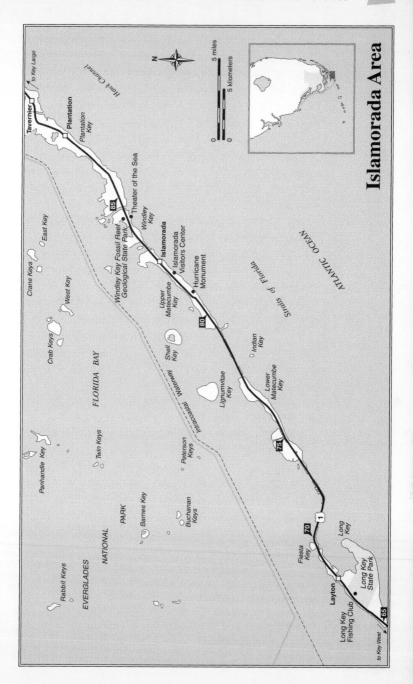

Islamorada Area

to Key Largo

Tavernier

Plantation

Plantation Key

Hawk Channel

N

5 miles

5 kilometers

0

0

Theater of the Sea

85

Windley Key

Crane Keys

East Key

West Key

Windley Key Fossil Reef Geological State Park

Islamorada

Islamorada Visitors Center

Hurricane Monument

Crab Keys

Upper Matecumbe Key

80

Straits of Florida

ATLANTIC OCEAN

FLORIDA BAY

Shell Key

Indian Key

Lignumvitae Key

Lower Matecumbe Key

Panhandle Key

Twin Keys

Peterson Keys

Intracoastal Waterway

75

Barnes Key

NATIONAL PARK

Buchanan Keys

1

Rabbit Keys

EVERGLADES

Fiesta Key

70

Long Key

Layton

Long Key State Park

Long Key Fishing Club

65

to Key West

quarried fill here to build foundations for his Overseas Railroad. One section, **Windley Key Fossil Reef Geological State Park**, has been further cut, revealing fossilized clams, corals, worm holes, and other archaeological treasures from the formerly submerged island. Short, easy-access trails through hardwood hammock lead to the quarry. A visitors center offers explanations and displays. Closed Tuesday and Wednesday. Admission. ~ MM 85.5, Windley Key; 305-664-2540, fax 305-453-1265.

This usually calm and beautiful sea was gathered up into a giant tidal wave on September 2, 1935, that swept away just about every living thing and manmade object in its wake, including a rescue train full of evacuees. A poignant stone memorial and the red caboose just down the street from the **Islamorada Visitors Center** are reminders of the storm that also destroyed the remarkable "railroad that went to the sea." Several other sites, which can be explored on short boat trips, remind visitors that this Upper Keys region offers far more than meets the eye. ~ MM 83.2; 305-664-4503, 800-322-5397, fax 305-664-4289; www.islamoradachamber.com, e-mail info@islamoradachamber.com.

Key Dives offers diving and snorkeling tours that go out to the lighthouse at Alligator Reef, named for one of the ships that ran aground here. Full rentals available. Sunset and chartered cruises for small groups are also an option. ~ MM 79.8, Islamorada; 305-664-2211, 800-344-7352 (dive center), fax 305-664-1007; www.keydives.com, e-mail info@keydives.com.

For a nice, friendly marine show where, if you're lucky, you might get to hold a hoop for a jumping dolphin or get a kiss from a seal, stop at **Theater of the Sea**, the oldest marine park in the world. It may now have fancier, more sophisticated competitors, but this place is still fun and quite personal. There are myriad sea

A NATURAL TRAGEDY

Stop for a minute at the **Hurricane Monument** to meditate on the terrible storm of Labor Day, 1935. Before the anemometer blew away, winds were recorded at 200 mph; the barometer fell to 26.35, one of the lowest pressures ever recorded in the Western Hemisphere. This slightly neglected but nevertheless moving monument was dedicated in 1937 to the memory of the 423 people who died in that storm. ~ MM 81.5, Islamorada.

creatures that can be touched, wild dolphins that join visitors for a "bottomless" boat trip and beautiful tropical grounds to explore. Visitors can also swim with dolphins, rays or sea lions here by reservation. Admission. ~ MM 84.5, Islamorada; 305-664-2431, fax 305-664-8162; www.theaterofthesea.com, e-mail info@ theaterofthesea.com.

Theater of the Sea offers a four-hour scenic cruise and snorkeling trip, **Adventure and Snorkel Cruise,** aboard the 48-foot powerboat "Cooter." Its route passes along the shore to Lignumvitae Key, then a short ocean cruise brings guests to historical Indian Key and Alligator Lighthouse. At Cheeca Rocks, a beautiful shallow reef ideally suited for snorkelers, snorkel equipment is provided or you can see the reef through the underwater viewers. The boat leaves twice daily from Snake Creek Bridge (MM 85) but tickets must be purchased at the Theater at least one day prior to sailing.

After a ten-minute boat trip to **Indian Key State Park Historic Site** you'll be presented with the remarkable story of the ten-acre island that was once the prosperous seat of Dade County. Beneath the nearby, usually calm waters of the Atlantic lie the most treacherous reefs off the Florida coast. The reefs were a source of income for Indians and then for Americans, who turned "salvaging" wrecked ships into profitable businesses. At that time the island town was a bustling place and boasted a grand hotel with a large ballroom, a bar and bowling alleys. One famous hotel guest was naturalist John James Audubon, who stayed over on his way to the Lower Keys. He filed one of the first complaints on record—the incessant dancing and partying made it hard for him to concentrate. Today, there is little sign of the merriment that had the bird man grinding his teeth. The town was destroyed in a grisly Indian attack in 1840. Rangers guide visitors on special tours down reconstructed village "streets" among the tall agave plants and other tropical growth. No tours Tuesday or Wednesday. Admission. ~ Indian Key; 305-664-2540, fax 305-664-0713.

◀ *HIDDEN*

It's another short boat trip to **Lignumvitae Key State Botanical Site.** This key encompasses 280 acres; its virgin sub-tropical forest is a reminder of how all the Keys probably appeared before people came in numbers. One-hour ranger-guided walks through this rare environment introduce such unusual trees as the gumbo-limbo, mastic and poisonwood. ~ 305-664-4815. The restored

◀ *HIDDEN*

Matheson House, built in 1919, has survived hurricane and time; it demonstrates how island dwellers managed in the early days of Keys settlement, dependent on wind power, rainwater and food from the sea. Closed Tuesday and Wednesday. Admission. ~ Lignumvitae Key; 305-664-2540, fax 305-664-0713.

Indian Key and Lignumvitae Key are accessible by private boat only. **Robbie's Rent** runs the shuttle service twice daily for the state park and recreation department. Island admission fee is included in the cost. For Indian Key, boats leave at 8:30 a.m. and 12:30 p.m. For Lignumvitae Key, 9:30 a.m. and 1:30 p.m. No access to the islands on Tuesday or Wednesday. Call in advance. ~ 305-664-9814, 877-664-8498, fax 305-664-9857; www.rob bies.com, e-mail robbies@robbies.com.

HIDDEN ►   The **Layton Nature Trail** is an almost-hidden loop trail from highway to bay, winding through a dense hammock of carefully marked tropical plants, such as pigeon plum, wild coffee and gumbo-limbo, that are unique to the Keys. For travelers in a hurry, the 20-minute walk provides a good introduction to the flora that once covered most of the Keys. ~ 67.5 Overseas Highway; 305-664-4815.

Located 18 feet below the surface of the Atlantic Ocean, the
HIDDEN ►   **San Pedro Underwater Archaeological Preserve** welcomes divers, snorkelers and observers in glass-bottom boats. The *San Pedro* was a 287-ton, Dutch-built galleon in the New Spain fleet that left Havana harbor on Friday, July 13, 1733, and met its doom when hurricane winds drove it onto the reefs. The shipwreck park, dedicated in 1989, provides a nice view of a variety of fish, crustaceans, mollusks and corals. Original anchors, ballast stones, bricks from the ship's galley and concrete cannon replicas enhance the park. ~ Located 1.3 nautical miles south of Indian Key; P.O. Box 1052, Islamorada, FL 33036; 305-664-2540, fax 305-664-0713.

West of Layton marks the site of the **Long Key Fishing Club,** established in 1906 by Flagler's East Coast Hotel Company. One aim of the group was to bring tourism to enjoy gamefish in this mecca for saltwater anglers. The president of the club from 1917 to 1920 was American author Zane Grey. ~ Near MM 67.

LODGING   The Islamorada business area includes another piece of Route 1 lined with mom-and-pop and various chain motels. If you prefer renting a home, condo or townhouse for a week, or even months, contact **Freewheeler Realty**. ~ 85992 Overseas Highway, MM 86, Islamorada; 305-664-2075, 866-664-2075, fax 305-664-2884; www.freewheeler-realty.com, e-mail info@freewheeler-realty.com.

Folks who enjoy being where the action is choose to stay at **Holiday Isle Resorts and Marina**, a great complex of lodgings, swimming pools, bars, restaurants and shops strung out along a stretch of Atlantic beach. The six-story main hotel and its three-story neighbor offer oceanfront rooms, efficiencies, apartments and suites with a peach and teal theme. Some are ordinary motel-type rooms; others are luxury apartments with kitchens, bars and wraparound balconies overlooking the ocean. ~ MM 84, Islamorada; 305-664-2321, 800-327-7070, fax 305-664-5171; www.holidayisle.com, e-mail info@holidayisle.com. DELUXE TO ULTRA-DELUXE.

Vacationers in search of sheer luxury favor **Cheeca Lodge**, a grand hotel perched on the edge of the Atlantic Ocean. Much of the original wood remains in the lodge, which has classy lobby areas, spacious rooms, two freshwater pools and a saltwater lagoon, indoor and outdoor dining, children's programs, a health spa, tennis courts and a nine-hole golf course. Villas are scattered around grounds shaded by a variety of tropical trees. A fine, long pier invites fishing and serves as a take-off point for scuba divers and snorkelers. ~ MM 82.5, Islamorada; 305-664-4651, 800-327-2888, fax 305-664-2893; www.cheeca.com, e-mail information@cheeca.com. ULTRA-DELUXE.

The Moorings is adored by the fashion industry, which uses its thousand-foot, porcelain-white beach for photo backdrops (*Vogue, Elle, Glamour*—they all shoot here).

Know those beach scenes in the *Victoria's Secret* and *J.Crew* catalogs? Plenty were taken at **The Moorings**, one of the Keys' most luxurious, least-known lodges. Guests will find The Moorings a place of quiet calm, hidden down a Keys sidestreet on an apron of ocean, its hammock grounds sprinkled with 18 conch cottages. Decor is a mix of tropical and safari chic with lots of wood—cypress, cherry, pine and ash—and splashes of sisal and Mexican tile. There's no room service or maid service (though either can be arranged), no radios or jet skis. But there's probably a gorgeous woman posing for a camera just down the beach. Some cottages require a two- or seven-night minimum. ~ 123 Beach Road, MM 81.5 oceanside, Islamorada; 305-664-4708, fax 305-664-4242; www.moorings village.com, e-mail moorings@bellsouth.net. ULTRA-DELUXE.

If you are traveling with your boat, you'll like knowing about **Bud N' Mary's Marina**, especially if you enjoy being in the middle of such sea-related activities as snorkeling, fishing and diving charters, party boats, glass-bottom boat tours, backcountry fishing trips and sunset and sightseeing tours. They have four motel units (two double beds, small refrigerator, television and telephone) for folks who love quick access to the sea and its offerings. There's also one efficiency above the tackle shop. ~ MM 79.8, Islamorada; 305-664-2461, 800-742-7945, fax 305-664-5592; www.budnmarys.com. MODERATE.

The incredibly hard wood of the lignumvitae tree, native to the Keys, was once used to make bowling balls.

At the **Islander Resort** you can snorkel in the clear ocean water off the fishing pier or swim in the freshwater and saltwater pools. The Islander offers 114 pleasant units with kitchenettes and screened porches. The 24-acre oceanside resort has a large private beach and is rich in tropical plants. This is a popular place for families. ~ MM 82.1, Islamorada; 305-664-2031, 800-753-6002, fax 305-664-5503; www.islanderflorida keys.com, e-mail islandsk@bellsouth.net. ULTRA-DELUXE.

The **Coral Bay Resort** offers spacious cottages nestled among thriving hibiscus and bougainvillea. Here you'll find a sandy beach, a heated swimming pool, chickee huts and a clear tidal salt pool complete with lobsters and stone crabs in the rocks. It's very popular with families. ~ MM 75.5, Islamorada; 305-664-5568, fax 305-664-3424; www.coralbayresort.com, e-mail coralbay@terra nova.net. MODERATE TO ULTRA-DELUXE.

DINING

The restaurant with the reputation is **Marker 88**, whose Continental cuisine has garnered raves from some of the nation's top culinary magazines. Entrées include fish Martinique topped with tomato concassé and sliced grilled bananas, and pan-seared yellowfin tuna steak flambéed with brandy and served with green peppercorn sauce. Nestled beside Florida Bay and shaded by waving palms, Marker 88 is informally elegant and intimate with a rich tropical ambience. The wine list is as impressive as the creative menu. ~ MM 88, Islamorada; 305-852-9315, fax 305-852-9069; www.marker88restaurant.com. MODERATE TO DELUXE.

Built of coral rock and stippled with oyster shells, the draw at the **Whale Harbor Restaurant** is the all-you-can-eat $25 seafood buffet. The doors open at 4 p.m. and folks drive from miles around for the plentitude: a 50-foot-long table offers shrimp, mussels, crab legs, scallops, oysters, baked snapper (ribs, roast beef and chicken for those who don't eat sea creatures), 85 side dishes and sweets for dessert. ~ MM 83.5, Islamorada; 305-664-4959, fax 305-664-0692; www.whaleharborinn@com. DELUXE.

The shimmering mermaid on the wall of the **Lorelei** may catch your eye, but it's the food that draws locals and tourists alike to this yacht-basin restaurant with a nice "early Keys" feel. They do all sorts of things with the catch of the day here—broil, blacken, coconut-fry, grill and meunière. There are traditional conch chowder and fritters, daily blackboard specials and a devastating Key lime for dessert. The Cabana Bar offers outdoor casual dining with a café-style menu. Open for breakfast, lunch and dinner. ~ MM 82, Islamorada; 305-664-4656, fax 305-664-2410; www. loreleifloridakeys.com, e-mail loreleimermaid@bellsouth.net. MODERATE.

Just before President George Bush was inaugurated in 1989, he went bonefishing in Islamorada and had dinner at Cheeca Lodge's main dining room, the **Atlantic's Edge Restaurant**. The appetizer was stone-crab pie with scallions and tomatoes, a sublime sample of the excellent gourmet dining at this elegant restaurant. Pan-seared foie gras is served with salt cod yucca fritter, grilled quail with herbed sausage stuffing, and blue crab fritters with Key Lime cocktail sauce. As if the food weren't enough, there's also a fine wine list. Dinner only. ~ MM 82, Islamorada; 305-664-4651, fax 305-664-2893; www.cheeca.com, e-mail concierge@ cheeca.com. MODERATE TO ULTRA-DELUXE.

For exceptional seafood, charbroiled steaks, chops and $3 margaritas, stop in at **Squid Row**. The eatery also offers daily grouper and yellowtail specials, and, for the ambitious patron who finishes off an entire seafood bouillabaisse entrée, a complimentary slice of Key lime pie. The restaurant's decor is nautical—or, more specifically, the interior tastefully resembles the inside of a ship, with an abundance of polished wood and an exposed wood-beam ceiling made to look like a hull. ~ MM 81.9, Islamorada; 305-664-9865. MODERATE TO ULTRA-DELUXE.

Morada Bay opened in 1997 and, instantly, the Keys had a fashion model scene. It's not that the models haven't been around—they have for several years, doing photo shoots across Route 1 at the very low-profile Moorings lodge. Morada Bay is

Text continued on page 112.

Kingdoms
Under the Sea

Many of the unique wonders of the Keys and Everglades begin at their shorelines. From the shallows of Biscayne Bay to the deeps at the brink of the Gulf Stream lies a vast underwater wilderness unlike any other natural region in the continental United States. Close in are vast carpets of sea grasses, birthplaces and nurseries for shrimp and fish and Florida spiny lobsters, temporary refuges for endangered manatees and sea turtles.

A few miles out lies the coral reef. Here divers can explore a beautiful, silent underwater world of brilliant colors and subdued hues, of curious shapes and vibrant darting creatures. In some places its long spiny fingers almost touch the sun-sparkling surface of the sea. In other regions twisting corridors lead to secret caves at depths almost beyond the reach of life.

The coral reef is actually a living kingdom made up of billions of little colonies of tiny animals called polyps that snare passing microorganisms with their tentacles. They live in small cups of limestone that they secrete around themselves. The unusual and varied shapes of these cups give them their names: elkhorn and staghorn coral, star coral and brain coral, lettuce, pillar and flower corals.

The coral castles with their exquisite sea gardens host many other sea creatures, such as snails, lobsters, mollusks, crabs, sea cucumbers, starfish, sand dollars and sponges. Around the walls, through the corridors and down the paths swim exotic fish, as many as 300 species of them. The corals grow very slowly, some less than an inch a year, as each new generation builds on the skeleton of its ancestors. Though sturdy in appearance, they are extremely fragile and can be destroyed by changes in water conditions and by careless divers and boaters. In the early Florida tourist days, huge sections of the reef were laid waste by entrepreneurs collecting sea life novelties for eager souvenir shoppers. Coral was harvested with crowbars and cranes; the queen conch population, symbol and food source for early settlers, virtually disappeared.

Many sections of this exotic underwater world are now protected, with tough penalties for even minor assaults on the fragile environment. Mooring buoys for divers and snorkelers have been placed in the most popular areas, to protect the reef from damaging anchors.

The northern end of the reef lies in **Biscayne National Park**. ~ Headquarters at Convoy Point, east of Homestead; 305-230-7275; www.nps.gov/bisc. East of Key Largo, **John Pennekamp Coral Reef State Park**, in combination with the **Key Largo Coral Reef National Marine Sanctuary**, encompasses about 178 nautical square miles of reef and sea grass beds. ~ MM 102.5; 305-451-1202. Southeast of Big Pine Key, the **Florida Keys National Marine Sanctuary** covers a five-square-mile area of spectacular coral formations and exceptionally clear waters. ~ Headquarters at 216 Ann Street, Key West; 305-292-0311. (For more information on the parks, see the area "Beaches & Parks" sections in this chapter.) Reef formations continue down through the ocean to the Dry Tortugas (see "Fort Jefferson" in Chapter Four).

Visitors don't have to be adept scuba divers to explore the wonders and surprises of this underwater world. Even first-time snorkelers reap rich rewards, floating on the surface in the shallowest areas where colors are often brightest and sea life most spectacular. Professional dive shops equip snorkelers and divers and, along with various park headquarters, advise on prime locations, water conditions and transportation options. (It is usually recommended that you avoid charters that transport both snorkelers and scuba divers at the same time.) Underwater visibility averages 40 to 60 feet and may reach 100 feet or more in calm summer weather. Some coral formations rise to within a few feet of the surface.

If you want to catch a glimpse of the reef without getting wet at all, board one of the glass-bottom boats setting out from several locations throughout the Keys, or stop at the living reef exhibit at Pennekamp Park or the Key West Aquarium.

Another underwater attraction is the host of wrecked ships (some claim there are more than 500 of them) that met their fates on the reef in the days before lighthouses marked safe passage through the Florida Straits. Tales of lost treasure and the challenge of archaeological discovery keep hopeful divers returning again and again.

the restaurant for The Moorings, though it is not so low-profile. The models not only love it here, but so do backcountry fishing guides, the local business elite, the wide-eyed tourists trickling over from neighboring motels to this brisk-white boathouse with shutters the color of hot-pink oleanders. There's a brick patio set with artsy wood tables, and a patch of white beach set with white adirondacks, all spread along a wide-open bay. The food is superb, from the tropical tapas (ahi tuna tartare and mascarpone-stuffed crabcakes) to the herb-crusted black grouper. ~ MM 81.6, Islamorada; 305-664-0604, fax 305-664-0669; www.morada bay-restaurant.com. MODERATE TO ULTRA-DELUXE.

Outdoor tables sit on a wooden deck that is laced with fishing nets and palm fronds. The waterside eatery overlooks mangroves and is fringed with palms. Decidedly casual and leaning toward tiki, the **Islamorada Fish Company** serves baskets of fried calamari, shrimp and fish. The coconut scallop shrimp is a house specialty. ~ 81532 Route 1, Islamorada; 305-664-9271, 800-258-2559, fax 305-664-5071; www.islamoradafishco.com. BUDGET TO MODERATE.

Lazy Days has been popular practically since its doors first opened in 1922. For lunch, consider the fried oyster sandwich or the steak Philly, and for dinner, go for the Japanese bread-crusted yellowtail or the cracked conch entrée. If weather permits, ask to sit on the outside veranda, as you'll be assured a great view of the ocean, which begins (or ends) mere feet away. ~ MM 79.9, Islamorada; 305-664-5256. MODERATE.

In a weathered old house overlooking Tea Table Relief, **Papa Joe's Landmark Restaurant** really is a landmark, with battered wood floors, pecky cypress walls and ancient air conditioners that chase away the island heat. Papa Joe's does fresh fish seven different ways, including coconut-fried, Oscar and meunière; they will cook your catch for a slightly lower price. They also serve many steak entrées and have a good early-bird menu. The adjoining waterfront bar is a scenic place to meet local characters. ~ MM 79.7, Islamorada; 305-664-8109, fax 305-664-3002. MODERATE TO DELUXE.

Little Italy is about as rustic as can be, with shell lamps and wine bottles lining the windows. The food is terrific and plentiful. Bowls come to your table brimming with Sicilian-style seafood like sautéed snapper heaped with fresh tomatoes, black olives, mushrooms, shrimp and scallops in a sherry and lemon butter sauce. There are also many chicken and veal entrées, and traditional favorites such as ravioli and lasagna. Breakfast, lunch and dinner served daily. ~ MM 68.5, Layton; 305-664-4472, fax 305-664-9643. BUDGET TO MODERATE.

SHOPPING

The Rain Barrel is an artist's village full of top-quality crafts and much more. Many of the craftspeople create their wares right in this tropical setting complete with waterfall. There are stained-glass artisans, jewelers, fine artists and potters, whom you can often see working at their crafts, as well as an outdoor café serving Mediterranean-style dishes. ~ MM 86.7, Plantation Key; 305-852-3084.

A faux castle with a mammoth faux lobster out front, **Treasure Village** is a collection of unique little gift and artisan shops plus one department-sized store. The latter, **Treasure Harbor Trading** (305-852-0511), features fashionable gifts with tropical themes, from clothing to music to home decor. ~ MM 86.7, Islamorada.

The **Shell Shack** is one of those places where you'll want to stop and pose for a photo and grin in your shorts and sunhat for the folks back home shivering in their woollies. The house is festooned with garlands of fishing buoys, while wooden fish traps form makeshift tables and trays that brim with seashells. For sale is

MORE THAN SPORTS

Housed in a huge remodeled boat warehouse, the **World Wide Sportsman** is a sort of theme park for sporting goods. Center stage inside is a full-scale replica of Hemingway's fishing boat, *Pilar*. A saltwater aquarium lines one wall, crowned with a faux mangrove tree. The ground floor holds fishing goods; the top floor offers outdoor clothing, bathing suits, an art gallery and a small cocktail lounge overlooking the bay. Exquisite, arty details set this place apart: mounted game fish on the walls, designed wrought-iron work on the doors in the shape of fishing poles and a row of rocking chairs on the back porch facing the marina. Seasonal hours. ~ 81576 Route I at MM 81; 305-664-4615, 800-327-2880, fax 305-517-2618.

Floridiana in the form of shells, wind chimes, T-shirts and such. ~ MM 83.5, Islamorada; 305-664-9467.

For trendy resort and swim wear and gifts stop at **Latitude 25**. ~ MM 82.7, Islamorada; 305-664-4421, 866-664-4421; www.latitude25clothingco.com.

Island Silver and Spice is the closest thing to a department store in the Keys, with top-quality tropical merchandise ranging from housewares and shoes to jewelry and artwork. ~ MM 82, Islamorada; 305-664-2714.

Angelika is upscale and boutiquish, a perfumed place of soft linen and flax wear for women, elegant hats, Sue Wong evening gowns, delicate lingerie, and silver jewelry beaded with stones. Most merchandise comes from small companies around the country. ~ MM 81.9, Islamorada; 305-664-9008.

NIGHTLIFE   A definite departure from the slew of tourists bars and nightspots that dot the Keys, **Hog Heaven** is a waterside biker bar teeming with locals. Its greatest appeal is its decent pub food served 'til 3:30 a.m. daily. Entertainment includes live bands and deejays, big-screen televisions, pool and video games. ~ MM 85.3, Islamorada; 305-664-9669.

Nightlife begins in the daytime at **Holiday Isle Resort,** with a host of party areas sporting such names as Jaws Raw Bar, Wreck Bar and the World Famous Tiki Bar. Signs also point you to "Kokomo," a beach bar named after the Beach Boys' famous song. There's canned and live music to suit a variety of tastes throughout the days and nights. ~ MM 84, Islamorada; 305-664-2321, 800-327-7070, fax 305-664-2703; www.holidayisle.com.

The original Long Key Lounge was wiped out by a hurricane in 1935.

The gorgeous ocean view and well-stocked raw bar offset the general chaos at **Wahoo's Bar and Grill**. This is a busy place where employees and charter-boat crew tend to hang out after their shifts. Sit inside or out. ~ MM 83.5, Islamorada; 305-664-9888, fax 305-664-0692.

Big Dick & the Extenders is the house band at **Woody's**, a bar, lounge and Italian restaurant with increasing *Animal House* atmosphere as the night wears on. The band plays fusion raunch rock-and-roll, swing and blues on weekends. Doors shut at 4 a.m., making it the latest closing night spot for miles around and the only game in town. Closed Sunday and Monday. ~ MM 82, Islamorada; 305-664-4335.

You can enjoy a quiet drink at a table overlooking the Atlantic in Cheeca Lodge's elegant **Curt Gowdy Lounge**. There's also deck seating available. ~ MM 82.5, Islamorada; 305-664-4651.

In 1960, Hurricane Donna blew what is now the **Cabaña Bar** out to sea. After it was towed back, the place became a mellow bayside lounge. Live musicians perform reggae and easy-listening "sunset music" nightly. ~ MM 82, Islamorada; 305-664-4338; www.loreleifloridakeys.com.

Inside World Wide Sportsman, the mother of all Keys sporting goods stores, the small and sophisticated **Zane Grey Long Key Lounge** retains the clubby atmosphere of a gentleman's bar. Grey, a writer who pioneered sportfishing in the Keys, established the original Long Key Fishing Club that this bar pays homage to. Patrons come for oversized chairs, the hand-hewn wooden bar, cigar smoking, martinis and fish tales. There's also live local musicians on the weekends. ~ 81576 Route 1 at MM 81; 305-664-4615, 305-664-4244.

ANNE'S PUBLIC BEACH Some of the best Keys finds are minute. Blink and you'll miss Anne's Public Beach, a serendipitous gem that can be accessed by keeping your eyes peeled for the sign and pulling off the road at the right spot. Lined with trees, the pretty beach stretches along a shallow-water swimming area; there's a boardwalk and a picnic area. Open sunrise to sunset. ~ Located on the oceanside of Route 1 at MM 73.5, Islamorada; 305-664-2345.

BEACHES & PARKS

◄ HIDDEN

LONG KEY STATE PARK Like the key on which it is located, this park is long and narrow—its shoreline of shallow flats and mangrove lagoons all shaped by the usually gentle Atlantic waters. Mahogany, Jamaica dogwood, gumbo-limbo and other tropical trees inhabit the tangled hammocks that, along with the mangrove swamps, can be crossed on boardwalks and viewed from an observation tower. Even though the traffic of Route 1 is closer than you might wish, you can actually camp right next to the ocean. This is a good place for children to wade or swim, and saltwater fishing is excellent adjacent to the park and in deep Gulf Stream waters of the Atlantic. Facilities include picnic areas, restrooms, a nature trail, a canoe trail, showers, an observation tower and canoe rentals. Day-use fee, $3.50 to $6 per

vehicle plus the $.50 Monroe County surcharge per person. ~
Located on the ocean side of Route 1 at MM 67.5; 305-664-
4815, fax 305-664-2629.

▲ There are 60 sites, including 50 with RV hookups; $31.49
per night.

▼▼▼▼▼▼▼▼▼▼▼▼▼
Marathon Area

Legend has it that a worker helping to construct the
awe-inspiring Seven Mile Bridge was inadvertently responsible for naming Marathon. Overawed by the challenge of spanning seven miles of open sea, the man simply called
the task a "marathon." The appellation stuck.

Until the Seven Mile Bridge project was actually completed,
the railroad line stopped at the outer edge of Vaca Key, said to have
been named for the cows that once grazed there. Railroad workers were the major citizens of early Marathon, and the terminal
contributed to a thriving local economy. But when the bridge was
completed, the port lost its importance and the railroad crews
moved on. Marathon quieted down, peopled mainly by fishermen
of both the commercial and sport varieties and folk attracted by
the laid-back life.

But Marathon is quiet no more. With over 12,000 residents,
it is the second largest community in the Keys, topped only by
Key West. Tourism and fishing are the chief businesses here; there
is seemingly not a species of southern sea creature that has not
been caught in the surrounding waters. Retirement and long-
term vacation living are popular, too. A number of small subdivisions have grown up around manmade canals that seemingly
give everybody a "waterfront" lot and a place to dock a boat.

The Marathon area actually encompasses a collection of islands
from Duck Key (below MM 60) to the beginning of the Seven Mile
Bridge (MM 47) and includes far more than the bustling, traffic-
filled, friendly metropolis and its occasional suburbs and resorts.
Just before the outskirts of the city lies the oceanfront community
of Key Colony Beach, a designed village where even the smallest
houses seem to have their own boat docks. And here and there
among these islands and from their bridges you'll encounter open
spaces and fine views of the ocean and Gulf.

SIGHTS

One of those views hits visitors immediately upon entering the
Marathon area via **Long Key Bridge**. If you have not yet been over-

whelmed by the realization that when you travel the Keys you're really heading out to sea, get ready. You'll certainly feel the impact after you leave Layton and cross the beautiful bridge over the point where the Atlantic Ocean meets the Gulf of Mexico between Long Key and the first little Conch Key. On most days, this meeting is calm and gentle. The horizon stretches blue on all sides as sea and sky meld. Travelers often stop at the little pull-offs on either end of this bridge—the second longest in the Keys—to take in the vastness of the water and the handsome bridge. Because the shore is sandy here, you will see people wading out in the shallow water or trying out their snorkeling and scuba gear.

After leaving the beautiful scenes at the Long Key Bridge, Route 1 continues through several small Keys, including Duck Key, once site of a salt-making enterprise and now inhabited by showy homes and a large resort, Hawk's Cay. Nearby **Grassy Key** is home of the **Dolphin Research Center**, where you can play and swim with the friendly creatures (30-day advance reservations are required and you must be at least 44 inches tall). Narrated sessions are given every half hour. Admission. ~ MM 59; 305-289-1121 or 305-289-0002, fax 305-743-7627; www.dolphins.org.

Continuing on Route 1, you will encounter population pockets and empty spaces, skirt the residential and vacation village of Key Colony Beach, and arrive finally at **Marathon**, the last town before the famous Seven Mile Bridge. Stop at the **Greater Marathon Chamber of Commerce and Visitor Center** for information on this bustling area, which boasts shopping centers, a modern airport, commercial boat yards and lots of facilities for travelers. ~ MM 53.5, Marathon; 305-743-5417, 800-262-7284, fax 305-289-

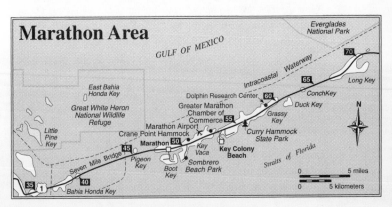

0183; www.floridakeysmarathon.com, e-mail info@florida keysmarathon.com.

HIDDEN ▶

Hidden from the casual observer, though actually located in the heart of Marathon, is **Crane Point Hammock**, headquarters of Florida Keys Land and Sea Trust. Considered by many to be the most environmentally and historically significant piece of property in the Keys, this bayside 63-acre nature preserve of tropical hardwoods and mangrove wetlands contains many exotic tree specimens, archaeological sites and a historic Bahamian conch-style house. A boardwalk over the tidal lagoon provides intimate views of native flora and fauna. Admission (includes Museum of Natural History and the Children's Museum). ~ MM 50.5; 305-743-3900, fax 305-743-0429; e-mail typcranept@aol.com.

If you head toward the ocean at MM 47.5, you'll end up around the commercial fishing docks, where you can watch the comings and goings of shrimp boats and other crafts. ~ 11th Street.

Crane Point Hammock is also home of the **Museum of Natural History of the Florida Keys**, which features a re-created coral reef, displays on pirate life and American Indian and shipwreck artifacts. They also have a shop with a wide selection of books on local wildlife, history and ecological information. ~ 5550 Overseas Highway; 305-743-9100, fax 305-743-8172; www.cranepoint.org.

Exhibits at the **Florida Keys Children's Museum**, also in Crane Point Hammock, include a tropical Caribbean lagoon, marine touch tank, iguana exhibit, historic sailing vessel and an American Indian hut built with palm fronds. Ideal for the entire family. ~ Crane Point Hammock; 305-743-9100, fax 305-743-8172.

HIDDEN ▶

Just beyond the docks at MM 47.5, **Boot Key** is popular with serious birdwatchers and is one of the few places where the official Hawk Watch counts are sometimes tallied during the fall hawk migration, when hundreds of raptors can be seen riding the thermals and kettling. The Key is accessible only when the draw bridge over the harbor is down. ~ Located on the oceanside at MM 50.

To fully experience the Marathon area, take to the water. As well as the distinctive diving and snorkeling trips to the reef, several sightseeing cruises are offered by local captains to Sombrero Reef and other popular destinations. Contact the Greater Marathon Chamber of Commerce for a list of some of the tour operators. ~ 305-743-5417, 800-262-7284, fax 305-289-0183; www.florida keysmarathon.com, e-mail visitus@floridakeysmarathon.com.

Reminiscent of old-time conch cabins, **Conch Key Cottages** are   **LODGING**
located on their own tiny island accessible by a short causeway.
This handful of rustic wooden cottages, boasting Dade County   ◀ *HIDDEN*
pine-vaulted ceilings, paddle fans, tile floors and fully equipped
gourmet kitchens, comes in a variety of sizes; some have jacuzzis
and screened porches and all are within easy access of a pleasant
little beach. There's a heated swimming pool and dock for all
guests to use. All units include use of a complimentary ocean
kayak for two. Unfortunately, the noise from busy Route 1 tends
to disrupt the peaceful atmosphere. ~ 62250 Overseas Highway,
Walker's Island; 305-289-1377, 800-330-1577, fax 305-743-8661;
www.conchkeycottages.com, e-mail info@conchkeycottages.com.
MODERATE TO ULTRA-DELUXE.

If you like a resort where everything is at your fingertips, the
60-acre **Hawk's Cay Resort** will fulfill your dreams. Here you
can sleep in a spacious room decorated in salmon and teal and
furnished with wickerwork rattan, dine in several very fine restaurants, bask beside one of the five pools or on a pleasant manmade beach, frolic with dolphins, play tennis and golf, or make
arrangements with the concierge for charter fishing, diving or just
about anything the Keys have to offer. The entire huge property
is elegant but casual. Two-bedroom villas are also available, as
well as a spa and a salon. ~ 61 Hawk's Cay Boulevard, Duck Key;
305-743-7000, 800-432-2242, fax 305-743-0641; www.hawks
cay.com, e-mail reservations@hawkscay.com. ULTRA-DELUXE.

Less than a mile south of the Dolphin Research Center, the
Bonefish Resort is charmingly raffish, Old Florida and affordable.
A dozen rooms of varying sizes are comfy. Some have kitchens.
Rooms 11, 12 and 14 are prime real estate, overlooking the ocean
with their own decks. Everyone is welcome to free use of paddleboats, kayaks and jacuzzis. ~ Route 1, MM 58, Grassy Key; 305-
743-7107, 800-274-9949, fax 305-743-9014; www.bonefish
resort.com, e-mail bonefishgk@bonefishresort.com. DELUXE.

Many motels and small hotels line the narrow but pretty
Atlantic Beach at Key Colony Beach. The **Key Colony Beach
Motel** offers 40 small, carpeted, functional rooms, and you can
dive into the large heated pool on those rare days when the ocean
is too cold. ~ 441 East Ocean Drive, Key Colony; 305-289-0411,
800-435-9811; www.members.aol.com/kcbmotel, e-mail kcb
motel@aol.com. MODERATE.

The **Ocean Beach Club** is a three-story coral affair with cool blue decor that suits its oceanside setting. Besides the rooms, there are deluxe-priced apartments with fully furnished kitchens, a small freshwater pool, a jacuzzi and lots of beach chairs for sunbathing on the rare (for the Keys) strip of sand. Guests can fish from the pier. ~ 351 East Ocean Drive, Key Colony; 305-289-0525, 800-321-7213, fax 305-289-9703; www.oceanbeach-club.com, e-mail obclub@bellsouth.net. DELUXE.

HIDDEN ▶   **Latigo** provides an unusually romantic two-night getaway for their guests—lodging and dining on a 56-foot yacht. After a sunset dinner cruise, the captain drops anchor for the night behind a small island cluster. Mornings are devoted to exploring the nearby coral reef. All meals and drinks are included in the rate; all cruises are for the reserving party only. ~ 1021 11th Street, Marathon; 305-289-1066, 800-897-4886; www.latigo.net, e-mail cruise@latigo.net. ULTRA-DELUXE.

When Hurricane Wilma hit the Keys, Coconut Cay Resort and Marina was reduced to **Coconut Cay Resort**. Still standing is the inland property, which includes nine double rooms and eleven dockside rooms along a canal. Several of these latter units come with free dockage for the boat traveler, and some also come with efficiencies. During your stay, take advantage of the heated pool and 4000-square-foot sunning desk, or charm the waters with a rented waverunner or kayak. ~ 7196 Overseas Highway, Marathon; 305-289-7672; www.coconutcay.com, e-mail info@coconutcay.com. MODERATE TO DELUXE.

◆◆

BODY SHOT

The elegant, world-class **West Indies Spa** is furnished with tasteful rattan, has plenty of places to chill and smells great—like cucumber, citrus and lily. Visitors are welcome to indulge in the spa's myriad beautification techniques, including facials, saunas, whirlpools, salon treatments and massages. My favorite: the Key's Style Margarita Salt Loofah, which begins in the tropical-rain room with a six-head Vichy shower, followed with a sea salt exfoliation, a soothing tequila gel and a cool lime body lotion finish. Cheers! This is a 50-minute body cocktail. ~ Hawk's Cay Resort, 61 Hawk's Cay Boulevard, Duck Key; 305-743-7000, 800-432-2242; www.hawkscay.com.

You can have a basic motel room or a fully equipped efficiency at the **Valhalla Beach Resort Motel** and feel as if you are on a ◄ *HIDDEN* private island with a quiet Atlantic inlet and waving palms. The nine units are strictly basic, but the tiny beach, boat ramp and docks, and considerable distance from traffic make this a quiet and special place. ~ MM 56.5, Marathon; phone/fax 305-289-0616. BUDGET TO DELUXE.

Immaculate, comfortable and cozy, the little blue and white **Anchor Inn** is one of a handful of a completely refurbished 1950s motels in Marathon. Choose from several adorable efficiencies or three fully equipped kitchen units with dining areas. The bathrooms and kitchens are brand-spanking new, and the interior decoration is homey but tasteful. There's no pool here, but public beaches and waterfront parks are within a 10-minute drive. ~ 7931 Overseas Highway, Marathon; 305-742-2213; www.anchor inn.com. BUDGET.

Don't be surprised if there's a Caddie with fins parked out front at the funky **Siesta Motel**, a restored 1950s motel with a large multi-colored gecko sculpture crawling up its sign. The Siesta is eye candy for vintage-travel connoisseurs: terrazzo floors, Dade County pine ceilings, tangerine-colored vinyl and pink and black tile bathrooms. There's no pool; guests may use the Faro Blanco pool and tiki bar. ~ 7425 Overseas Highway, Marathon; 305-743-5671, fax 305-946-8220; www.siesta motel.net. BUDGET.

Built as a fishing camp in the 1940s, the 28-unit **Crystal Bay Resort** has been refurbished. The modest, homey cottages are cute and clean. Each has its own small porch or patio, and kitchen units are available. The sprawling grounds are fantastic, with white gay-nineties-style lamps, a fish pond, reading hammocks and aviaries housing a scarlet macaw. There's a pool and 200 feet of sandy beachfront. ~ 4900 Overseas Highway, Marathon; 305-289-8089; www.crystalbayresort.com, e-mail info@ crystalbayresort.com. MODERATE.

Only a five-minute boat ride from shore, **Pretty Joe Rock** is ◄ *HIDDEN* among Marathon's best kept—and priciest—secrets. For $3000, you can spend the weekend on this tiny island, in a restored thousand-square-foot, two-bedroom, two-bath cottage. Built by an adventuresome woman pilot in the 1950s, this Old Florida

Text continued on page 124.

Days of
   the Dolphins

As far back as the shadowy times of prehistory, humans have been fascinated by dolphins. In Greek mythology, Apollo once took the form of a dolphin to lead a boat to Delphi. Various coastal communities around the world have greeted the dolphin as a bearer of good fortune, guider of lost ships, saver of human lives. Though scientists cannot interpret the actions of dolphins in terms of human emotions, it is easy to see why these lovely marine mammals have captivated the imagination for so many centuries. Stand on a Florida beach and watch a pod of dolphins surface and dive, or leap gracefully above the waves. Or sail into the Gulf of Mexico, accompanied by dolphins who dart in and out of your path, seemingly playing with you as you tack and turn. Though much of the dolphin's life remains a mystery, there is no question that they are highly intelligent.

Dolphins, like whales, are cetaceans. The greatest confusion, perhaps, comes from distinguishing dolphin from porpoise. To the casual observer, the most obvious physical difference is that most dolphins have a pronounced beak and a dorsal fin with a curvature toward the tail, while none of the porpoises has a discernible beak, and all but one have a triangular dorsal fin. Also, dolphins have cone-shaped teeth, while porpoise teeth are spade-shaped.

Dolphins live a complex social life, often traveling in large herds broken down into family units called pods. Mothers keep an eye on their calves for up to five years, displaying deep affection throughout infancy. Researchers report that dolphins forced to live alone display unhappiness. Adolescents isolate themselves into groups of their own sex, not returning to socialize with the whole group until they become mature adults. No wonder we are tempted to think of them in human terms!

Yet however much we might like to identify with dolphins, and though their brains are similar in size to ours, dolphins possess many abilities that we can only envy. Most impressive is echolocation, the use of a biological sonar that allows dolphins to locate food and interpret other objects, no matter how dark or murky the water, by sending out and echoing back their curious clicks and squeals and whistles. And unlike us, they can dive to great depths for long periods of time without developing painful, life-threatening bends. Located on the tops of their heads are the nostrils, remarkable blowholes with two internal passages, one for each lung.

Though fewer dolphins ply the waters surrounding South Florida than once swam here, sharp-eyed visitors can still reap their share of sightings in the wild. Besides, the Florida Keys have long been one of the centers for the study and training of these sea mammals. At the **Theater of the Sea**, the oldest marine-mammal facility in the world (established in 1946), you can learn about the Atlantic bottlenose dolphins, California sea lions, sea turtles and other marine creatures that inhabit the 17-acre park's three-acre natural saltwater lagoon. You also get to wade with baby dolphins. Admission. ~ MM 84.5, Islamorada; 305-664-2431, fax 305-664-8162; www.theaterofthesea.com. Several motels and resorts boast their own private dolphin pets who put on shows for or swim with their guests.

Swim with a dolphin? Yes, it is possible (for a handsome fee), and it can be a rewarding and, some say, almost mystical experience well worth the price. At the **Dolphin Research Center**, the income from fees and admission helps support an extensive program of therapy for kids with special needs, teaching and research. Admission. ~ MM 59, Grassy Key; 305-289-1121; www.dolphins.org, e-mail drc@dolphins.org. You also can make a swim appointment at **Dolphins Plus**, an education and research center. It is next door to Island Dolphin Care, a non-profit organization that works on dolphin-assisted therapy for disabled children. Admission. ~ MM 99.5, Key Largo; 305-451-1993, fax 305-451-3710; e-mail info@ dolphinsplus.com. **Dolphin Connection**, based at Hawk's Cay Resort, offers several encounter programs, including a behind-the-scenes look at training as well as supervised swims. Admission. ~ MM 61, Duck Key; 305-289-9975, 888-814-9154; www.dolphinconnection.com. **The Dolphin Cove Center**, which provides dolphin/human therapy to special-needs children, also offers in-water encounters to the public (fee). ~ MM 102, Key Largo; 305-451-4060, fax 305-451-4021; www.dolphinscove.com.

As interest in dolphins increases, critics of human-dolphin encounters express concern about possible harmful effects on these sensitive animals in the wild; the federal government has launched an education campaign that encourages people to admire from a distance (it is illegal to feed wild dolphins). The research centers will share information on these subjects with you.

Keys construction has weathered numerous hurricanes. The interior now features finished wooden floors, trendy bamboo and rattan furniture, full bar, kitchen, washer/dryer and jacuzzi. A deck overlooks lobster-filled waters. Boat, snorkeling equipment and fishing tackle are included. ~ Banana Bay Resort and Marina, 4590 Overseas Highway, Marathon; 305-743-3500; www.bananabay.com, e-mail info@bananabay.com. ULTRA-DELUXE.

Electricity, fresh water, and telephone and cable television lines are piped underwater from the main key to Pretty Joe Rock.

The 20 clean and functional rooms and efficiencies at **Bonefish Bay Motel** offer a cozy base of operations. Located just north of Vaca Cut, the '50s-style motel has a pool and access to a dock. ~ 12565 Overseas Highway, MM 53.5, Marathon; 305-289-0565, 800-336-0565, fax 305-289-3475; www.bonefishbay.com, e-mail reservations@bonefish-bay.com. MODERATE.

At roadside, it looks like the front of an ordinary motel. But don't be fooled by the plain exterior. Follow the lane that leads to the bay, and you'll find yourself in a shady oasis. This is **Banana Bay Resort**, ten secluded acres that will make you forget the endless stream of cars buzzing by at the doorstep on Route 1. The 65 rooms are decorated in Caribbean plantation style; most have private verandas. The resort offers an exercise room, a freshwater pool with restaurant and lounge, tennis courts, boat and watersport rentals and charters for fishing, sailing and diving. There's a poolside continental breakfast buffet included in the rate. A small, private island with a two-bedroom conch cottage is also available, at ultra-deluxe rates. ~ MM 49.5, Marathon; 305-743-3500, 800-226-2621, fax 305-743-2670; www.bananabay.com, e-mail info@bananabay.com. DELUXE TO ULTRA-DELUXE.

Sombrero Resort and Lighthouse Marina offers waterfront efficiencies that have kitchenettes, as well as one-bedroom condos. Everything about the place is appropriately light and airily tropical, from the sparkling pool to the cheerful tiki bar. There are four tennis courts along with a pro shop, fitness center, sauna and 79-slip marina. Children are encouraged, making it a good family lodging. ~ 19 Sombrero Boulevard, Marathon; 305-743-2250, 800-433-8660, fax 305-743-2998; www.sombreroresort.com. ULTRA-DELUXE.

HIDDEN ▶   For kayaks or bikes to rent, or arranged fishing trips, try the **Sombrero Reef Inn & Fishing Lodge**, situated in an oceanside motel. There are four rooms for rent, each with private bath and entrance, air conditioning, views of the ocean and good breezes. Full kitchens and waterfront patios are also available. ~ 500 Sombrero Beach Road, Marathon; 305-743-4118; www.som breroreefinn.com, e-mail matt@sombreroreefinn.com. DELUXE TO ULTRA-DELUXE.

If you're looking to explore the open seas, or if sportfishing gets your pulse racing, a good bet is **Captain Pip's Marina & Hideaway**. Guest are assigned their own 18- or 21-foot boat, and Pip's is always happy to arrange half- or full-day guided fishing and diving trips. The guest rooms, efficiencies and suites allow up to six people, and come with wicker furniture, ceiling fans, Cuban tile floors, refrigerators, microwaves and coffeemakers. ~ 1410 Overseas Highway, Marathon; 305-743-4403, 800-707-1692; www.captainpips.com, e-mail captpips@aol.com. ULTRA-DELUXE.

Knights Key Inn is a three-story unit of older vacation apartments with kitchens, almost hidden alongside a neighboring campground, where you can dock your boat for free. You have a great view of the Seven Mile Bridge. Rooms are old-fashioned with a slightly nautical decor. There is a small picnic area with a pool and palm trees. ~ 40 Kyle Way West, MM 47, Marathon; 305-289-0289, 800-743-4786; www.keysdirectory.com/knights keyinn. DELUXE.

◄ HIDDEN

They call the **Porto Cayo at Hawk's Cay Resort** a formal dining room, which makes it a Keys rarity, but it's not so formal that you and your family can't relax and enjoy it. The linen cloths and potted plants create a nice ambience for enjoying the gourmet menu. Dinner entrées include baked manicotti and spaghetti bolognese. Hours vary in the off season, so call ahead. Closed for special events. ~ MM 61, Duck Key; 305-743-7000, fax 305-743-5215. MODERATE TO DELUXE.

DINING

As its name suggests, this large nautical-themed restaurant is at the **WatersEdge**. It's on an inlet, rather than the open ocean, and overlooks an informal marina area. However, the setting is attractive, and the activity surrounding the boats moored just outside the windows is endlessly entertaining. The restaurant is actually part of Hawk's Cay Resort, but is several blocks away— far enough to allow hotel guests to feel they've "gone out" to dinner. The American menu is varied and interesting, with an emphasis on fresh seafood. There's also a children's menu and an all-you-can-eat soup and salad bar. Dinner only. ~ 61 Hawk's Cay Boulevard, Duck Key; 305-743-7000, fax 305-743-5215; www.hawkscay.com, e-mail reservations@hawkscay.com. MODERATE TO DELUXE.

Tucked away in the Rainbow Bend Resort and overlooking the Atlantic Ocean, the **Hideaway Café** is a local favorite for gourmet dinners and romantic outings. Diners feast by candlelight on crisp, white tablecloths in the small and intimate dining room. Fare is Continental: roast duck, escargots, rack of lamb, *chateaubriand*, fresh local seafood and *coq au vin*. There's also a great wine list. Dinner reservations are recommended. Breakfast and dinner only. ~ MM 58, Grassy Key; 305-289-1554; www.hideawaycafe.com. DELUXE TO ULTRA-DELUXE.

Don Pedro demonstrates a creative use of a strip shopping center unit. Cuban cuisine is the feature of this sparkling blue-and-gray eatery located on an insignificant corner. All the entrées, such as *lechón asado* (roast pork), *churrasco* (Argentine steak), *boliche asado* (pot roast), and *picadillo* (a tasty ground beef dish), come with yellow rice, black beans, fried bananas and crispy Cuban bread. The very filling meals may be accompanied by steamy, thick Cuban coffee or homemade sangria and topped off with a dessert of flan, a traditional baked custard. Closed Sunday. ~ MM 53, Marathon; 305-743-5247, fax 305-743-0518; www.donpedrosrest.com. BUDGET TO MODERATE.

HIDDEN ►

Turn toward the ocean at the Trailerama sign on Route 1, and at the water's edge you'll find **Burdine's Chiki Tiki Bar and Grille**, a friendly outdoor joint overlooking Boot Key Harbor. Decorated with lobster buoys and license plates, Burdine's is a local favorite where singer-songwriters occasionally entertain in the afternoons. The fish sandwiches are great, as are the skewered tuna and shrimp. The menu also includes chicken fajitas and hamburgers. The cook's own invention, fried Key lime pie, is pretty good—if you can stomach pie filling inside a tortilla. ~ 1200 Oceanview Avenue, Marathon; 305-743-9204; www.burdines waterfront.com. BUDGET TO MODERATE.

The best food in Marathon is at **Barracuda Grill**. The dining room is small and minimalist, mostly white, with low-lit art parked on the walls and a sleek bar in the back. Sizzling offerings include

"Voodoo Stew" with fish, calamari, scallops and shrimp. Other great plates feature chicken, lamb, pork and beef. There's a good selection of wines. Seasonal hours, call ahead. ~ MM 49.5, Marathon; 305-743-3314. DELUXE TO ULTRA-DELUXE.

Takara Japanese Restaurant & Sushi Bar is a local dive serving up outstanding fresh raw fish. Make it past the unassuming exterior and treat your palate to a sampling from the long list of modestly priced sushi, sashimi, nigiri, teriyaki and tempura. Hot or cold *sake* is a perfect accompaniment to your meal. Closed Sunday. ~ 3740 Overseas Highway, MM 49.5, Marathon; 305-743-0505. BUDGET TO MODERATE.

Don't panic when you read "dolphin" among the special dinner entrées. This refers to a popular tropical game fish, not to the gentle mammal. It would make things easier if only restaurants would agree, once and for all, to stick to its other name, mahimahi.

You'd better like seafood if you stop at the **Cracked Conch Cafe,** which claims to have been "cracked up and conched out since 1979." Concessions are made for landlubbers, however, in the steak and chicken entrées. The main thing, of course, is the mollusk that comes out of the pretty pink shell—chowdered, frittered, cracked, burgered and sautéed. This is an unpretentious little place that is Keys to the core—that is, it sports a spacious bar and is not air-conditioned. But it's wide open to whatever breezes can be captured, and there's open-air seating out back next to a fountain. ~ MM 49.5, Marathon; 305-743-2233; www.conch-cafe.com, e-mail deconda@excite.com. MODERATE.

Not into seafood? Located poolside at the Sombrero Resort, **Marathon Pizza and Pasta** serves up homemade cooked-to-order ◄ HIDDEN Italian favorites in a cozy, friendly dining room. The New York–style pizzas feature the standard toppings, along with some unusual choices such as steak and gorgonzola cheese. You'll also find good soups, salads, pastas and homemade desserts. Closed Sunday. ~ 19 Sombrero Boulevard, Marathon; 305-743-9993. MODERATE.

Located in Banana Bay Resort and Marina, the **Banana Cabana Restaurant** retains an old Florida Keys charm. The waitstaff and the dining room's somewhat mismatched but immaculate decor strike a comfortable chord with locals and visitors alike. The terrific Continental cuisine prepared with a Caribbean flair includes sautéed yellowtail with capers, lemon butter and garlic. Or try coconut-encrusted chicken breast, topped with pineapple mango glaze. Outside, tables by the lit, aquamarine pool encourage a leisurely meal, finished off with turtle cheesecake. There's also an impressive wine list and the popular Sunset Tiki Bar. ~ 4590 Overseas Highway, MM 49.5, Marathon; 305-289-1232; www.bananabay.com. MODERATE TO DELUXE.

HIDDEN ▶ If you wind down 15th Street past where you think it ends, you'll come to **Castaway**, a no-nonsense eatery on the working wharf where locals have been coming for several decades. There's a wide variety of seafood on the menu, with chicken, steak and vegetarian dishes, but the big come-on here is shrimp "steamed in beer—seconds on the house." They ply you with luscious hot buns dripping with honey even before you begin. Lunch served Monday through Friday. ~ Turn toward the ocean just below MM 48; 305-743-6247, fax 305-743-6249; e-mail lobstercrawl@aol.com. MODERATE.

Seven Mile Grill is a solid choice for diner fare with a tropical flair. This local hotspot may make ample use of its frier, but it also dishes up homemade soups such as shrimp bisque and conch chowder. For entrées, consider stuffed crabs or steamed shrimp in beer, topped off with a slice of the grill's award-winning Key lime pie. Open for breakfast, lunch and dinner. Closed Wednesday and Thursday. ~ MM 47.5, bayside, Marathon; 305-743-4481.

SHOPPING The gift shop at the **Museum of Crane Point Hammock** carries a little bit of everything—sea life figurines, jewelry, T-shirts and the ever-popular snow globe. ~ MM 55.5, Marathon; 305-743-9100; www.cranepoint.org.

AUTHOR FAVORITE

Keys Fisheries Market and Marina, located on the gulfside docks, is the largest seafood producer in the Keys. They also cook on the premises. Fresh lobster, shrimp, fish—even the elusive golden crab—are served up in both basic and elaborate ways, including the lobster reuben, smoked fish spreads and bisques. Order from a pick-up window, eat at one of the shaded picnic tables and watch the tarpon roll in the warm waters off the dock. I loved the grilled hog snapper sandwich, served with fries and slaw. They stock a decent selection of California, French and New Zealand wines. ~ End of 35th Street, Marathon; 305-743-4353; www.keysfisheries.com, e-mail keysfisheries@comcast.net. MODERATE.

Don't miss **The Quay Shops,** a little cluster of weathered-gray   ◄ *HIDDEN*
boutiques that includes **Bayshore Clothing** for tropical fashions
and **It's a Small World** (305-743-8430) for out-of-the-ordinary children's togs and toys. ~ MM 54, Marathon.

The **Bougainvillea House Gallery** is a local-art buyer's paradise. Featuring fine art and jewelry, the artists' cooperative exhibits the work of 30 artists. Oils, watercolors, ceramics, photography and blown glass are among the mediums represented.
Most of the subject matter relates to the Keys. ~ 12420 Overseas
Highway, MM 53.5, Marathon; 305-743-0808; www.bougain
villeahousegallery.com.

Anthony's features a vast array of women's swimsuits, as well
as trendy name-brand sportswear, lingerie and sleepwear. ~ 5800
Overseas Highway, Suite 25, MM 50, Marathon; 305-743-5855.

If you are doing your own cooking, or you'd just like to peruse
the catches of the day, explore the collection of **seafood markets**
along the wharves at the end of 11th or 15th Street. These are
outlets for some of the area's serious commercial fishing. ~ On the
oceanside near MM 48.

The **WatersEdge** overlooks the water beside the showy marina at   **NIGHTLIFE**
Hawk's Cay. There's a casual mood and live music on Friday and
Saturday nights. Open approximately November through
August. ~ MM 61, Duck Key; 305-743-7000; www.hawks
cay.com.

For Force 5 blues try the **Hurricane Bar.** Decent bands rou-
tinely take the stage, cranking Cajun, rock, jazz, Delta blues and
zydeco, multiple nights a week. Dinners are served until midnight.
~ MM 49.5, 4650 Overseas Highway, Marathon; 305-743-2220.

Friday and Saturday happy hour offers live entertainment
and hors d'oeuvres at **The Tiki Bar.** ~ Holiday Inn, MM 54,
Marathon; 305-289-0222.

At the **Quay,** you can enjoy the sunsets, full seafood meals
and tropical drinks at this brightly decorated Gulfside spot. ~
MM 54, Marathon; 305-289-1810.

For a true "come as you are" type of atmosphere, the **Dockside Lounge** at the Sombrero Marina can't be beat. An eclectic mix
of patrons, nightly live music and drink and food specials make
for a winning combination that yields a raucous time in this sleepy
slice of the Keys. ~ MM 50, Marathon; 305-743-0000.

For a nightcap and some entertainment in more posh surroundings, the **Banana Bay Resort** has three bars on its premises: a main bar, a pool bar and a tiki bar with an Alice in Wonderland chess set. You'll be rubbing elbows with fellow tourists as you listen to live bands and belt out a few tunes on karaoke night. ~ MM 49.5, Marathon; 305-743-3500.

Several arts organizations are active in the Marathon area, sponsoring concerts and plays year-round. For information contact the Marathon Community Theatre. ~ P.O. Box 500124, Marathon, FL 33050; 305-743-0994.

You'll find a down-home place with a mix of locals and tourists who've steered in from Route 1 at the **Barracuda Grill.** There's live entertainment on some weekends and spontaneous karaoke whenever the spirit moves a customer so inclined to sing. Closed Sunday. ~ MM 42, Marathon; 305-743-3314; www.barracudagrill.com.

BEACHES & PARKS

HIDDEN ▶

CURRY HAMMOCK STATE PARK 🧍 🚲 Unspoiled and uncrowded, this unassuming park offers hiking and biking trails as well as beach and picnic facilities. The beach is narrow and natural, covered with sea grasses and shrubs, with an ideal shoreline for exploring during low tide. From mid-August through November, it is a major thoroughfare for migrating birds, including merlins, ospreys, hawks and turkey vultures. The peregrine falcon, once extinct as a breeding bird east of the Mississippi, makes magnificent October showings here thanks to the efforts of local conservation groups. ~ Located oceanside at MM 56; 305-289-2690.

SOMBRERO BEACH PARK 🏊 This community park is a generous area with a plethora of plants and trees and a wide sandy beach, offering one of the few public beaches around. It is a good place for some sun and relaxation and an ideal romping spot for children. Swimming is pleasant in usually clear, calm ocean water. There are covered picnic areas, barbecues, restrooms, showers and a playground. ~ Sombrero Beach Road at MM 50 in Marathon; 305-743-0033, fax 305-743-3667.

Lower Keys Area

The Lower Keys, which begin at MM 40 just below the Seven Mile Bridge and extend to around MM 5, are *different.* They are different in geological makeup, in flora and fauna and even in ambience and pace from the rest of the Keys. Geologically, their fossil coral base is layered with a limestone that's called oolite (for its egg-shaped granules). Some of the islands of the Lower Keys are forested with sturdy pine trees, others with tall tropical hardwoods where orchids and bromeliads thrive. A number of endangered species, including the unique Key deer, struggle for survival on these low-lying islands.

Big Pine Key is the largest of the islands and second in area only to Key Largo in the entire Keys. Wildlife refuges and shopping centers share this island, the former protecting much of the unique plant and animal life, the latter offering necessary services for the people who choose to live in what seems a quieter, lonelier region than those on either side.

The Lower Keys boast the best public beach south of the mainland and access to a fine protected section of coral reef offshore in the Atlantic. Though there are pockets of development, from collections of little frame houses to assorted elegant residences, frenetic modernization seems to have been held at bay. With some unassuming screened-in eateries, scattered modest lodgings and significant protected wild areas, this region offers more chances to experience the "old Keys" than any other.

SIGHTS

Perhaps the most impressive sight in the Lower Keys is its initial access, the magnificent **Seven Mile Bridge**, spanning the sea between Marathon and Sunshine Key. The bridge that carries the Overseas Highway today is the "new" bridge, built in 1982 to replace the terrifyingly narrow but equally impressive structure that parallels it on the Gulf side. The old bridge, referred to as "the longest fishing pier in the world," crosses **Pigeon Key**. From the new bridge the Key appears something very desirable, palmy and perfect, with handsome yellow and white conch houses sparkling in sunlight. There is water everywhere, the green of the gulf merging with blues of ocean. One assumes that many a motorist, bound for Key West, has looked over at Pigeon Key with astonishment.

It's unlikely that Henry Flagler's crew felt the same way about Pigeon—nearly 400 holed up here in camps while they toiled on the railroad from 1908 to 1935. The camps were hot and muggy and swarming with mosquitoes much of the year, and people went crazy. There is the story of the bridge foreman's wife, who had an affair with the camp cook. When the pair was discovered, the wife took a rope to the second floor of her house, looped it around a ridge beam, and hung herself. In recent years ghost experts have been brought in and some say they can feel the spirit of the departed wife, especially in the second-floor attic of the 1912 **Bridge Tender's House**.

To visit the old camp complex, visitors board a vintage trolley train over to Pigeon Key, watch a film on the island's history, then explore the seven buildings that date from 1912.

Start in the 1912 **Assistant Bridge Tender's House**, renovated to look as it did in 1912: painted deep yellow and propped on cone-shaped pilings. There's a museum inside with a model of the old seven mile bridge and photographs of those early times and residents who lived here from 1938–41 when Pigeon Key was a fish camp. Admission. ~ Visitors Center is at MM 47, at the west end of Marathon and across from Pigeon Key; 305-289-0025; www.pigeonkey.org, e-mail pigeonkey@aol.com.

Unlike the upper and middle Keys, most of the Lower Keys seem to lie at right angles to the highway. Their geology, and hence their vegetation and wildlife, differ in many respects from that of their neighbors to the northeast. **Bahia Honda Key**, for example, features some white-sand beaches; many unusual species of plants and birds are found throughout the Lower Keys. ~ MM 36.7.

As you look across to the southern peninsula of Bahia Honda Key, you will see a magnificent section of the old **Flagler Bridge**, with the railroad trestle on one level and the automobile highway arching above it, a masterpiece of engineering for its day.

If you survey the sky on the Gulf side, you'll catch a glimpse of **Fat Albert** floating high above the water. A large, white, blimp-shaped radar balloon, he's diligently on the lookout for illegal drug traffickers and other inappropriate interlopers. To keep him from being *too* diligent, he is moored to a missile tracking station on Cudjoe Key.

At MM 33 you arrive at **Big Pine Key**. Stop at the **Lower Keys Chamber of Commerce** for information about this area. Big Pine Key is second only to Key Largo in size, but its character is quite different. Here there are blooming subdivisions, pine trees, good-sized shopping centers and freshwater sink holes formed in the oolic rock foundation of the island. The contest between development and the wild is apparent. Closed Sunday. ~ MM 31; 305-872-2411, 800-872-3722, fax 305-872-0752; www.lowerkeys chamber.com, e-mail lkchamber@aol.com.

Lower Keys

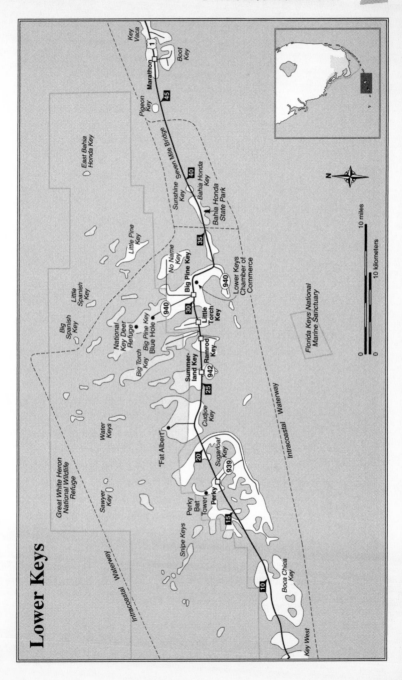

Not far from the town of Big Pine lies a good-sized freshwater rock quarry pond called **Blue Hole**, the only one of its kind in the entire Keys. It is inhabited by several alligators, who often lie near the shore, as well as turtles and various wading birds and fish. ~ Key Deer Boulevard, two and a quarter miles north of Route 1. The nearby **Jack C. Watson Nature Trail** meanders through a typical Big Pine Key habitat of palms and slash pine and skirts a unique hardwood hammock. **The Fred Manillo Nature Trail** provides benches and a turning deck for people with disabilities.

HIDDEN ▶   Only reachable by boat, **Looe Key** has been absorbed into the large **Florida Keys National Marine Sanctuary**, but it is still an exceedingly popular diving site. The spectacular coral formations of this five-square-mile area and the crystal-clear waters make it delightful even for novice snorkelers. Several wrecked ships also lie within the sanctuary, including the 1744 British frigate HMS *Looe*. Those floating yellow buoys mark marine-life protected areas. ~ Located 6.7 nautical miles southeast of Big Pine Key; headquarters at 216 Ann Street, Key West; 305-292-0311, fax 305-292-5065; www.fknms.nos.noaa.gov. Call the Chamber of Commerce for snorkeling and diving information.

HIDDEN ▶   Enjoy a sea kayaking adventure in the Great White Heron and the Key Deer wildlife refuge by calling **Reflections Nature Tours**. Their wildlife and educational trips give you a chance to see coral and sponges in the shallow water of the red mangroves. Biking and hiking tours are also available ~ P.O. Box 431373, Big Pine Key, FL 33043; 305-872-4668; www.floridakeyskayaktours.com.

HIDDEN ▶   If you take a detour toward the Gulf on lower Sugarloaf Key, you'll get a glance at the **Perky Bat Tower**. This Dade County pine curiosity was built in 1929 as the brainchild of Richter C. Perky, who hoped to get the menacing mosquito population under control by importing a population of insect-devouring bats to take up residence in this louvered bat condo. Some say the bats never arrived, others claim that they came and, not satisfied with their carefully designed accommodations, took off for preferable climes. At any rate, the novel structure still stands and is on the National Register of Historic Places. ~ Off Route 1 at MM 17.

LODGING   Generic motels and small resorts appear here and there in the Lower Keys; rates are often lower than in nearby Key West. If you look hard, you'll also discover that some of the very best lodgings in this area are the hidden ones. Be aware, however, that Monroe County's efforts to maintain enough affordable housing for locals reduces the availability of certain types of vacation rentals. This primarily affects your ability to rent a home or apartment for less than 28 days. The pool of vacation properties in Big Pine Key, which has relatively few hotel/motel rooms, has dropped dramatically. Your best bet here is to make arrangements well in advance.

There are three handsome duplex cabins on the Gulf side of **Bahia Honda State Park**. Though the cabins are not really hidden because you can see them from the highway, many visitors are unaware that the six grey frame units on stilts are available for rental. The fully equipped lodgings with spacious decks can accommodate up to six people. Make reservations by phone up to 11 months ahead. ~ MM 36.7, Bahia Honda Key; 305-872-2353, 800-326-3521; www.dep.state.fl.us/parks. DELUXE.

If you'd like to rent a vacation home away from the highway, contact **Big Pine Vacation Rentals**. All the homes are on the waterfront, either on open water or canals, all with boat dockage. A 28-day minimum stay is required. ~ MM 29.5, Big Pine Key; 305-872-9863; www.vrbo.com, e-mail bpvacation@aol.com. MODERATE TO DELUXE.

The motto of **Barnacle Bed and Breakfast**, "barefoot oceanfront living with panache," says it all. The owners built their ele-   ◄ HIDDEN

AUTHOR FAVORITE

All my environmentalist instincts emerge when I visit **National Key Deer Refuge**. The Key deer are a miniature subspecies of white-tailed deer that grow to be less than three feet tall at the shoulder. In the 1940s, the population almost disappeared, inspiring the establishment of the 8600-acre refuge. I've frequently spotted America's tiniest deer in the wilderness areas of the refuge, especially in the early morning or late afternoon. Visitors should be warned that there are heavy fines for feeding or harming these endangered, fragile animals. Trail and viewing areas open shortly before dawn to take advantage of prime deer-viewing time. The visitors center is closed weekends but trails are open daily. ~ Big Pine Key Area on Key Deer Boulevard, one-quarter mile north of Route 1, MM 30.5; 305-872-2239, fax 305-872-3675; nationalkeydeer.fws.gov, e-mail r4rw_fl.nkd@fws.gov.

gant home in the shape of a six-pointed star, creating a collection of interestingly designed, distinctive rooms around a central atrium where gourmet breakfasts are served. Guests stay in either of two rooms with private baths in the main house or in the efficiency in the many-angled annex. Kayaks and bicycles are available for guests free of charge. Children must be 16 years or older to stay here. ~ 1557 Long Beach Drive, one and a half miles from MM 33, Big Pine Key; 305-872-3298, 800-465-9100, fax 305-872-3863; www.thebarnacle.net, e-mail barnacle@att global.net. DELUXE.

For the past three decades, unsuspecting tourists have been pleasantly surprised by the comfort and amenities of **Big Pine Key Fishing Lodge.** This no-frills, family-owned-and-operated "fishing lodge" has more than a hundred RV sites (most with full hookups), several dozen tent sites, five mobile-home units and six efficiencies. The mobile homes and efficiencies come in a variety of configurations, up to and including three-room units with full kitchenettes. The facility also includes a great pool, picnic area, recreation room, dock and marina. A three-day minimum stay is required. ~ MM 33, Big Pine Key; 305-872-235, fax 305-872-3868. MODERATE.

HIDDEN ►   **Deer Run Adult Guest House** offers three rooms with separate entrances and private baths in a very attractive Florida-style house with high ceilings, Bahama fans and good views of the ocean. A 52-foot veranda overlooks the sea and the natural grounds where Key deer roam. The owner has cleverly decorated the outdoor area with driftwood and other jetsam deposited by the Atlantic currents onto the beach. Outdoor hammocks, chaise longues and a barbecue grill help you feel at home. Guests have free access to bicycles, a canoe and an outdoor hot tub. Adults only. Two-night minimum. ~ Long Beach Drive, two miles from

TOP OF THE POLES

By now you have probably noticed that some of the telephone poles along the Overseas Highway seem to be topped with great piles of sticks and twigs. These are **osprey nests**. If you look closely, you will occasionally see a bird with its young. Ospreys are regular residents of the Keys; some seem uninhibited by the cars and 18-wheelers that constantly whiz beneath them.

MM 33, Big Pine Key; 305-872-2015, fax 305-515-0208; www.
floridakeys.net/deer, e-mail deerrunbb@aol.com. DELUXE.

The windswept, old-time one- and two-bedroom cottages at
the **Old Wooden Bridge Fishing Camp** are especially popular   ◀ HIDDEN
with anglers and divers who don't need a lot of amenities other
than a comfortable plain cabin, a full kitchen and access to the
water. Rental boats are available, or you can stroll on over to the
Bogie Channel Bridge for some great fishing. ~ Punta Risa at
Bogie Channel; take Wilder Road at MM 30 and follow signs to
No Name Key; 305-872-2241, fax 305-872-5557; www.old-
woodenbridge.com, e-mail oldwood0@bellsouth.net. DELUXE.

The family that owns **Parmer's Resort** has been adding more
and more units to this attractive collection of quiet rooms, apartments and efficiency suites for more than two decades. The result is an assortment of older and newer individually designed
units, each named for an indigenous bird or fish. Tropical landscaping and a pool enhance the locale. For a treat, request "Sail
Fish," a large efficiency with a pretty porch right beside Pine
Channel. ~ At end of Barry Avenue, a half mile off Route 1 toward the bay at MM 28.5, Little Torch Key; 305-872-2157, fax
305-872-2014; www.parmersresort.com, e-mail info@parmers
resort.com. MODERATE TO ULTRA-DELUXE.

"Tropical paradise" is a worn-out phrase, but it really fits
Little Palm Island. This five-acre island of waving palms and   ◀ HIDDEN
green lawns features 14 luxurious two-suite bungalows, each one
facing the water. You'll enjoy generous thatched-roof quarters
with abundant windows, British Colonial decor, a private sundeck and outdoor bamboo shower, meals in the excellent restaurant, boat transportation from Little Torch Key and enough
quiet to calm the most jangled nerves. If you want to fish, tour
nature preserves, dive or sightsee, Little Palm will make the
arrangements; but if you want to stay around, you can sail,
windsurf, browse in the gift shop, get a massage in the full-service spa or just luxuriate on the island once enjoyed by Harry
Truman and other notables. ~ Offshore at MM 28.5, Little Torch
Key; 305-872-2524, 800-343-8567, fax 305-872-4843; www.lit-
tlepalmisland.com, e-mail getlost@littlepalmisland.com. ULTRA-
DELUXE.

There's nothing special about the motel rooms at **Looe Key
Reef Resort & Dive Center**, but it is very popular with divers,

having a dive shop, boat ramps and dive trips to Looe Key Sanctuary available for guests. There is also a restaurant, lounge and swimming pool. ~ MM 27.5, Ramrod Key; 305-872-2215, 800-942-5397, fax 305-872-1848; www.diveflakeys.com, e-mail looekeydiv@aol.com. DELUXE.

Sugarloaf Lodge is one of the "full-service" resorts with average but pleasant motel rooms and efficiencies facing the water. Full service here means a pool, restaurant and lounge, a marina, mini-golf and tennis. It's also very convenient to Key West. ~ MM 17, Sugarloaf Key; 305-745-3211, 800-553-6097, fax 305-745-3389; www.sugarloaflodge.com, e-mail information@sugarloaf lodge.com. DELUXE.

DINING

The **Key Deer Bar & Grill** is plain but a little less so than some of the other popular Lower Keys eateries. Fresh fish is served broiled, fried, blackened or sautéed. They also have steaks, baby back ribs, prime rib featured Friday and Saturday nights, pizzas. There's a daily happy hour from 4 to 7 p.m., with free pizza at 5 p.m. ~ MM 31, Big Pine Key; 305-872-1014, fax 305-872-1015. MODERATE.

Since 1936, the **No Name Pub** has been establishing its name as a choice dive among dives. The interior is covered in dollar bills signed by customers past, and the pub proudly proclaims, "Our decor is early and late American clutter." There's also outstanding pizzas, fish sandwiches, chargrilled burgers, seafood baskets and, of course, plenty of ice-cold beer to wash it all down. ~ North Watson Boulevard, MM 30, Big Pine Key; 305-872-9115; www.nonamepub.com.

The **Good Food Conspiracy** offers a dose of healthy eating at its simple little outdoor lunch counter with additional seating in a backyard garden. You'll nosh on soups as well as whole-wheat pita sandwiches filled with organic turkey, sprouts and veggies and cheese melts. There's also a juice bar for fresh smoothies and green drinks as well as a health food store. Lunch only. ~ MM 30, Big Pine Key; 305-872-3945. BUDGET.

HIDDEN ►

To get away from it all in style, plan to dine at the restaurant on **Little Palm Island**. You have to call ahead for a reservation; they will tell you when the boat will pick you up to take you to the lovely, luxurious island resort. If you're wise, you'll go in time to watch the sunset while sipping a cocktail beside the sandy beach or partaking of one of the items from the Continental menu that changes daily, but might include jumbo lump crab cake or seared filet mignon. They also provide a "wellness menu," with items like somen noodles with ginger broth and chicken. Sunday's offering is a decadent brunch buffet. ~ Offshore from Little Torch Key, MM 28.5; 305-872-2551; www.littlepalmisland.com, e-mail getlost@littlepalmis land.com. ULTRA-DELUXE.

> For the gourmet adventurer, Little Palm Island can provide a mobile meal for the traveler on the go.

Folks flock to **Boondocks Grille & Draft House** for baskets of breaded onion rings but stay for the seafood. This elevated, open-air tiki hut specialize in fresh local seafood, including crab cakes, peel-and-eat shrimp, and stone-crab claws. Fish is grilled, blackened or fried, and served with salad or vegetables and potato or rice. ~ MM 27.5, Ramrod Key; 305-872-4094, fax 305-872-5602. MODERATE.

Though concentrating on fish, the **Square Grouper** has a wide-ranging menu that includes peppercorn-encrusted New York strip, seafood stew and the always-popular grouper sandwich, served with shoestring onions and a deadly homemade Key lime tartar. And in case the name didn't tip you off (a "square grouper" is a bale of marijuana dropped into the sea by drug runners fleeing authorities), the Grouper maintains a laid-back—though classy—environment, complete with ceiling fans and couches. ~ MM 22.5, Cudjoe Key, Little Torch Key; 305-745-8880. BUDGET TO DELUXE.

Mangrove Mama's is such a wildly decorated, side-of-the-road, banana tree–surrounded eating establishment that you probably wouldn't stop unless someone recommended it—and plenty of Lower Keys folks do just that, with great enthusiasm. The menu, though brief and to the point, is somewhat fancier than you'd expect, with such treats as baked stuffed shrimp, fresh seafood specials and hand-cut steaks. The Key lime pie is superb and the herb teas are as pleasant a surprise as the handsome brick fireplace, used on very rare chilly nights. Mama's has the occasional band on Friday nights. ~ MM 20, Sugarloaf Key; 305-745-3030, fax 305-745-3076. MODERATE.

SHOPPING   For all the basic necessities, the main place for shopping in the Lower Keys is the **Big Pine Key Shopping Plaza**. ~ On Key Deer Boulevard just off Route 1 at MM 30, Big Pine Key.

Standing high on stilts, **Out of the Blue** is a pretty pink "earth-friendly" building that welcomes visitors with the sound of wind chimes and houses several levels of gifts and services for "conscious living"—jewelry, pottery, crystals, gifts, books and lots of other things. Bring your kids to play, or get a massage for yourself. ~ MM 29.7, Big Pine Key; 305-872-8864.

NIGHTLIFE   The **Key Deer Lounge** has live entertainment on weekend nights and occasional special events such as Halloween parties and the

HIDDEN ►   like, as well as a pool table so you can entertain yourself. ~ Key Deer Bar & Grill, MM 31, Big Pine Key; 305-872-1014, fax 305-872-1015.

For an evening with the locals, drop by the **No Name Pub**, a funky, run-down eating and drinking establishment with a carved-up wooden bar, over 20 kinds of beer and a jukebox; it claims to have the "best pizza in the known universe." This is a fun place that just about anybody can direct you to. ~ North Watson Boulevard, MM 30, Big Pine Key; 305-872-9115; www.nonamepub.com.

At **Coconut's Lounge** there's live weekend entertainment including pop, rock and country-and-western bands. ~ MM 30.5, Big Pine Key; 305-872-3795.

Friday and Saturday there's live rock-and-roll performed by local bands at **Looe Key Reef Resort**. ~ MM 27.5, Ramrod Key; 305-872-2215.

The **Tiki Bar** is a typical resort-motel nightspot. This one has entertainment on Saturday night. ~ Sugar Loaf Lodge, MM 17, Sugarloaf Key; 305-745-3211.

HIDDEN ►   About a mile off Route 1 and perched on the end of a side street, the **Geiger Key Smokehouse** is a waterside tiki bar where the locals hang, especially on weekends when there's live music and a Sunday barbecue. With a dearth of tourists, the prices are low, the atmosphere is genuine Keys and the salty characters are in full bloom. ~ MM 10.5, Big Coppit Key; head toward the ocean at the Circle K and follow signs; 305-296-3553; www.geigerkey marina.com.

VETERANS BEACH (LITTLE DUCK KEY PARK) 🏊 🐟 This little park on the ocean provides a place for a roadside rest and a swim just after you cross the Seven Mile Bridge, heading down the Keys. It's only a tiny strip of shallow beach with a few windblown trees, but the beach is sandy, the swimming better than many places and the water usually clear enough for snorkeling. There are restrooms and a picnic area. ~ Located on the oceanside of Route 1 at MM 40.

**BEACHES
& PARKS**

BAHIA HONDA STATE PARK 🏊 🐟 This state park offers what many consider the best swimming beaches in the Keys—wider and leading into deeper water than most. Remnants of the undeveloped Keys remain in this beautiful park—silver palms, satinwood, dwarf morning-glories and a large number of shore and wading birds, as well as rare birds such as the white-crowned pigeon. You may camp in the wide open spaces (best choice during mosquito season) in view of a handsome segment of Henry Flagler's original old bridge, or in the shady hardwood hammock at Sandspur Beach. Fishing is excellent, both in the bay and the ocean; guides are available during tarpon season. Swimming is also excellent, both in the Atlantic Ocean and Gulf of Mexico. Facilities include picnic areas, restrooms, vacation cabin rentals, a bathhouse, nature trail, a concession stand, a marina, a snorkel shop and limited groceries. The Nature Center has information on guided nature and history walks through the park. Day-use fee, $5 per vehicle, plus the $.50 Monroe County surcharge per person. ~ Entrance on ocean side of Route 1 at MM 36.7; 305-872-2353.

> Snorkeling tours depart daily from Bahia Honda State Park. Equipment rental and instruction are provided.

▲ There are 80 camp sites (64 with water and electricity); $31.49 per night. Reservations: 800-326-3521.

The Middle Keys are famous for bridge fishing. It's free and you do not need a license; just pick up some simple gear at a bait and tackle, the K-Mart or even a gas station. Favorite spots include both ends of the **old Seven Mile Bridge**, the **Long Key Bridge** and both bridges at **Tom's Harbor**.

Outdoor Adventures

**SPORT-
FISHING**

You can also go sportfishing on a pricey, custom-designed charter or by joining one of the numerous party boats on a scheduled trip. Everything from bait, boat, guide, rods and reels are provided; just bring food and drink. A good place to find charters operating throughout the Keys is www.weeklyfisherman.com.

KEY LARGO AREA Among many, many other charter services, **The Sailor's Choice** is a good choice for families or first-time fishers. They take large groups out for deep-sea fishing daily, in search of yellowtail, mutton, grouper and dolphinfish. ~ MM 100 at the Holiday Inn; 305-451-1802. Family-friendly **Charters Unlimited** will take you trolling for grouper in the Key Largo shallows. Captain Dick Magaldi offers half- and full-day trips that can include snorkeling to keep the little ones occupied. ~ MM 104 at the Caribbean Club; 305-451-9289.

ISLAMORADA AREA There are dozens of sportfishing outfits to choose from in Islamorada, including the party boat **Miss Islamorada**, for full-day offshore snapper fishing. Private charters can also be arranged. ~ MM 79.8 at Bud and Mary's Marina; 305-664-2461, 800-742-7945. **Holiday Isle Resorts & Marina** will make arrangements for backcountry and offshore fishing trips and charters for yellowtail, grouper, marlin, tuna, mahimahi and sailfish. Maximum of six people. ~ MM 84.5; 305-664-8986 ext. 642; www.holidayisle.com.

Two more reliable charters are the bayside **Couple-A-Bucks Charters** ~ MM 84 at the Whale Harbor Marina, 305-852-4384, www.coupleabucks.com; and the oceanside **Reel & Reef Charters** ~ Holiday Isle Resort, MM 84.5, Islamorada, phone/fax 305-853-0636, www.floridakeyscharter.com. Both offer half- and full-day charters, expert guides and tailored trips to suit your fancy.

MARATHON AREA Charter booking services are offered by **The World Class Angler** for flats, bridge, offshore or reef fishing. Depending on the kind of fish you're after, they can arrange for one of their 200 guides to show you where to go. ~ 5050 Over-

IT'S SNUBA, NOT SCUBA!

SNUBA is the latest thing in underwater exploration. This is a shallow-dive system where the air supply (read tank) follows on the surface, allowing you to dive down to 25 feet. **SNUBA Tours of Key Largo** can arrange this; lessons are also available. ~ MM 103.2; 305-451-3252, 800-966-3483.

seas Highway, Marathon; 305-743-6139, fax 305-743-0392. **Marathon Lady Party Boats** offers day and (seasonally) night fishing trips in and around the Florida Keys for local reef-bottom fishing. ~ MM 53 at Vaca Cut; 305-743-5580; www.marathon lady.com. For flats and offshore fishing, join Captain Barry Meyer on the **Magic**. He'll trailer his boat to meet you anywhere in the Keys for tarpon, permit or bonefish. ~ MM 52; 305-743-3278; www.barrymeyer.com.

LOWER KEYS AREA   You can test your angling skills with **Captain Dave Wiley**. He will guide you in and around the Great White Heron Wildlife Refuge for shark, barracuda and bonefish. ~ MM 27.5, Ramrod Key; 305-872-4680, 800-833-9857; www.key westflats.com. Try backcountry fishing with **Tim Carlile**; they specialize in tarpon and bonefishing and will take you Gulfside. ~ Sugarloaf Marina, MM 17, Sugarloaf Key; 305-745-3135; www.sugarloafkeymarina.com.

On any calm and beautiful day the sea to the east of Florida's Upper Keys is dotted with boats. They belong to the scuba divers and snorkelers who are captivated by the beauty of the continental United States' only living reef. Others search the remains of ships wrecked on that same lovely reef. Many communities in the Keys have dozens of scuba shops and dive centers designed to meet the needs of both novice snorkeler and sophisticated diver.

DIVING

KEY LARGO AREA   Route 1 in the Key Largo area seems like one continuous dive shop. To meet your diving needs, try **The Coral Reef Park Company, Inc.** The dives here are geared for the novice, and instruction ranges from resort to dive master courses. You'll see a variety of tropical marine life, including sea turtles, moray eels and an occasional nurse shark. ~ John Pennekamp Coral Reef State Park, MM 102.5; 305-451-6322; www.penne kamppark.com. **Ocean Divers** is another choice for a range of chartered dives including wreck, shell and deep-sea trips all within Florida Keys National Marine Sanctuary. ~ MM 105.5; 305-451-0037; www.oceandivers.com.

Quicksilver Catamaran Charters runs half-day dives to John Pennekamp Coral Reef State Park, evening snorkles (summer only) and hour-and-a-half sunset sails (winter, spring and fall). Gear is available for rent; pack your own food and drink. ~ MM 100, Key Largo; 305-451-0105; www.quicksilversnorkel.com.

ISLAMORADA AREA Holiday Isle Resorts & Marina has a full-service dive center offering two trips daily, one snorkeling and one diving. The dive includes a visit to the wreck of the *Eagle*, a 287-foot freighter. Reportedly, there is a resident jew fish roughly the size of a VW bug. ~ MM 84; 305-664-3483, 800-327-7070 ext. 644. The guides at **Rainbow Reef Dive Center** will take you to a variety of explore spots from Pennekamp State Park to Alligator Reef, where you'll dive coral and artificial reefs, wrecks, ledges and walls. They also provide courses—open water through instructor. Night and lobster dives are available year-round. ~ MM 83.5, Islamorada; 305-644-4600, 800-457-4354; www.rainbowreef.us.

MARATHON AREA For trips, lessons and equipment contact **Tilden's Scuba Center**. The morning dive might take you out to a wreck for exploration and in the afternoon, you might end up in Samantha's reef or Coffin's Patch for some of the most magnificent coral you've ever seen. ~ MM 49.5, Marathon; 305-289-1021; www.tildensscubacenter.com. The staff at **Hall's Diving Center** runs a full-service operation. In addition to lessons and certification, Hall's offers dive charters for reef diving. Trips are half-day, consisting of one-hour dives at two sites. ~ MM 48.5, Marathon; 305-743-5929, 800-331-4255; www.hallsdiving.com.

LOWER KEYS AREA Looe Key Reef Resort and Dive Center is a full-service dive center that offers a five-hour, three-location trip to the Looe Key Sanctuary reef. For beginners, there's expert instruction. ~ MM 27.5, Ramrod Key; 305-872-2215, 800-942-5397; www.diveflakeys.com. Another full-service center is **Cudjoe Gardens Marina and Dive Shop**. Up to six people can get on board their operations to Looe Key's protected finger reefs. Open-water courses are taught and boat rentals and repair are available. ~ MM 21, Cudjoe Key; 305-745-2357. **Innerspace Dive Shop** has excellent SSI, NAUI and PADI certification courses. For advanced divers and snorkelers, the main attraction is the Looe Key reefs, which are strictly no-touch sanctuaries. They also run trips to *Adolphus Busch*, a new wreck dive. As many as six people can go at a time. ~ MM 29.5; 305-872-2319, 800-538-2896.

Women-owned and -operated **Venus Charters** offers women-friendly boat trips around Key West. Captain Karen Luknis leads snorkeling, dolphin watching, fishing and nature trips to the ocean and the back waterways of the Lower Keys. ~ 305-292-9403.

KEY LARGO AREA   In Key Largo the best prices for boat rentals are at John Pennekamp Coral Reef State Park's **Coral Reef Park Company**. Boats range from 18- to 28-foot center counsel crafts and can be rented by the half- or full day. Snorkeling and glass-bottom boat tours of the coral and fish life are also available. ~ MM 102.5; 305-451-1621; www.pennekamppark.com.

ISLAMORADA AREA   **Holiday Isle Resorts & Marina** offers motorboats suitable for snorkeling and fishing expeditions. ~ MM 84; 305-664-2321. There are also 16- to 23-foot motorboats at **Robbie's Boat Rentals**, which can be rented on a half- or full-day basis. ~ MM 77.5; 305-664-9814. **Bud N' Mary's Marina and Dive Center** has charter and fishing trips. ~ MM 79.8; 305-664-2461. **Long Key Watersports** rents motorboats, waverunners and kayaks. ~ MM 68.2, Long Key; 305-664-0052. **Bay and Reef Company** offers private boat tours aboard their 21- and 24-foot motorboats. Each excursion is customized and may include fishing, snorkeling or bird-watching, along with eco-tours of Florida Bay, the Everglades and Cape Sable. ~ MM 82, oceanside, Islamorada; 305-393-0994; www.bayandreef.com.

Canon Beach, in John Pennekamp Coral Reef State Park, features remnants of an early Spanish shipwreck just 100 feet off-shore.

MARATHON AREA   In Marathon you rent 18- to 25-foot power-boats at half- or full-day and weekly rates from **Fish 'n Fun Boat Rentals**. ~ MM 53.4; 305-743-2275; www.fishandfunrentals.com. **Jerry's Charters** is another option for outboard motorboats, as well as pedal boats, kayaks and waverunners. ~ Banana Bay Resort Marina, MM 49.5; 305-743-7298; www.jerryscharters.com.

LOWER KEYS AREA   You can rent brand-new angler offshore powerboats at **Dolphin Marina**. ~ MM 28.5, Little Torch Key; 305-872-2685. Or try **Cudjoe Gardens Marina**. ~ MM 21; 305-745-2357.

Sprouting like kudzu along Route 1 are kayak rental shops and stands. Most offer some kind of organized trips as well as rental to those who want to do their own thing.

KEY LARGO AREA   **Coral Reef Park Company, Inc.** offers canoes and kayaks for exploring the park. ~ MM 102.5, John Penne-kamp Coral Reef State Park, Key Largo; 305-451-1621.

ISLAMORADA AREA   Sprouting like kudzu along Route 1 are kayak rental shops and stands. Most offer some kind of organized trips as well as rental to those who want to do their own thing. **Florida Keys Kayak and Sail** offers 19 guided tours, combining kayaking, hiking and snorkeling. Destinations include area wrecks, geographic and historic sites, mangroves and mudflats. ~ MM 77.5, Robbie's Marina, Overseas Highway, Islamorada; 305-664-4878; www.floridakeyskayakandski.com.

MARATHON AREA   In Marathon, you can rent kayaks at **Ocean Paddler South**, which also has outlets in Summerland Key and Islamorada. ~ MM 48.5; 305-743-0131; www.oceanpaddler.com. **Marathon Kayak** offers rentals as well as three- to six-hour guided tours. ~ Sombrero Resort, 19 Sombrero Boulevard, Marathon; 305-743-0561; www.marathonkayak.com.

LOWER KEYS AREA   Operating with knowledgeable local guides, **Reflections Nature Tours** offers morning, afternoon and sunset group tours of the mangrove/flats environment in and around Great White Heron and Key Deer wildlife refuges. If you wish to venture farther, you can do the powerboat - kayak combo (maximum two people), taking the powerboat deep into the refuge and then kayaking and wildlife watching. Other options include nature walks or bike tours (November through April). ~ P.O. Box 431373, Big Pine Key, FL 33043; 305-872-4668; www.florida keyskayaktours.com. **Outdoor Adventures** offers two-hour trips to natural salt ponds and mangroves. ~ MM 5.2, Stock Island; 305-295-9898.

SAILING   **KEY LARGO AREA**   In Key Largo the best prices for boat rentals are at John Pennekamp Coral Reef State Park's **Coral Reef Park Company**. Snorkeling and glass-bottom boat tours are also available. ~ MM 102.5; 305-451-6300. **Caribbean Watersports** offers two-hour enviro-tours into Everglades National Park aboard either Zodiac inflatables or Hobie Cat sailboats. Other recreational sports such as kayaking, snorkeling and waverunning can be arranged. ~ MM 97 at the Westin Beach Largo Resort, 305-852-4707; www.caribbeanwatersports.com. The 40-passenger, 50-foot **Quicksilver Catamaran** offers morning and afternoon snorkel trips to John Pennekamp Coral Reef State Park. A cooler is provided and passengers may bring a lunch and beverages. The nightly sunset cruise includes champagne. Snorkel gear is available; ask for a children's discount. MM 100,

Overseas Highway, Holiday Inn Docks, Key Largo; 305-451-0105; www.quicksilversnorkel.com.

ISLAMORADA AREA Keys visitors are increasingly interested in exploring the fragile ecosystems that surround the islands and Florida mainland. **Easy Adventures** emphasizes sightings of birds, dolphins, manatees and other wildlife, marine-science studies and photography from a comfortable, 22-foot canopied motorboat. Two-, four- and eight-hour charters are geared toward families. They also offer fishing and snorkeling. The captain and guide is Anne Baxter, a former Everglades National Park ranger. ~ MM 81.6 at the Worldwide Sportsman Arena, Islamorada; 305-451-8393; www.keysboats.com.

MARATHON AREA **Hootmon Sailing Charters** is available for a sunset champagne cruise every evening. ~ MM 49.5 at the Banana Bay Resort, Marathon; 305-289-1433. **Florida Keys Sailing** offers guided trips and sailboat rentals; boats range from 15 to 36 feet. ~ 2470 Dolphin Drive, Marathon; www.sailfloridakeys.com.

LOWER KEYS AREA Enjoy an unforgettable five-hour tour aboard the *Emerald See,* **Strike Zone Charters'** 40-foot catamaran. Snorkel over the reef, visit the "backcountry" and relish a fish cookout on a private island. ~ MM 29.5, Big Pine Key; 305-872-9863, 800-654-9560; www.strikezonecharter.com.

Windsurfers can find boards and lessons at **Caribbean Watersports**. MM 97 bayside, at the Sheraton Beach Resort, Key Largo; 305-852-4707, 800-223-6728; www.caribbeanwatersports.com.

WIND-SURFING

One of the best ways to capture the essence of the Keys is to just laze away a few days aboard a slow-moving, pontoon houseboat. Pontoon houseboats can be rented from **Houseboat Vacations of the Florida Keys.** Available for a minimum of three

HOUSE-BOATING

SUNKEN TREASURE

The 510-foot **Speigel Grove,** a retired U.S. Navy Landing Ship Dock, is the largest ship ever intentionally sunk to create an artificial reef. An excellent multilevel dive, the ship is home to slews of fish and other marine life. Accessible to divers and snorkelers, the *Speigel Grove* was sunk in 2002 about six miles off Key Largo in 130 feet of water.

nights and three days. ~ MM 85.9, Islamorada; 305-664-4009; www.thefloridakeys.com/houseboats.

GOLF

At Key Colony Beach, near Marathon, the public may play at the nine-hole KCB. ~ MM 53.5; 305-289-1533.

TENNIS

Many Keys resorts provide tennis for their guests. Tennis courts are available to nonmembers at the **Sugarloaf Fitness Resort**. Neat but relaxed, the club also offers a heated swimming pool, a jacuzzi, a bar and a restaurant, sand volleyball and a gym. Fee. ~ MM 19.5, 19269 Bad George Road, Sugarloaf Key; 305-745-2289. The **Islamorada Tennis Club** is open to the public with both clay and hard courts and night lighting. ~ MM 76.8; 305-664-5340.

BIKING

Bikeways parallel Route 1 intermittently down through the Keys. Bicycling the 2.2 miles over the **old Seven Mile Bridge** is a stellar way to access Pigeon Key. (Cars aren't allowed, and the walk can be a bit strenuous for some, especially in the heat.)

Bike Rentals **Bike Marathon** will rent and deliver bicycles (one-week minimum) to you at your Marathon area hotel, resort or campsite. Consider a bike ride during sunset, and watch for local wildlife. Reservations are recommended in the high season. ~ 305-743-3204. You can rent a wide range of bikes, from single-speed cruisers with baskets and mountain bikes to children's bicycles at the **Equipment Locker Sport & Bicycle**. Locks come with rentals. ~ MM 53, Marathon; 305-289-1670.

HIKING

Residential development and the lack of sandy beaches limit hiking possibilities in the Keys.

KEY LARGO AREA A hiking/biking path runs from Mile Marker 106 in upper Key Largo for about 20 miles. This is a walking route parallel to Route 1. It ties in with a short nature trail, passes the John Pennekamp Coral Reef State Park, follows an old road to a county park and leads to some historic sites.

▼ ▼ ▼ ▼ ▼ ▼ ▼ ▼ ▼ ▼ ▼
Transportation

CAR

Route 1 from Miami and the slightly more northerly scenic **Card Sound Road**, which veers off from Route 1 at Florida City, lead to Key Largo, where Route 1 becomes the **Overseas Highway**, continuing on through the Keys all the way to Key West.

Note: Mile markers, often called mile posts, can be seen each mile along Route 1 in the Keys. They appear on the right shoulder of the road as small green signs with white numbers, beginning with Mile Marker (MM) 126 just south of Florida City and ending at MM 0 in Key West. When asking for directions in the Keys, your answer will likely refer to a mile marker number. We use them throughout the Keys, except for Key West, where street addresses are used.

AIR

Many visitors to the Keys choose to fly to Miami (see Chapter Two for more information). However, there are two small airports in the Keys located in Marathon and Key West. The **Florida Keys Marathon Airport** is Florida's most attractive little airport, with a green tin roof and parade of palm trees. A lobby is cooled by ceiling fans with canvas sailboat mast-style blades.

Servicing the Upper Keys, **The Airporter** provides regularly scheduled shuttle service from Miami International Airport to Key Largo, Homestead, Islamorada and other areas. ~ 305-852-3413, 800-830-3413. **Upper Keys Transportation, Inc.** provides car service to Miami International Airport 24 hours a day with personally scheduled reservations. ~ 305-852-9533, 800-749-5397.

BUS

Greyhound Bus Lines (800-231-2222; www.greyhound.com) services a few Keys locations. They are in Key Largo at MM 99.6, 305-296-9072; in Big Pine Key at MM 31, 305-296-9072; and in Marathon at MM 50.5, 305-296-9073.

CAR RENTALS

Avis Rent A Car (800-331-1212), **Budget Rent A Car** (800-527-0700) and **Enterprise Rent A Car** (800-325-8007) are located at the Marathon Airport. In Key Largo, call **Enterprise Rent A Car** (800-325-8007).

TAXIS

In Marathon, call **Action Express Taxi**. ~ 305-743-6800.

AERIAL TOURS

Sight sharks and stingrays—from a safe distance. Wildlife excursions in the air are offered at **Fantasy Dan's Airplane Rides**. Sunset and champagne flight are available by reservation. ~ MM 17, Sugarloaf Key Airport; 305-745-2217.

FOUR

Key West

The Spanish called it *Cayo Hueso*, Island of the Bones. That's what the amazed explorers found when they first landed here— human bones scattered about—but no one ever discovered where they came from. Were they Indian bones? The remains of some grisly massacre? No witness ever came forward to tell the tale. Be that as it may, the word *hueso* was eventually anglicized to "west," and the name "Key West" has stuck through the town's curious and colorful history.

Though not quite in the tropics, Key West is to all appearances a tropical island. Lying low on a shimmering sea, it boasts backyards lush with hibiscus, oleanders, frangipani and kapok and mango trees. Its generous harbors are filled with hybrid fleets of battered fishing craft, glass-bottom boats and handsome yachts. Date and coconut palms rustle like dry paper in the usually gentle and dependable breezes that come in off the sea. Heat pervades, but even in midsummer it's seldom unbearable. Key West is a small-town sort of place where narrow streets are lined with picket fences and lovely old frame houses. At the same time, it's a traveler's haven with classy hotels and happy hours. The cul-de-sac of the Overseas Highway, it's unlike any other city in the United States.

Four miles long from east to west and two miles in width, Key West provides more contrasts than one could dream up for any town, especially one located on a little island over a hundred miles out to sea from mainland Florida. Once the wealthiest city per capita in the country, it was at a later date also the poorest. Men have made fortunes here and have lost them, too, leaving legacies of fine, ornate houses along with quaint, weathered shanties. The military presence has waxed and waned repeatedly as the needs of war have demanded, each time leaving its mark on the architecture and society of the island as well as on the archaeology beneath the sands. Tourists have descended in hordes, then gone away, depending on the economic status of the nation.

During its trauma-filled history, the city has nearly been destroyed several times—by hurricane, by fire, by economic crises. But Key West has always risen phoenix-like from the ashes of defeats that would have flattened a less determined population. Closer to Havana than to Miami, its residents are descendants of the English, Cuban, Bahamian, African and myriad other folk who have found this tiny place to be an appealing home.

Some of the first residents, after the American Indians, were the English Bahamians who came to make their fortunes salvaging the ships that met their doom on the Atlantic reefs. These folks were called "conchs" after the large shells they used for food, decoration and musical instruments. Later came the sponge fishermen who, for a while, provided 90 percent of all sponges sold in the United States. Cigar makers from Cuba numbered as many as 6000, producing millions of hand-rolled cheroots in the late 19th century. Hordes of workers came to continue Henry Flagler's railroad past the Seven Mile Bridge out to Key West about 30 miles away.

Numerous well-known artists and writers, most notably Ernest Hemingway, Tennessee Williams and Elizabeth Bishop, have found Key West a place of inspiration. For half a century, Pulitzer Prize winners have come and gone, including poet Wallace Stevens, who wrote that Key West "looked like something in a dream."

Tennessee Williams was one who found not only creative inspiration but social tolerance. One of Key West's first gay literary figures, he was lured by its feverish ambience and beautiful young sailors. Since his arrival in the 1940s, Key West has been a playground for homosexuals. Today, gays account for about 25 percent of the city's population, serve on the city council and are largely responsible for the island's wonderful flamboyancy. Each year, more than 400,000 gay men and women visit the island. And though AIDS has recently tempered what has been called "the wildest tropical port on the gay sexual tour," the gay scene still swings on the 700–800 block of Duval Street.

With the new millennium Key West experienced some substantial changes. Paradise is now firmly planted on the map as a tourist destination, and the incredible level of popularity has triggered the attention of corporate moneymakers. Increasingly, big-name national clothing and other chain shops and restaurants are vying for tourist dollars, especially along Duval Street. High-priced leases have made it nearly impossible for the smaller, independent businesses to stay in the game.

The big guns have brought new rules and regulations, sales quotas, service-worker scripts, and the like. Sadly, the laidback, individualistic atmosphere of old Key West is yielding to the pressures of the "real world," as the locals call the rest of the United States. Cell phones, traffic congestion and almost-proper business attire have infiltrated everyday island life. Gargantuan cruise ships visit daily, docking on the Gulf side of the island and unloading passengers by the thousands for a few hours of sightseeing and shopping. Anything from T-shirts to tanzanite can be found along the heavily touristed cruise-ship corridors radiating from Mallory Square.

Virtual Key West exists on the internet, including the island's famous sunset, and a summer of taping by MTV has put the image of Wyndam's Reach Resort into the heads of untold numbers of young folks.

Good-bye Jimmy Buffet; hello Backstreet Boys.

Real-estate prices here are outrageous, and many properties have been purchased by well-to-do folks looking for second homes or investments. Spiffy renovation projects abound, and rebuilt conch structures throughout Old Town boast fresh coats of designer-color paints. New construction continues with timeshares, hotels and high-priced condominiums cropping up along the water, in the salt ponds, and even between the county jail and the dump.

Of course, expansion and gentrification carry a heavy price. Going fast are the funky houses with hippy murals painted on the sides and the traditional "lived-on" porches, complete with upholstered chairs and old soda-pop signs. Bohemian types struggle to earn a living. And rising property taxes have pushed out many of the native "conchs."

The good news is the arts have exploded. The new money has brought more urban, sophisticated tastes. The symphony, the pops orchestra, the film society—arts groups that were previously inconceivable on an island are now a real part of Key West. (Even an opera company is on the way.) Today, glitzy, high-priced fundraisers for arts and cultural organizations are commonplace, and visitors as well as locals enjoy traveling exhibits and bigger names at the area's museums and theaters.

Bahama Village, where much of the island's African-American population resides, has challenged gentrification with the formation of a land trust and a resurgence of interest in their cultural heritage, establishing both a museum and an ethnic festival.

In recent years the local culture has been enriched by newcomers from Eastern Europe and the former Soviet Union, many of whom were funneled by labor brokers to Key West in the mid-'90s as low-wage employees—a practice which caused quite a political (and legal) stir. Increasingly, however, this group is freeing itself from these practices, becoming a visible thread in the local fabric, opening shops and restaurants, and moving from the kitchens and laundry rooms of resorts up to the front desks. Pierogies, anyone?

Many other groups also have woven color and contrast into the rich island tapestry. Jazz performers, county-and-western singers and classical musicians have contributed to the sounds of the town. Loafers have discovered Key West

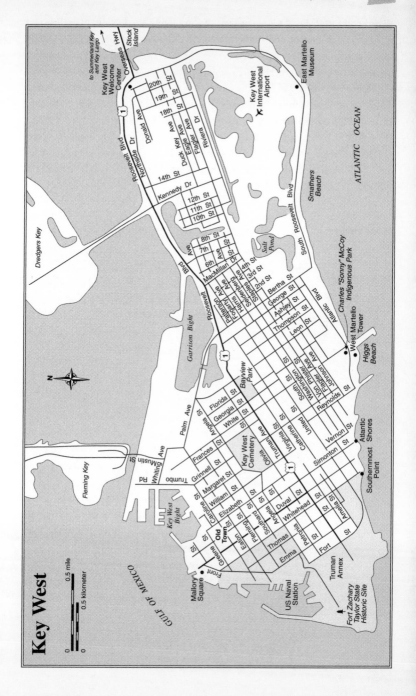

Key West

0   0.5 mile

0   0.5 kilometer

GULF OF MEXICO

ATLANTIC OCEAN

to Summerland Key and Key Largo

Overseas HWY

Stock Island

Key West Welcome Center

East Martello Museum

Roosevelt Blvd

Northside Dr

Donald Ave

20th St

19th St

18th St

Duck Key Ave

Eagle Ave

Flagler Dr

Riviera Dr

Key West International Airport

14th St

Kennedy Dr

12th St

11th St

10th St

Smathers Beach

8th St

7th St

6th St

MacMillan Dr

5th St

4th St

3rd St

2nd St

Ave

Roosevelt Blvd

Patterson Ave

Fogarty Ave

Harris Ave

Seidenberg Ave

Staples Ave

Salt Pond

South Roosevelt Blvd

Charles "Sonny" McCoy Indigenous Park

Bertha St

George St

Ashley St

Thompson St

Leon St

West Martello Tower

Higgs Beach

Garrison Bight

Atlantic Blvd

N

Bayview Park

Florida St

Georgia St

White St

Seminole St

18th St

Watson St

South St

Pohalski St

West Phila Ave

Von Phister St

Flagler Ave

Johnson St

Reynolds St

Palm Ave

Ashby St

Frances St

Grinnell

Key West Cemetery

Olivia Ave

Truman Ave

Virginia St

Catherine St

United St

Vernon St

Simonton St

Atlantic Shores

Southernmost Point

Fleming Key

Whiting Ave

Trumbo Rd

Margaret St

William St

Caroline St

Elizabeth St

Eaton St

Fleming St

Southard St

Angela St

Duval St

Whitehead St

Petronia St

Amelia St

Thomas St

Emma St

Fort St

Key West Bight

Old Town

Greene St

Front St

Mallory Square

US Naval Station

Truman Annex

Fort Zachary Taylor State Historic Site

Dredgers Key

Fleming Key

to be a comfortable spot for idling away the hospitably hot days. Fortunetellers and spiritualists, magicians and tattoo artists offer their shows and services around the island. Street performers come in every level of talent and weirdness, including one who hoists a grocery cart with his teeth.

Indeed, travelers will find that Key West has much to tantalize the senses. Today's Key West is foremost a tourist town, one of the nation's chief travel destinations. Whatever your interest, you will soon discover something to your liking, whether it be tours, nightlife, souvenir shops, art events, festivals, a nightly sunset celebration or courtyard cafés drenched in tropical foliage. Lately, young Europeans have been lured by those cafés, and by the island's bohemian lifestyle, heeding the billboards that beckon travelers to "go all the way" to this tip of the Florida boot.

Key West

While it's easy to stay busy here, it's just as easy to miss some of Key West's most enchanting features. For Key West has held on to many of its contrasts. While you might want to do all the routine visitor activities, you would also be wise to allow yourself enough time to stroll among the old houses, to admire the tropical trees, to taste some *bollitos* at a neighborhood grocery, to fire the imagination with retold tales of pirates and preparation for wars. Plan to tour the cemetery, watch for birds, meet the fishing fleet, explore the fort, talk to folks who live here, and you will begin to get a feel for this most unusual and varied town.

Key West is basically divided into two sections—Old Town, the place where tourists spend most of their time—and the "new town," where residents live and shop and carry out their daily lives.

The initial impression of Old Town is usually one of narrow streets, big old houses crowded together, highrise hotels that block the view, too many T-shirt shops and tourists and plenty of confusion. But don't be dismayed. Key West is easy to get to know, and there are all sorts of tours and printed guides and maps to help you. Once you are oriented, you'll have time to enjoy the salt air, to catch a bit of history, to appreciate the brilliant tropical trees whose blossoms gather in a carpet beneath your feet.

Unless you were born here, you will never get to be a genuine "conch," but it will probably not take you long to find plenty to your liking in the great variety of this island city that has never had a frost.

SIGHTS   It's easy to get around Key West; the entire island is only about four miles long and two miles wide. Stop in at the **Key West Wel-**

come Center for a taste of the area. ~ 3840 North Roosevelt Boulevard; 305-296-4444, 800-284-4482, fax 305-292-8981; www.keywestwelcomecenter.com.

By following Route 1 you will arrive in **Old Town,** the historic and main tourist area of Key West, just about where North Roosevelt Boulevard becomes Truman Avenue. This is a helter-skelter sort of place, with grand old Victorian houses, inviting alleys, junky souvenir shops, rocking-and-rolling bars, classy hotels, intimate guest houses, crowded marinas, street hawkers and incredible sunsets all tossed together into a colorful, noisy, artsy collage.

Away from Old Town, the remainder of the island includes settled residential areas, predictable shopping and a number of interesting sights that should pull you away from the tourist trappings. Here you are likely to run into those actually born in Key West, who proudly refer to themselves as "conchs." The original settlers were named after the giant shells that were so much a part of their sea-oriented lives.

Although Old Town is small enough for pleasant walking, and the whole island for biking, it helps to get oriented on one of several available tours. Besides, you'll pick up some very interesting history of this unique island city. The trackless **Conch Tour Train** has been orienting visitors for over 30 years with narrated 14-mile island tours, leaving at regular intervals daily. Fee. ~ Two depots, one near the Welcome Center at 3850 North Roosevelt Boulevard (ticket sales only) and one at 303 Front Street (passenger pick-up spot); 305-294-5161, 800-868-7482, fax 305-292-8993; www.historictours.com, e-mail keyott@historictours.com.

Old Town Trolley Tour meanders through the historic old streets during a 90-minute narrated excursion. There are nine stops for those looking to fit in a little shopping or just want to

FANTASY FEST

The last week of October brings Key West's most popular event—Fantasy Fest. A Mardi Gras–style party that runs through Halloween, Fantasy Fest attracts all sorts of people in all types of costumes primed for a wild time. Just keep in mind that this small island can only hold a limited number of people, and during Fantasy Fest, it's advisable to make your reservations early if you hope to take part in the festivities.

stretch their legs. Fee. ~ Leaves every 30 minutes from the Welcome Center and Mallory Square; 305-296-6688, fax 305-292-8939; www.historictours.com, e-mail keyott@historic tours.com.

HIDDEN ▶   For a more indigenous excursion, join the **Lloyd's Tropical Bike Tour**. It is hosted by Lloyd Mager, an environmentalist who, during his many years in Key West, has never owned a car or a motorbike. The casual, stress-free 120-minute ride meanders down hidden side streets, visits little-known oddities (including several local people) and explores the island's luxurious foliage. A passionate guide, Mager started his tours because he "couldn't stand that someone would leave here never smelling a gardenia or tasting a mango or feeling the thrill of Key West by bike." ~ 305-294-1882.

If you'd rather get oriented on your own, stop at the **Key West Chamber of Commerce** and pick up a *Pelican Path* walking guide. There are many historical and hidden gems and a few strange stops, including a lane called Love and Grunt Bone Alley, where grits and grunts were once eaten. ~ 402 Wall Street; 305-294-2587, 800-527-8539, fax 305-294-7806; www.keywestchamber.org, e-mail info@keywestchamber.org.

To watch cigars hand-rolled and sold, stop by **Rodriguez Cigar Factory**. Closed Sunday. ~ 113 Kino Plaza; 305-296-0167.

A wonderful example of bureaucratic snafus is the **U.S. Custom House and Post Office**, an imposing three-and-a-half-story red brick Romanesque revival structure, which, according to local tour guides, was built to specifications dictated by Washington in 1891. It has four full-size fireplaces and a steeply pitched roof designed to shed snow. (Well, it worked.) It now houses the **Key West Museum of Art & History**, which has changing displays of local, regional and Caribbean art. The admission fee includes an audio tour. ~ 281 Front Street; 305-295-6616;www.kwahs.com.

History buffs will enjoy searching for the gun turret from the **Battleship** USS **Maine**. Not exactly hidden, but somewhat hard to find, this is a little monument dedicated to the memory of Union soldiers who fought during the Civil War. ~ Front and Greene streets in the park in front of the Custom House.

Although Key West's first lighthouse was built in 1825, a hurricane swept it away some 20 years later. A new structure was built inland in 1847 and guided ships through the water until 1969.

Today, along with the adjacent lighthouse keeper's house, it contains the **Lighthouse Museum** operated by the Key West Art and Historical Society. For a panoramic view of this flat little island, climb the 88 steps to the top. See the huge Fresnel lens that cost $1 million back in the mid-19th century, vintage photographs and nautical charts, ship models and memorabilia from area lighthouses. Admission. ~ 938 Whitehead Street; 305-294-0012; www.kwahs.org.

Though many famous authors have spent time in Key West, none has left as strong a mark as Ernest Hemingway. He and his wife Pauline bought a fine old coral-rock house in which they lived from 1931 until the end of their marriage in 1940. Today, the **Ernest Hemingway Home and Museum** is a tribute to "Papa's" life and work, for it was here that he created such masterpieces as *To Have or Have Not* and *For Whom the Bell Tolls*. Tours are given

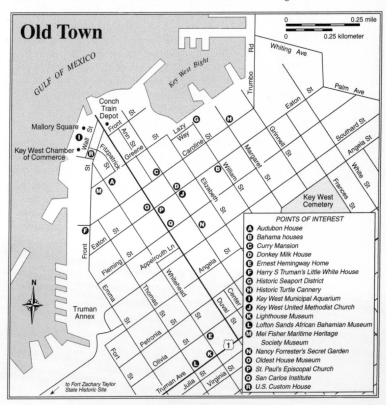

Old Town

0   0.25 mile
0   0.25 kilometer

GULF OF MEXICO

Key West Bight

Whiting Ave

Palm Ave

Eaton St

Trumbo Rd

Conch Train Depot

Mallory Square

Key West Chamber of Commerce

Front St

Ann St

Greene St

Lazy Way

Caroline St

Grinnell St

Southard St

Angela St

Margaret St

William St

Elizabeth St

White St

Frances St

Key West Cemetery

Fitzpatrick St

Eaton St

Fleming St

Appelrouth Ln

Whitehead St

Angela St

Front St

Thomas St

Emma St

Center St

Duval St

Truman Annex

Petronia St

Olivia St

Truman Ave

Julia St

Virginia St

to Fort Zachary Taylor State Historic Site

N

POINTS OF INTEREST

Ⓐ Audubon House
Ⓑ Bahama houses
Ⓒ Curry Mansion
Ⓓ Donkey Milk House
Ⓔ Ernest Hemingway Home
Ⓕ Harry S Truman's Little White House
Ⓖ Historic Seaport District
Ⓗ Historic Turtle Cannery
Ⓘ Key West Municipal Aquarium
Ⓙ Key West United Methodist Church
Ⓚ Lighthouse Museum
Ⓛ Lofton Sands African Bahamian Museum
Ⓜ Mel Fisher Maritime Heritage Society Museum
Ⓝ Nancy Forrester's Secret Garden
Ⓞ Oldest House Museum
Ⓟ St. Paul's Episcopal Church
Ⓠ San Carlos Institute
Ⓡ U.S. Custom House

The most notable feature of Old Town is the architecture. Many of the beautiful old houses you see were built of wood by ships' carpenters in a blend of styles that came to be known as conch-style houses. Influenced by the varied backgrounds of their owners and the demands of the hurricane-prone climate, the result is an eclectic architectural heritage unique to this island city.

BAHAMA HOUSES   For an introductory sampling of these conch houses, start at the corner of Eaton and William streets, where two Bahama houses stand side by side. These dwellings are the only ones known to have been shipped in their entirety to Key West from the Bahamas. Built in the mid-1800s by master shipbuilders, they feature unusual siding, mahogany window sashes and broad verandas. ~ 730 Eaton Street and 408 William Street.

CONCH-STYLE HOUSES   Next door, the **Samuel Filer House**, built around 1885, is a study in black and white contrasted with an etched cranberry glass transom and double-screen door. ~ 724 Eaton Street. Only the front of the **Bartlum/Forgarty House** was floated over from the Bahamas on a schooner. The mid-19th-century dwelling is constructed with wooden pegs. ~ 718 Eaton Street.

DONKEY MILK HOUSE   No gimmicks, only immaculately preserved history awaits at the **Donkey Milk House** just down the street. The 1866 Classic Revival house is named for the donkey-drawn carts that once gathered in the courtyard to collect milk for their local deliveries. The home's original owner was Peter Williams, a U.S. marshal who saved his house from Key West's devastating 1886 fire by dynamiting Eaton Street. In 1890, after his wife bore their second set of twins, he purchased another house, wheeled it across the island and attached it to the back of

daily, reflecting on Hemingway's works and his rigorous lifestyle. Through the marvelous house and luxuriant grounds roam sleek six-toed cats, said to be descendants of Hemingway's own; they lie irreverently on his works, snooze on his Spanish furniture and stalk the rooms that still reflect the writer's colorful personality. An on-site bookstore sells Hemingway's works as well as prints inspired by the literature and the house itself. Admission. ~ 907 Whitehead Street; 305-294-1136, fax 305-294-2755; www.heming wayhome.com, e-mail hemingwayhome@prodigy.net.

this one. Where the two houses meet, it's impossible to tell. Tours by appointment only. Admission. ~ 613 Eaton Street; 305-296-1866, fax 305-296-0922.

HOUSE OF WORSHIP   A little further along Eaton Street you'll spot the **Key West United Methodist Church**. This impressive building has two-foot-thick walls that were made from solid limestone quarried right beside the sanctuary. Built between 1877 and 1892, the handsome church has a native mahogany ceiling and a teakwood chancel. Viewing is possible by appointment only. ~ Eaton Street at Simonton Street; 305-296-2392, fax 305-296-4702.

OLDEST HOUSE   At the next block turn right on Duval Street, where the **Oldest House Museum** sits. This nine-room pine home was built in 1829 by a ship's carpenter for Captain Francis and Emeline Watlington and their nine daughters. Learn about life on this salt-marsh, mosquito-infested island at a time when the treatment for yellow fever was a mustard poultice and provisions arrived via schooner. A professional wrecker, Watlington saved lives and salvaged cargo from ships wrecked on the reef. The museum documents this fascinating trade, which attracted honest men as well as unscrupulous opportunists. Admission. ~ 322 Duval Street; 305-294-9502, fax 305-294-9501.

HOUSE OF LUXURY   Continue along Duval to Caroline street and take a right to find the Queen Anne–style **Curry Mansion**. With delicate double balustrades, beveled glass and fan windows, ornate trim and 23 rooms, this opulent abode presents a three-story display of millionaire life at the turn of the 20th century. Only the Bahama-style hinged shutters are common to other, less ostentatious homes of early Key West. The showcase house is open for daily self-guided tours, showing off the luxurious appointments and fine 19th-century furnishings. Admission. ~ 511 Caroline Street; 305-294-5349, fax 305-294-4093; www.curryman sion.com, e-mail frontdesk@currymansion.com.

You may have to wait in line to have your picture taken at the spot marking the **Southernmost Point**. "Ninety miles to Cuba," reads the sign beneath the kitschy-looking striped buoy surrounded by folks with cameras. ~ Ocean end of Whitehead Street.

The **Audubon House & Tropical Gardens** is a fine sample of early Key West architecture; its restoration inspired a city-wide interest in preserving other historic structures. Furnished with fine antiques of the 18th and 19th centuries, the three-story frame house is held together entirely by wooden pegs and is an excellent example of the shipbuilders' craft. It now serves as a museum housing an extensive collection of works by John James Audubon, the famous painter and naturalist. A lush one-acre tropical garden surrounds the house and features the **John Malcolm Brinnin Commemorative Pond**. Named after the late Key West poet and biographer, the garden features a reflecting pool and exquisite landscaping of plants, fruit trees, herbs and orchids. The gift shop offers museum-quality prints, art objects, jewelry and posters. Admission. ~ 205 Whitehead Street; 305-294-2116, fax 305-294-4513; www.audubon house.com, e-mail tomaudubonhouse@earthlink.net.

You really are allowed to lift a gold bar at the Mel Fisher Maritime Heritage Society Museum, though you can't take it with you.

At the **Key West Municipal Aquarium** you can touch a starfish or watch a shark being fed. Opened in 1935, the aquarium was the first visitors' attraction built in the Keys. Today the exhibits include a turtle pool, shark tanks, live coral and many other samples of Atlantic and Gulf underwater life. The "Atlantic Shores" exhibit is a red mangrove ecosystem complete with wildlife and a touch tank. Guided tours and feedings take place four times a day. Admission. ~ 1 Whitehead Street; 305-296-2051, fax 305-293-7094; www.keywestaquarium. com, e-mail aquarium@historictours.com.

If you've ever wondered how much a gold bar weighs or if rubies still sparkle after spending centuries on the bottom of the sea, visit **Mel Fisher Maritime Heritage Society Museum**. The place literally dazzles with gold chains, jewel-studded crosses and flagons, and great piles of gleaming coins—all treasures gathered by Fisher and his crew of divers from the sunken ships *Atocha* and *Margarita*. You really are allowed to lift the gold bar, though you can't take it with you. Admission. ~ 200 Greene Street; 305-294-2633; www.melfisher.org, e-mail info@melfisher.org.

Every visitor to Key West inevitably witnesses the **Sunset Celebration at Mallory Square**, a Key West institution that will make you feel like you're part of a Mayan ritual. You'll find bagpipers, jugglers, fire-eaters and people who think it's fun to stand on one foot for half an hour. As the great moment nears, a cheer rises from the crowd, reaching fever pitch as the sun hits the horizon. ~ Northwest end of Duval Street.

HIDDEN ▶ Located at a former turtle cannery site, the **Historic Turtle Cannery & Maritime Museum** features photographs and a history of Key West's turtling industry, which in the mid-1800s slaughtered huge numbers of the now-protected green turtles for soups and steak. Exhibits include turtle shells and skulls as well as the biology and conservation of sea turtles today. Feed a live turtle (most likely one undergoing rehabilitation for injuries) in the abandoned turtle kraals in the afternoon. ~ Land's End Marina, 200 Margaret Street; 305-294-0209; e-mail tina824@aol.com.

Duval Street is the main street of Old Town, though it cannot be compared to any other Main Street in America. It begins on the gulf and ends at the ocean, yet walking it one has little sense of the water. Instead Duval seems one long masquerade of old and new architecture, thin white porches and lavish gingerbread, flowering trees of outlandish proportions, store windows with strange and fabulous displays, metal blenders groaning from smoothie stands, guitar players hoping for a dollar, hucksters whispering toward restaurants and stores.

Key West is at its best and worst on Duval Street, though some locals would say mostly worst. It is not uncommon to hear Conches say they "haven't ventured on Duval in years," though one should be skeptical of such talk, Key West being such a small island. Truth is the two ends of Duval couldn't be more different. "Upper Duval," on the southeast end, is quieter and classier, with its string of galleries and cafés and bistros, pretty inns and their lush gardens, and a wine bar where one can sip a glass of gewürztraminer beneath the Christmas palms.

"Lower Duval," to the northwest, is tumultuous and tacky. T-shirt shops seem to mutate here every few months, and there are many bars and lots of gaseous cars cruising with their bass at full bore. Some blame Lower Duval's demise on the cruise ships that dock down here several times a week, disgorging passengers in search only of a beer and a T-shirt. They find both at the Hard Rock Cafe.

The oldest church in Key West was established in 1832. It was prophetically dedicated to St. Paul, the quintessential shipwreck victim. Two later churches on the site were swept away by hurricanes (a third burnt down). In 1919 a magnificent white masonry structure went up, and that one, **St. Paul's Episcopal Church**, lasted. Embellished with noteworthy stained-glass windows and sporting an 8000-pound, 2000-pipe organ, today's church is a peaceful place to spend a quiet moment away from the antics of Duval Street. ~ Duval and Eaton streets; 305-296-5142, fax 305-294-6687.

Some Key West sights are so hidden that they can't be seen—at least not often, according to the guides at **Key West Ghost Tours**, a group that has tapped into the island's spooky history and paranormal past. Leaving from the La Concha Hotel nightly, the lantern-lit tour is a 90-minute, one-mile stroll around Old Town, with factual and fantastic commentary about Key West's spirits, including "Robert the Doll" and the island's own necrophiliac, Dr. Von Cossel. Trained guides don period costumes. Fee. ~ Crowne Plaza La Concha Hotel, 430 Duval Street; 305-294-9255, fax 305-294-5175; www.hauntedtours.com, e-mail keysghoul@aol.com.

Enrico Caruso once sang at the **San Carlos Institute**, and Cuban patriot José Martí delivered many rousing speeches from the balcony of the auditorium. This is actually the fourth San Carlos Institute, others having succumbed to fire and hurricane. Founded in 1871 to teach Cuban immigrants the language and customs of their adopted country, to preserve the history and heritage of the land they had left behind, and to plan the campaign that would free Cuba from Spain's domination, the institute now houses a museum and a library as well as hosting special events and theatrical performances. The pale yellow building, with its turrets and columns and gingerbread and its 16-foot-high doors of Cuban cedar, had deteriorated badly, but was recently restored, and is now open for tours. Closed Monday. ~ 516 Duval Street; 305-294-3887, fax 305-371-6117; e-mail rapenalbert@aol.com.

About 60 butterfly species flutter freely about the **Key West Butterfly & Nature Conservatory**, a state-of-the-art solarium and nature exhibit. Flowering plants, waterfalls and trees create

GRAVE HUMOR

"I Told You I Was Sick," reads the straightforward message immortalized on a gravestone in the **Key West Cemetery**. Due to the rocky geology of the island, many of the stone-encased caskets rest above ground, often carrying curious and, what seem now, humorous messages. History abounds in this enchanting and poignant spot, too, as in the special memorial to those who died at the sinking of the U.S. Battleship *Maine* in Havana harbor in 1898. You may stroll the cemetery until 6 p.m.; The Historic Preservation Society (305-292-6718) gives tours on Tuesday and Thursday. ~ Angela and Margaret streets; 305-292-8177.

the fairytale-esque walk-through habitat. A learning center examines all things butterfly—from anatomy and physiology to feeding and migration. The facility also houses live birds, including red-factor canaries, Zebra finches, Cordon-Blue finches and "button" or Chinese-painted quail. The gift shop features butterfly items from around the world. Admission. ~ 1316 Duval Street; 800-839-4647, 305-296-2988; www.keywestbutterfly.com, e-mail info@keywestbutterfly.com.

Once home to the island's shrimp fleet, the revitalized **Key West Bight** and the **Historic Seaport District** now bustles with maritime, retail and entertainment activity. This is the place where Key West's tall ships, including the *Schooner Appledore* and the historic *Western Union*, embark for sunset sails and snorkeling trips. Stroll the Harborwalk, where restaurants range from fishing shacks to fine dining, with dozens of equally diverse shops and boutiques in between. Bars with live entertainment, art galleries, and charter fishing companies also do business here. ~ Historic Seaport at the Key West Bight; 305-293-8309; www.keywestseaport.com.

Over 125 of the Keys' indigenous plants grow at the **Charles "Sonny" McCoy Indigenous Park**, a showplace for trees and plants native to the region. You may wander inside the gates of the park during the daytime and learn to recognize the lignum vitae, silver palm and a number of tropical trees native to the Keys. There is a fish pond hidden away in the back. Closed weekends. ~ Atlantic Boulevard at White Street; 305-293-6418.

Also on the grounds is the **Wildlife Rescue of Florida Keys**, where injured wildlife is rehabilitated and then released back into the wild. From an observation platform that offers a view of the island's freshwater pond, you can see heron, ibis, gallinule and migratory birds that gather here. ~ McCoy Indigenous Park, White Street and Atlantic Boulevard; 305-294-1441, fax 305-294-8082.

The historic **West Martello Tower** is the enchanting home of Key West Garden Club's **Joe Allen Garden Center**. The remains of the once-upon-a-time fort, with its crumbling brick walls and arches and its massive banyan trees and old palms, create a pleasant, restful environment for numerous bromeliads and other tropical flora usually confined to greenhouses, and spectacular seasonal

Text continued on page 166.

Fort
Jefferson

L ike a scattering of tiny emerald beads, a cluster of coral reel islands dot the Gulf of Mexico 68 miles west of Key West. Ponce de León named them "Tortugas" for the turtles he found there, sailors called them "Dry" because they hold no fresh water. But the Dry Tortugas do hold a national park centered around a magnificent 19th-century fort.

To see **Fort Jefferson** from the air, surrounded by azure sea, walled moat and white sand, is like conjuring up a fairy tale, enriched with popular legends of pirate treasure. Walking through the open sally port and arched hallways, one steps into a vast area whose silence is broken only by seagull cries and the calls of migratory birds. ~ For information, contact the park at 305-242-7700, fax 305-242-7711; www.nps.gov/drto, e-mail drto_information@nps.gov.

Fort Jefferson, from its perch on Garden Key, appears much as it did in its brief 19th-century heyday. German and Irish craftsmen, with the assistance of slaves, created the spectacular brick- and stonework from millions of bricks brought by sailing ships from Pensacola and Virginia, and granite and slate brought from New England. The eight-foot-thick walls stand 50 feet high and feature handsome arches and wide views of sea approaches. Fort Jefferson's half-mile hexagonal perimeter made it the largest link in the chain of coastal fortifications built from Maine to Texas in the first half of the 19th century. It encompasses almost all the land of its tiny key, creating the illusion that it floats on the glistening tropical sea.

Though at first glance the fort seems complete, it was never actually finished. Begun in 1846, work continued for 30 years, but Fort Jefferson's importance came to an end with the invention of the rifled cannon. When federal troops occupied the fort throughout the Civil War, they discovered its foundations were not built on solid coral reef as was originally thought, but on sand and coral boulders. The walls began to show cracks as foundations settled with the shifting of the sea floor.

Fort Jefferson's most inglorious claim to fame came in 1865. To this lonely and inescapable reef were sent the "Lincoln Conspirators," four men convicted of complicity in the assassination of President Abraham Lincoln. Most noted of these was Dr. Samuel Mudd, the physician who had innocently set the broken leg of John Wilkes Booth following the shooting of the president. Sentenced to life imprisonment at Fort

Jefferson, Mudd was eventually pardoned following his gallant efforts at treating the almost 300 garrisoned men who were struck with yellow fever at the fort during the 1867 epidemic. Today visitors can explore Mudd's cell and envision the bleakness of his fate.

The Army formally abandoned Fort Jefferson in 1874, following more yellow fever and a serious hurricane; it never saw any military action. And many military men may have felt grateful, for duty at Fort Jefferson, where water was scarce, mosquitos thick and hurricane winds ferocious, was not coveted. But fortunately for historians and travelers, President Franklin D. Roosevelt proclaimed Fort Jefferson a national monument in 1935, thus preserving its unique heritage and its spectacular architecture.

To visit Dry Tortugas National Park and Fort Jefferson, you can go by ferry boat (three hours) or seaplane (45 minutes) from Key West. Contact the park (305-242-7700) or the Key West Chamber of Commerce (305-294-2587, 800-527-8539; www.keywestchamber.org) for further information.

Seaplanes of Key West provides service to the Dry Tortugas. ~ 305-294-0709, 800-950-2359, fax 305-296-4141; www.seaplanesofkeywest. com, e-mail info@seaplanesofkeywest.com.

Yankee Fleet offers daily runs between Key West and Dry Tortugas National Park. Continental breakfast, a full picnic lunch, the use of snorkel gear and a 40-minute tour of the fort are included in the fare. ~ Key West Bight Marina, Key West; 800-634-0939; www.yankeefreedom. com, e-mail carol@yankeefreedom.com.

Sunny Days Catamarans (305-293-6100, 800-236-7937, fax 305-293-9848; www.drytortugasferry.com, e-mail cattours@aol.com) offers daily ferry trips to Dry Tortugas National Park and Fort Jefferson. The fee includes roundtrip transport, continental breakfast, lunch, drinks and snorkel gear.

You can spread a picnic, pitch a tent in the shade of tropical trees or sunbathe on the tiny, pristine beach, but you must bring everything with you, for only restrooms are available on the island. An excellent self-guiding tour, introduced by an explanatory slide show, orients visitors to the wonderful wild fort that you may roam to your heart's content. Snorkelers need only wade out waist-deep from the little beach to behold the colorful array of marine creatures that dart among the patches of living coral in the crystal-clear Gulf water.

displays. Closed Sunday and Monday. ~ Atlantic Boulevard and White Street; 305-294-3210; www.keywestgardenclub.com.

St. Mary Star of the Sea is the second-oldest Catholic church in Florida. Built at the turn of the 20th century of Miami oolite quarried in the Keys, the interesting building features pressed-tin arches and metal columns. On the grounds stands a small **grotto** in honor of the Lady of Lourdes, built many years ago by a nun, who prayed it would provide protection from hurricanes. So far, the grotto seems to have served the purpose she planned, receiving credit from many believers for the absence of any killer storms since the sister's dedicated work was undertaken. Sunday noon mass in Spanish. ~ 1010 Windsor Lane; 305-294-1018.

HIDDEN ►   Located in a historic home in Bahama Village, the **Lofton B. Sands African Bahamian Museum & Resource Center** preserves and educates the public about the history and cultural contributions of Key West's African-Bahamian community. Historic documents and artifacts as well as a research archive are housed here. Watch for traveling exhibits and special programs. Closed Sunday and open by appointment. ~ 325 Julia Street; 305-293-9692.

From the top of the citadel of the **East Martello Museum** you can get a magnificent view of the island and the Atlantic, just as the Union Army builders of this 1862 Civil War brick fortress planned. Today the historic structure houses 11 rooms and a large collection of Key West artifacts and serves as both a museum of Key West history and a gallery displaying the work of Keys artists. The fort's tower alone, with vaulted ceilings and spiral staircase, is worth a visit and, at the top, it affords you a view of the Gulf and the Atlantic. Admission. ~ 3501 South Roosevelt Boulevard; 305-296-3913, fax 305-295-6649; www.kwahs.com, e-mail cpennington@kwah.org.

Climb to the top of the East Martello Museum's tower and you'll be rewarded with a view of the Gulf and the Atlantic.

Few developments have caused so much controversy on this tiny island as the **Truman Annex**. Owned for decades by the Navy, the quiet, shady 103-acre parcel was the last big piece of undeveloped land on Key West when it was auctioned in 1986 to a wealthy Sikh from Maine. Since then, expensive condominiums, a complex of Victorian-style houses, marinas and luxury hotels have been built. Although this is a gated community, there is a walking guide to this former naval station. ~ Main pedestrian entrance is at Caroline and Whitehead streets.

Located here is **Harry S Truman's Little White House**, built in 1890, where presidents Truman, Eisenhower, Kennedy and Carter vacationed. The handsome white clapboard building has two facades and spacious porches enclosed with wooden louvers. There are also two rooms of presidential exhibits, one of which is dedicated entirely to President Truman. Admission. ~ 111 Front Street; 305-294-9911; www.trumanlittlewhitehouse.com.

Drive through the Truman Annex and you will find the **Fort Zachary Taylor State Historic Site**, a treasure trove of Civil War weaponry and memorabilia. The excavations of the 1845 fort have revealed beautiful mid-19th-century arched brickwork, parade grounds and the largest collection of Civil War cannons in the U.S. The park itself has an excellent swimming beach. Day-use fee, $3.50 to $6 per vehicle, plus $.50 Monroe County surcharge per person. ~ Southwestern point of the island, at the end of Southard Street; 305-292-6713, fax 305-292-6881; www.fort taylor.org.   ◄ HIDDEN

The Botanical Garden Society maintains a small but nicely laid-out and well-marked **Botanical Garden** where you can get acquainted with many of the trees and other indigenous flora that grow in this distinctive region. There are two freshwater ponds, and if you look hard enough, you may catch sight of a rare butterfly. Closed Wednesday. ~ College Road and Aguero Circle, Stock Island; 305-296-1504; www.keywestbotanicalgarden.org.   ◄ HIDDEN

You won't find signs for **Nancy Forrester's Secret Garden**, a well-hidden spot of interest to environmentalists and plant fanciers. More than 25 years ago, Nancy began to create an informal rainforest for herself, and later opened it to the public. Narrow paths wind through the property, leading to small glades where benches and tables invite you to relax and enjoy the sounds of silence. Traipse down the lane that looks like a private drive beside a real estate company and you'll find the small wooden gate. You're welcome to bring your own lunch. Admission. ~ One Free School Lane, which leads off Simonton Street in the 500 block; 305-294-0015; www.nffgarden.com.   ◄ HIDDEN

The lobby at the **Historic Gato Cigar Factory** houses an excellent interpretive exhibit on Key West's most successful cigar manufacturer, Eduardo Hidalgo Gato, and the influences of his industry on the island. Vintage photographs, cigar labels and historic narratives reveal that at the turn of the 20th century, Key   ◄ HIDDEN

West was the world's leading producer of clear Havana cigars, with tobacco from Cuba rolled by Cuban workers on this American island. Today the restored cigar factory serves as headquarters for Monroe County government. Closed weekends. ~ 1100 Simonton Street.

For picture-window views of the coral reef in the Atlantic, and late-afternoon sunset cruises, climb aboard the glass-bottom sightseeing boat **Pride of Key West**. Admission. ~ North end of Duval Street; 305-296-6293, fax 305-296-4527; www.seathereef.com, e-mail glassbottomboat@sprynet.com.

LODGING   In Key West you can find countless accommodations—from bare-basics motels to outrageously expensive resorts. Unfortunately, bare basics often carry a moderate price tag in Key West, now that the island is wildly popular year-round. Some of the best values can be found at the island's varied guesthouses, many with whimsical architecture splashed with tropical colors and surrounding exquisite little courtyards. A number of the guesthouses cater to gays only, so be sure to ask about the house policy. If you want help finding a place to stay, contact **See a Room Key West**. Closed Sunday. ~ 800-916-2030, fax 305-872-5591; www.seearoomkeywest.com.

Also try **Vacation Key West**, an island-based wholesaler that offers discounts of 20 to 30 percent on lodging throughout the Keys. ~ 100 Grinnell Street; 305-295-9500, 800-595-5397, fax 305-296-3731; www.vacationkw.com, e-mail info@vacationkw. com. For reservations at one of the island's inns, contact the **Key West Innkeeper's Association**. ~ 922 Caroline Street; 305-295-1334, 800-492-1911.

The **Hilton Key West Resort and Marina** posts some of Key West's highest rates, for which you get a waterfront locale and sprawling marina, shops and eateries and fine dining, and rooms that are modern and minimalist, with eggshell walls and wall-to-wall teal carpets. For a more secluded spot, you can board a little boat over to Sunset Key, where there are gingerbread homes for rent through the Hilton's **Sunset Key Guest Cottages**. Or you can simply lie in a chair on the beach at Sunset, order a cocktail from the bar, and try to choose between swimming in the salty ocean or the large heated pool. ~ 245 Front Street; 305-294-4000, 800-221-2424, fax 305-294-4086; www.keywestresort.hilton.com; www.sunsetkeycottages.hilton.com. ULTRA-DELUXE.

Quietly dominating the edge of Old Town, the soft pink, metal-roofed **Hyatt Key West** is a maze of well-lit stairs and balconies. The cool pastel decor suits the location beside a small private beach and marina. A pool, a jacuzzi, an exercise room, a fine restaurant, an indoor/outdoor lounge and numerous water-sports rentals and tours make this one of the choicest lodgings—and one of the most convenient for Key West sightseeing. ~ 601 Front Street; 305-296-9900, 800-554-9288, fax 305-292-1038; www.hyatt.com. ULTRA-DELUXE.

The Historic Florida Keys Preservation Board honored the **Cuban Club Suites** its "Five Star Award of Excellence," a fitting honor for this restoration of one of Key West's most important historical structures. The second-floor balcony affords views of Duval Street similar to those seen by the island's first Cuban émigrés, whose primary social/political club operated from this building in the 1900s. Today the suites are furnished in a tropical Victorian style, with cathedral ceilings; amenities include fully equipped kitchens and lavish bathrooms. Suitable for up to six people, units run larger than many Old Town residences. Children over 16 only. ~ 1108 Duval Street; 305-296-0465, 800-833-0372, fax 305-292-7665; www.keywestcubanclub.com, e-mail info@key westcubanclub.com. ULTRA-DELUXE.

The lushest place on the island is surely **The Gardens Hotel**. Now a small, luxurious European-style hotel, it was once the Peggy Mills Botanical Garden. The late Mills, known around town as Miss Peggy, searched the world for rare species, importing orchids

AUTHOR FAVORITE

One of the friendliest places in town, the **Pier House Resort and Caribbean Spa** has long been one of Key West's most popular hotels. It sprawls along the Gulf with rambling tin-roofed villas and acres of docks. Here you get all the goodies of an elaborate resort—superb restaurants, lively nightspots, a therapeutic spa—with that classic laidback Keys mood. A small beach is soft and picturesque, the swimming pool expansive, and the grounds jungly. Old Town shops and sights are a short stroll away. ~ 1 Duval Street; 305-296-4600, 800-327-8340, fax 305-296-9085; www.pierhouse.com, e-mail info@pierhouse.com. ULTRA-DELUXE.

from Hawaii and Japan, and palms and canopy trees from Latin America. She also brought in 87,000 bricks to create the footpaths that now curl through the garden. Five handsome buildings of crisp white, including Mill's original 1870s house, offer elegant rooms with French doors, wood floors, marble baths and porches. Continental breakfast can be taken in the glass sunroom or on the veranda. There's a pool and jacuzzi. ~ 526 Angela Street; 305-294-2661, 800-526-2664, fax 305-292-1007; www.gardens hotel.com, e-mail reservations@gardenshotel.com. ULTRA-DELUXE.

Constructed just after the Great Fire of 1886, **Eaton Lodge** sports a distinctive diamond-patterned balustrade along the balcony and veranda. The nonsmoking rooms and suites are furnished in authentic period pieces with colorful comforters on the beds—maybe carved mahogany or wrought-iron four-posters—all have refrigerators and private baths. Each opens onto a wonderful garden that was created by Genevieve Warren, one of the home's earliest owners. Its winding pathways lead past a fish pond, around a whirlpool spa to the side of the old cookhouse and onto a brick-paved terrace, where morning breakfast, which includes homemade tropical fruit bread, is served. It's hard to believe that the quiet of this lush and peaceful oasis is just steps away from the hustle and bustle of Duval Street. ~ 511 Eaton Street; 305-292-2170, 800-294-2170, fax 305-292-4018; www.eaton-lodge.com, e-mail eatonlodge@prodigy.net. ULTRA-DELUXE.

A two-and-a-half-story Greek Revival Victorian mansion, Eaton Lodge has been featured in every major publication from *National Geographic* to the *New York Times*.

Built in 1890 and featuring a handsome metal-roofed turret on one corner, **The Artist House** is one of many conch houses turned hostelry. Guests may have one of six rooms with private bath, refrigerator and antique or period reproduction furnishings, including four-poster or genuine brass beds. A jacuzzi and sundeck are set among lush tropical plantings in the garden; breakfasts are extended continental. Rich period wallpapers and superb restoration make this an elegant lodging. ~ 534 Eaton Street; 305-296-3977, 800-582-7882, fax 305-296-3210; www.artisthousekey west.com, e-mail ahkwinc@aol.com. ULTRA-DELUXE.

With its vast jungle garden and unusual assortment of lovely rooms, **Island City House** is unquestionably one of the best guesthouses in Key West. Choose from the 1880s Arch House with its studio suites and gingerbread trim; the 1880s Island City House mansion with its creaky wood floors and homey antiques; or the 1980s Cigar House with its spacious modern suites overlooking the pool and jacuzzi. All rooms have kitchens, though a cart loaded with fresh fruit and pastries beckons from the garden every morning. ~ 411 William Street; 305-294-5702, 800-634-8230, fax 305-294-1289; www.islandcityhouse.com, e-mail info@islandcityhouse.com. ULTRA-DELUXE.

Westwinds is a historic bed and breakfast with 26 guest rooms scattered among four cream-colored conch houses. In the rooms, you'll find wicker furnishings, a ceiling fan, air conditioning and a phone; only one of the buildings has rooms with televisions. Guests enjoy lounging around the exotically landscaped pool area. It is here that the continental breakfast is served in the morning. No children under 12 are allowed. ~ 914 Eaton Street; 305-296-4440, 800-788-4150, fax 305-293-0931; www.westwindskeywest.com, e-mail frontdesk@westwindskey west.com. DELUXE.

A Cuban cigar factory in the 1880s, **Simonton Court** is now a gardeny compound spread across two acres of bougainvillea and hibiscus, lattice and brick lanes. There are 26 rooms in ten cottages and buildings, including the two-story inn with floors of Dade County pine; the luxurious mansion with period antiques, spacious verandas and marble baths; and cottages of pink clapboard. All the rooms are immaculately restored and have refrigerators, TVs and VCRs; some have kitchenettes. Plunge pools and swimming pools are set among the trees, and it is very quiet here. No children allowed. Popular with gay and straight travelers alike. ~ 320 Simonton Street; 305-294-6386, 800-944-2687, fax 305-293-8446; www.simontoncourt.com. ULTRA-DELUXE.

Locals like Fleming Street. It has the library, a bike lane, many canopy trees and the famous Fausto's Food Palace. It also has the pink-washed **Ambrosia House Tropical Lodging**, with seven comfortable rooms, all variously themed. The Jungle Room, for instance, has wall-to-wall Dade County pine, a poster bed draped in silky netting, and animal print bedspreads and cushions. Mini-fridges and coffeemakers come with every room, and there's a rambling wood deck out back with a pool and hot tub. Its sister property across the street, the **Ambrosia Too**, boasts 12 townhome and cottage units and two pools. ~ 622 Fleming Street; 305-296-9838, 800-535-9838, fax 305-296-2425; www.ambrosiakeywest.com. DELUXE TO ULTRA-DELUXE.

After a major renovation of this 1880s-era classic revival compound of four buildings, the **Marquesa Hotel** has landed securely on the National Register of Historic Places. Each of the 27 rooms is luxurious and formal, with antique appointments, pastel walls, gleaming white woodwork and distinctive fabrics. Every corner is a masterpiece of workmanship. The property includes an award-winning restaurant and two sparkling pools in a tropical garden. ~ 600 Fleming Street; 305-292-1919, 800-869-4631, fax 305-294-2121; www.marquesa.com. ULTRA-DELUXE.

There's a funky, European air about **Eden House** that recalls a time when Key West was laid-back, diverse and loaded with characters. Think clean and comfortable, with patchwork hints of resort luxury. With 40 units, the place meanders through the better part of a block, and includes a pool (with a daily complimentary happy hour deckside), jacuzzi, waterfalls, sundeck, porch swings and thick foliage. The staff is fun and friendly. ~ 1015 Fleming Street; 305-296-6868, 800-533-5397, fax 305-294-1221; www.edenhouse.com, e-mail mikeeden@keysdigital.com. MODERATE TO ULTRA-DELUXE.

The charming main house, with its ten cozy rooms and comfortable furniture, gives **Merlin Guesthouse** a warm, centralized feel even though the doors to most guest rooms line up motel-style, facing a well-traveled street. The lush tropical garden extends the compound's living area and provides intimate out-of-doors nooks and crannies. Enjoy extreme privacy as well as a sense of community with the owners and other guests. ~ 811 Simonton Street; 305-296-3336, 800-642-4753, fax 305-296-3524; www.merlinguesthouse.com, e-mail merlinguesthouse@snappydsl.net. MODERATE TO DELUXE.

One of the island's lushly planted resorts, **Paradise Inn** is full of light and space—its winding limestone and brick paths, bubbling whirlpool and pool open to sunshine. There is much floral exotica: pink tabebuias and night-blooming jasmine, purple-flowered sky vines trailing along gingerbread piazzas, and ylang-ylang trees whose heady blossoms smell like Chanel No. 5. Families like it here; the rooms are spacious suites or cottages with one or two bedrooms and baths of marble and an extended continental breakfast is included in the rate. There's plenty of on-site parking, too—a rare and welcome feature in Key West. ~ 819 Simonton Street; 305-293-8007, 800-888-9648, fax 305-293-0807; www.theparadise inn.com, e-mail paradise@theparadiseinn.com. ULTRA-DELUXE.

Ethereal peach buildings trimmed in white gingerbread stand along a pretty beach at **Wyndham Reach Resort**. This balmy address has lovely terraced suites with Mexican tile floors, ceiling fans, wet bars, commanding views of the ocean, a swimming pool and a health club. ~ 1435 Simonton Street; 305-296-5000, 800-996-3426, fax 305-296-3008; www.reachresort.com. ULTRA-DELUXE.

The **Curry Mansion Inn** provides 28 rooms with private baths. Most are in the beautiful backyard guest wing that surrounds the pretty deck and pool, eight are in the Victorian home across the street and four are in the fine old historic mansion itself. Furnishings are mostly fine wicker, and every bed is covered with a handmade quilt. Rooms in the annex are all pastel and white, creating a cool, fresh feel even on the hottest summer day. Rates include happy hour and a full, tropical breakfast with various freshly baked breads. ~ 511 and 512 Caroline Street; 305-294-5349, 800-253-3466, fax 305-294-4093; www.currymansion.com, e-mail frontdesk@ currymansion.com. ULTRA-DELUXE.

The Curry Mansion's architectural details echo many ports of call, including New England (the widow's walk) and New Orleans (those ornate trellises are balustrades).

The owners of **La Te Da** have exquisitely restored every inch of every building, including 15 spacious and plush guest rooms tucked within a helter-skelter maze of porches, balconies and sundecks. There are three bars and a fancy restaurant that starts indoors beneath twinkling chandeliers and continues around a sparkling pool. Still remaining is the balcony where José Martí campaigned in 1890 for funds to support the Cuban revolution. Gay-friendly. ~ 1125 Duval Street; 305-296-6706, fax 305-296-3981; www.lateda.com, e-mail latedakw1@aol.com. DELUXE.

Unless you're up for sleeping on a seawall or pier, you can't spend a night any closer to Cuba than at the **Southernmost Hotel in the USA**—it really is what it says. Accommodations are ordinary but gleaming, and the large motel has pseudo-gingerbread trim, two heated pools and a tropical deck with a tiki bar and a pool bar, all contributing to its being a comfortable lodging handy to Key West tourist sights. ~ 1319 Duval Street; 305-296-6577, 800-354-4455, fax 305-294-8272; www.southernmostresort.com. DE-LUXE TO ULTRA-DELUXE.

An elegant bed and breakfast by the sea, **Dewey House** is a Queen Anne confection with ocean-view rooms that's just steps away from bustling Duval Street. Every morning breakfasts of mango, papaya and puffy croissants are set on the terracotta terrace overlooking tiny, palmy South Beach, where locals perform their sunrise yoga. Every afternoon there are cheese and wafers and either iced or hot tea. Luxurious Dewey House features rooms of deep green and honey, high ceilings and wrought-iron poster beds, baths with round whirlpool tubs behind glass doors, and French doors opening to wood-deck balconies. To preserve the air of refined indulgence, no children under 18 are allowed. ~ 506 South Street; 305-296-5611, 800-354-4455, fax 305-294-8272; www.southernmostresort.com. ULTRA-DELUXE.

La Mer Hotel is one of many restored Victorian conch-style houses. This one has contemporary furnishings and definite flair, with many tropical plants, oceanview balconies and porches. Both a continental breakfast and high tea are served daily. Adults only. ~ 506 South Street; 305-296-5611, 800-354-4455, fax 305-294-8272; www.lamerhotel.com, e-mail info@southernmost resorts.com. DELUXE TO ULTRA-DELUXE.

Coconut Beach Resort is a timeshare, but not in the sense that springs to mind, with bleak, child-battered rooms and salesmen staring hungrily at you from a lobby corner. Coconut Beach is run as a hotel, a savvy, seabreezy place of whitewashed and gabled houses running along the ocean, its vast sundeck framing a swimming pool and waterfall, its raised trellised walkways ambling around rare and exotic flora. Rooms range from studios to two-bedroom suites, all decorated in contemporary styles of tiled floors and blond rattan furniture, and most looking out across ocean. ~ 1500 Alberta Street; 305-294-0057, 800-835-0055, fax 305-294-5066; www.coconutbeachresort.com, e-mail cbrkw@ flakeysol.com. ULTRA-DELUXE.

HIDDEN ►

A member of the international Youth Hostel Association, the **Key West International Youth Hostel and Seashell Motel** has budget-priced dorm rooms for males, females and mixed couples in a quiet residential neighborhood; motel rooms are moderate to deluxe. All ages are welcome. There are full kitchen facilities and lockers and bicycles to rent. ~ 718 South Street; 305-296-5719, fax 305-296-0672; www.keywesthostel.com, e-mail keyhostel@bellsouth.net. BUDGET TO MODERATE.

Even if you don't choose to stay at the **Wyndham Casa Marina Resort,** you should drop in and indulge in the Sunday brunch or at least explore the lobby of this 1921 landmark. This handsome Spanish-style hotel radiates historic elegance. The pine floors gleam like glass. The French doors leading to a spacious loggia and the fine dining room's restored mahogany coffered ceiling pay tribute to Flagler's dreams for the Keys. A beachfront restaurant and bar, two pools and a jacuzzi, a health club, lighted clay tennis courts, a water sports center and an airport shuttle add modern luxury. ~ 1500 Reynolds Street on the ocean; 305-296-3535, 800-626-0777, fax 305-296-3008; www.casamarinakeywest.com. ULTRA-DELUXE.

The Wyndham Casa Marina Resort was created as the final resort along Henry Flagler's railroad in 1921.

Looking more like it should be in Disney World than Key West, the **Sheraton Suites** sports a cluster of faux Bahamas-style buildings coated in radiant peach and purple. In the lobby, teal benches and purple chairs look cartoonish; at the meandering pool, water cascades from fake boulders; and in the rooms, blue waves dance on the pastel bedside stands. All 180 rooms are 508-square-foot suites offering living rooms with sofa beds, microwave ovens, louvered doors and two televisions. Many have jacuzzi tubs and some have balconies. The public beach is just across the street and there's a day-and-night shuttle to Duval Street. ~ 2001 South Roosevelt Boulevard; 305-292-9800, 800-452-3224, fax 305-294-6009; www.sheratonkeywest.com, e-mail info@sheratonkeywest.com. ULTRA-DELUXE.

DINING

Marvelous Gulf views, candlelit tables and soothing piano music are reasons for reveling at **One Duval,** the only four-diamond restaurant in Key West. As an added treat, the cuisine is consistently outstanding, relying heavily on innovative treatments of local seafood, fruits and vegetables. Musts here are the conch chowder and the snapper in parchment with citrus butter. Dinner only. ~ 1 Duval Street; 305-296-4600, fax 305-296-7569; www.pierhouse.com, e-mail info@pierhouse.com. DELUXE TO ULTRA-DELUXE.

A rowdy, noisy, casual atmosphere is usual at the **Half Shell Raw Bar**, and, like as not, you'll find someone's faithful pooch tethered to the large anchor outside. There's no air conditioning, but open windows and the waterfront location coax in the ocean air. Under a wall collage of license plates and currency, patrons gobble up the freshest seafood and down huge quaffs of cold beverages. ~ Land's End Village, 231 Margaret Street; 305-294-7496. MODERATE.

Right next to Moore's Paint & Body Shop, a half-block north of Sloppy Joe's, is an easy-to-miss restaurant. Called simply **Thai Cuisine**, the indoor/outdoor eatery serves traditional Thai dishes in a bright, airy and decidedly ethnic atmosphere. Pad thai, roast duck basil, and snapper curry are among the menu's 70-plus items, featuring ingredients like coconut milk, green curry paste, clear noodles, lime, fresh basil, and mangrood leaves. A great choice for vegetarians. No lunch on Saturday and Sunday. ~ 513 Greene Street; 305-294-9424. MODERATE.

The marriage of German cuisine and island ingredients is surprisingly successful. The menu at **Martin's** offers traditional *sauerbraten* with *spatzle* and red cabbage alongside innovative dishes such as fresh sautéed grouper topped with a dijon crust and served with champagne kraut and rosemary potatoes. Nestled on an artsy lane, this spot has a tiny romantic dining room, canopied garden tables and a darling outdoor bar stocked with delicious dark *biers*. Martin's is known for fabulous Sunday brunch and homemade desserts. Dinner only. ~ 416 Appelrouth Lane; phone/fax 305-296-1183. DELUXE.

Completed in 1998, the city's Harbor Walk curves around Key West Historic Seaport, past a section of newish eateries. The **A & B Lobster House** has had a vantage over this portion of the bight since the 1950s. Thanks to a classy restoration that revitalized the restaurant's swanky appeal, the A & B offers elegant dining and a harbor view that Key Westers have held dear for half a century. On an island where chefs lean toward Caribbean cuisine, Chef Konrad Jochum presents refreshingly simple, traditional fare (à la some New England fishhouse); his plump oysters Rockefeller and seafood cream-sherry pan roasts are exquisite. Fresh ingredients, including aged Black Angus steaks and Maine lobster, are flown in. Downstairs is **Alonzo's**, a more casual oyster bar. ~ 700 Front Street, upstairs; 305-294-5880;

www.aandblobsterhouse.com, e-mail info@aandblobsterhouse.com. MODERATE TO ULTRA-DELUXE.

B.O.'s Fish Wagon looks like a heap of flotsam washed up on   ◄ *HIDDEN* a street corner—and it is, nets and buoys and license plates all huddling beneath a thatched roof of questionable integrity. But it's well known as the place for a great Key West lunch, or at least an entertaining one, the many culinary options include shrimp and softshell crab sandwiches, oyster po'boys, chili, barbecues and *picadillo*. ~ 801 Caroline Street, at William Street; 305-294-9272. BUDGET TO MODERATE.

Pepe's Café and Steakhouse is like a wonderful old boathouse,   ◄ *HIDDEN* outfitted in battered wood walls, tiller-top tables and rumpled fishing snapshots. Opened in 1909 by a Cuban fisherman, it moved from prominent Duval Street to a lonesome byroad. All the better: except for locals, few know of the eatery's great burgers and baked oyster. There are also pork chops, steak, seafood and creamed chip beef on toast for breakfast. A bougainvillea-covered patio offers outdoor dining. ~ 806 Caroline Street; 305-294-7192, fax 305-294-3580; www.pepescafe.net. MODERATE.

For a filling and tasty meal, try **El Siboney**, a Cuban restau-   ◄ *HIDDEN* rant where they serve generous portions of *ropa vieja* (it means "old clothes," but it's really a beef dish), stuffed shrimp and some fine pork dishes—all with black beans and rice. Other side dishes include *plátanos* and *casava*, a sometimes tasteless starchy yucca dish, but here well seasoned and worth a try because it's good for you. White lace cloths add a touch of class to this plain fam-

---

AUTHOR FAVORITE

Trendy **nine one five** specializes in tapas-style dishes and is one of the few restaurants open late (until midnight during the week and 1 a.m. on weekends). Order several small dishes from a list of dozens influenced by Mediterranean and Asian cuisines, as well as traditional American foods. Try imported chorizo with drunken goat and *manchego*, serrano ham with long-stem artichokes, dates stuffed with garlic and wrapped in bacon, and spicy pork kabobs with mango chutney. The wine list is extensive; if you'd prefer something nonalcoholic, the homemade lemongrass soda is refreshing. Dine inside or out. Dinner only. ~ 915 Duval Street; 305-296-0669. DELUXE.

ily place. ~ 900 Catherine Street; 305-296-4184. BUDGET TO
MODERATE.

Welcome to neighborhood café dining at its finest. With just
seven tables and a tiny bar, **Mo's** is a whirlwind of kitchen clat-
ter, great smells and the sounds of people having fun. It's famous
for appetizers such as country patés and baked cheddar. Entrées
include fresh spinach salad with Mo's dijon dressing, vegetarian
casseroles, seafood lasagna and sumptuous roast lamb. Rena's
apple pie is to die for. Closed Sunday. ~ 1116 White Street; 305-
296-8955. BUDGET TO MODERATE.

Finnegan's Wake is a piece of the Ould Sod transported directly
across the water complete with a huge, dark-wood, mirrored bar
that surely was stolen from some Irish pub.
There's a great selection of beers that includes
Guinness and Harp Ale, and a rosy-cheeked bar-
tender who can drop into a brogue as thick as Irish
stew. The menu is more Irish than Paddy's pig; try
potato leek soup, Dublin pot pie or County Cork
corned beef and cabbage. In spite of all the boisterous
fun that goes on in the bar area, the dining room is
comfortable and spacious, and there's a shaded outdoor
eating area. ~ 320 Grinnell Street; 305-293-0222, fax 305-293-
8593; www.keywestirish.com. MODERATE TO DELUXE.

Though conch is a staple
on South Florida menus,
this tasty mollusk
(endangered in the
U.S.) is likely imported
from the Caribbean.

In a tiny white building near the cemetery, **Seven Fish** offers
bistro fare. Prices are good, and the menu is eclectic, with meat-
loaf and mashed potatoes listed alongside tuna sushi. Nightly
specials include three fresh fish entrées and dishes such as angel
hair pasta with fish, clams, shrimp and marinara sauce. Decor is
Deco minimalist, with exposed wood rafters and a gleaming little bar. Tables are tightly arranged, so go early or late if elbow
room is important to you. Dinner only. Closed Tuesday and the
month of September. ~ 632 Olivia Street; 305-296-2777; www.
7fish.com. MODERATE.

Often when celebrities attach their name to a place it ensures
mediocrity. Not so with **Kelly's Caribbean Bar, Grill & Brewery**,
owned by actress Kelly McGillis and husband Fred Tillman. Their
island fare is colorful, zesty and inventive, their home-brewed beer
truly tasty, and their courtyard setting spacious and well-liked by
locals. Some of our favorite dishes: jumbo coconut shrimp with a
pineapple dipping sauce and Caribbean apple chicken with mashed

potatoes. ~ 301 Whitehead Street; 305-293-8484, fax 305-296-0047; www.kellyskeywest.com. DELUXE.

Antonia's is in a big, handsome, open room with a high ceiling of polished wood and a long, glittery bar attended by pretty people. Much pasta and wine is consumed at Antonia's, and many business deals consummated. There is no lunch, but there is a man in the window all day, his floured hands kneading and rolling and cutting pasta. You can have a half or full order of pasta, but otherwise things are elaborate and pricier: grilled rack of lamb chops with mustard and rosemary, beef tenderloin and veal medallions. ~ 615 Duval Street; 305-294-6565, fax 305-294-3888; www.antoniaskeywest.com. ULTRA-DELUXE.

Duval is tourist territory, but that doesn't stop the locals from crowding into **Camille's** for breakfast every morning—or evening, depending on your lifestyle. You can go light with fruit, yogurt and fresh-baked muffins, or sumptuous with egg combinations, waffles or french toast, an omelette or a bagel and smoked salmon. Sandwiches are available, too, but definitely take a back seat to the breakfast goodies. The decor is sort of fun and funky—movie posters and publicity stills, masks and stained glass. ~ 1202 Simonton Street; 305-296-4811, fax 305-296-2221; www.camilleskeywest.com. MODERATE TO DELUXE.

When you pick up a menu and see words like *mesclun, ancho* and *risotto*, you know you're in for an inventive evening, food-wise. **Cafe Marquesa** doesn't disappoint. With dishes such as barbecued Key West prawns with white bean mash, oven-roasted plum tomatoes and grilled corn relish, you can see that this is no café, this is fine dining at its best. You and I know that *haricot vert* is just a green bean, but it tastes better in French and when served up with seared mahimahi with papaya-cucumber salsa and black-bean flan. The tiny but toney Marquesa's ambience, with its smoke-free air, its elegant tables and trompe l'oeil wall, is as entrancing as its imaginative, changing menu, and the service is knowledgeable and discreet. Dinner only. ~ 600 Fleming Street; 305-292-1244, fax 305-294-2121; www.marquesa.com. ULTRA-DELUXE.

The boisterous burgers-and-ribs joint that was Compass Rose has been reinvented as **Michaels**, calm and candlelit, a balmy patio beneath pink frangipani and coconut palm, with a little water garden and fountain. Steak is the star at Michaels, USDA Prime beef that's grilled to order and accompanied by garlicky mashed potatoes. Everything else is very good, too, from the seared duck to the veal chop stuffed with basil, mozzarella and prosciutto. Dinner only. ~ 532 Margaret Street, at Southard Street; 305-295-1300; www.michealskeywest.com. ULTRA-DELUXE.

HIDDEN ▶ **Blue Heaven** has become an institution thanks to its funky Bahama Village location, chic artsy waitstaff, and authentic Caribbean menu. Dine inside or out in the rustic yard (complete with free-roaming chickens) on Caribbean barbecue shrimp (deglazed with Red Stripe beer and served with corn muffins) or a vegetarian feast of basmati rice, black beans, plantains, fresh veggies and red-onion marmalade. For dessert feast on flaming Bananas Heaven, with spiced rum and homemade vanilla ice cream. A favorite for breakfast and Sunday brunch. Closed Labor Day to mid-October. ~ 729 Thomas Street; 305-296-8666, fax 305-296-9052; www.blueheavenkw.com. ULTRA-DELUXE.

HIDDEN ▶ Across the street from Blue Heaven, **Johnson's Café** is a neighborhood gem. You can sit outside, observe the Petronia Street scene and chow down on soul food, like the signature double fried pork-chop sandwich. Order at the window and sit down to an oil-cloth and hot sauce dining experience. Lunch only; days and hours vary, so call ahead. ~ 801 Thomas Street; 305-293-2286. BUDGET.

HIDDEN ▶ The best roll-up sandwiches on the island are at **Lobo's,** which offers 30 combinations of veggies, cheeses, meats, salads and seafood wrapped in a flour tortilla. Creative choices include the Wild Mushroom, a grilled portobello with tabouleh, jack cheese and fresh basil mayo, and the Thai Hot Tuna, a tuna salad with mango chutney, avocado and sprouts combo. The salads, quesadillas and burgers are also outstanding. Outside seating only. Open Sunday in season. ~ 5 Key Lime Square; 305-296-5303. BUDGET.

If it weren't for the intoxicating aroma of garlic and olive oil and
HIDDEN ▶ herb-spiked sauces, you might drive right by **Mangia Mangia,** hidden as it is in a quiet neighborhood. But find it you should, because the pasta is the freshest around. The rigatoni with jumbo shrimp is topped with a salad of radicchio, arugula and Belgian endive. The *bolito misto de mare* is a combination of seafood and *pappardello* pasta in a clam broth with white wine and herbs. It's served inside or in a courtyard of many palm trees, with oil lamps flickering on your table. Dinner only. ~ 900 Southard Street; 305-294-2469. MODERATE.

Relax in **Ambrosia**'s traditional Japanese atmosphere and   ◄ *HIDDEN*
pace yourself for indulgence. From the first bite of *hijiki* to the
last spoon of green tea creme brulée, the food here satisfies the
senses. Chef Masa's rolls of exotic seafood, rice and caviar, and
precision-sliced local tuna are tasty works of art. The beef tataki
and other cooked dishes are equally exquisite. During the off season, no lunch is served and the restaurant is closed Sunday. ~
1100 Packer Street; 305-293-0304, fax 305-296-6389. DELUXE.

Pisces is so small and unspectacular on the outside, it's impossible to imagine that inside this boutique restaurant—small,
intimate and candlelit with artwork by Andy Warhol—awaits
the most elegant of spaces, with arches, crisp white linens and
twinkling crystal lamps, offering rich, tropical cuisine of the most
sensational order. From the roast half duckling with fresh rasp-
berry sauce to the lobster flambéed in cognac with saffron butter, every inspired dish tastes as luscious as it looks. Dinner only.
Closed Sunday. ~ 1007 Simonton Street; 305-294-7100; e-mail
pisces@bahamasvacationguide.com. ULTRA-DELUXE.

Key West supports at least five sushi restaurants. For less expensive but excellent sushi and Japanese food, **Origami** is rela-   ◄ *HIDDEN*
tively informal and offers tropical courtyard seating. Dinner only.
~ 1075 Duval Street; 305-294-0092. MODERATE TO DELUXE.

A sign of these celebrity-driven times, **Shula's on the Beach** is   ◄ *HIDDEN*
owned by former NFL coach Don Shula. The pricey restaurant
serves lots of certified Angus steaks as well as fresh seafood and
chicken entrées. Decorated with memorabilia from Shula's career
with the Miami Dolphins, the 180-seat dining room offers indoor
and outdoor seating overlooking the beach. Dinner only. ~ Wyndham Reach Resort, 1435 Simonton Street; 305-296-6144; www.
donshula.com. DELUXE TO ULTRA-DELUXE.

SUBLIME SUNSETS & SEAFOOD

Louie's Backyard consistently ranks among the top restaurants in the
Keys. Over the years, the eatery's open-air seating and stunning views
have made it a hotspot for romantics, while its inspired menu has continued to seduce the palates of passionate foodies. Try for seating on the
outside deck, where you can enjoy fresh seasonal meats and seafood
while admiring the approach of sunset. Reservations recommended. ~
700 Waddell Avenue; 305-294-1061; www.louiesbackyard.com. DELUXE
TO ULTRA-DELUXE.

HIDDEN ▶   **The Rusty Anchor** is run by a local family who have turned a one-time leaky-floored shrimpers' bar into a favored eating spot for locals from Key West and elsewhere. Charter boat captains send their customers here because, as one said, "It's just the best," a good example of the word-of-mouth publicity that keeps folks coming. The location is unlikely, proving that the reputation of good seafood, well-prepared conch fritters and, surprisingly, barbecued baby back ribs, are all it takes to make a one-room eatery a success. Closed Sunday. ~ On the corner of Old Shrimp Road, Stock Island; 305-294-5369, fax 305-296-7536; www.rustyanchor. com. MODERATE.

HIDDEN ▶   **The Hogfish Bar and Grill,** located on the water at Safe Harbor Marina, has retained the funky relaxed quality that made Key West famous. Rustic and friendly, with a breeze cooling the covered open-air dining area, this is one of the few places that regularly offers hogfish (a delicious snapper) as well as a killer Sunday barbecue. The entire menu is simple but good—burgers, steamed shrimp, Italian sausage sandwiches—and daily specials. There's a bar on site, and live entertainment Thursday through Sunday. ~ 6810 Front Street, Stock Island; 305-293-4041. BUDGET TO MODERATE.

SHOPPING   Key West is the place to spend your money. The Old Town streets in the waterfront area are a mass of shops and boutiques offering everything from imported flamingos to artful fabrics. Visitors do most of their shopping in the dozens of glitzy and funky shops in Old Town; practical shopping is available in several centers in the newer areas.

Not quite all the sponge fishermen are gone from Key West, as explained on a continuous video at the **Sponge Market**. "Sponge King" C. B. McHugh demonstrates the harvesting and treating of sponges and tells their history on the film; the store has bins of these marvelous nonpolyfoam wonders and other gifts. ~ 1 Whitehead Street; 305-294-2555.

HIDDEN ▶   **The Restaurant Store** caters to commercial kitchens and home chefs who will go crazy over all the great gadgetry and great prices. ~ 111 Eaton Street; 305-294-7994, 800-469-7510; www. keywestchef.com.

Peppers of Key West can raise beads of sweat on even the coolest cucumbers. This hot-sauce boutique has over 400 brands of the fiery condiment and specializes in Caribbean sauces. Customers are encouraged to test the products at the tasting bar. Related books, kitchen gadgets and local pepper art are also sold here. ~ 602 Green Street; 305-295-9333; www.peppersofkeywest.com.

Located in a historic old one-time waterfront grocery, the **Key West Art Center** is a cooperative for local artists. Works for sale include paintings and drawings of seascapes, sunsets and Key West street scenes, as well as sculpture and other art. ~ 301 Front Street; 305-294-1241.

Vintage-fabric connoisseurs and pillow freaks take note: The **Seam Shoppe**, a working upholstery shop, stocks bolts of stunning, ultra-cool textiles, as well as tassels, braid and piping—and will create custom pillows from any of them. Owner Cindy Meyer collects mint-condition original fabrics and replicas; classic designs include giant tropical flora and animal-pattern motifs. Just window shopping is a trip down memory lane. Closed Sunday. ~ 1114 Truman Avenue; 305-296-9830; www.tropicalfabricsonline.com.

◀ HIDDEN

One of the most expensive and exclusive cigar stores in the Keys, **Tropical Republic Fine Cigars** carries hundreds of brands of major stogies as well as obscure and hard-to-find "boutique" cigars. In addition to a full line of smoking accessories, there's fragrant pipe tobacco and imported cigarettes. Try its proprietary Gurkha-made cigar, infused with Captain Morgan Spiced Rum. ~ 112 Fitzpatrick Street; 305-292-9595.

Pelican Poop Shoppe is housed in the building in which Hemingway wrote his masterpiece, *A Farewell to Arms.*

Brightly colored tropical resortwear is for sale at **Key West Fashions**. ~ 201 Simonton Street; 305-294-9535.

Kino Sandals has been making their uncomplicated footwear for men, women and children for almost as long as anyone can remember. Seasonal Sunday closures. ~ 107 Fitzpatrick Street; 305-294-5044.

Right smack dab in Old Town, the **Fairvilla Megastore** is geared for lovers, with a broad selection of intimate apparel, erotic toys, massage oils and the like. Serious buyers and browsers rub shoulders in this place, which is as much an attraction as an actual shop. ~ 520 Front Street; 305-292-0448; www.fairvillaonline.com.

For a wild selection of arts and crafts culled from across the Caribbean, stop in at the **Pelican Poop Shoppe**. Centered around a tropical garden atrium, you'll find painted-metal Siamese fighting fish, decorated wind chimes and papier-mâché flamingos as well as Haitian and porcelain ceramic art. ~ 314 Simonton Street; 305-296-3887; www.pelicanpoop.com.

Though he's usually on the road performing and recording, Jimmy Buffett and his eclectic blend of Caribbean and cowboy music have become a trademark of Key West, where the singer got his start. Now Buffett fans can pop into his local **Margaritaville Store** for all kinds of memorabilia from tapes to T-shirts. ~ 500 Duval Street; 305-296-1435, 800-262-6835, fax 305-296-1084; www.margaritaville.com, e-mail info@margaritaville.com.

In the same complex, **Fast Buck Freddie's** is a wonderful hodge-podge of a department store left over from the days before malls. Browse through racks of trendy tropical clothing, funny posters, fine candies, swimwear, home furnishings and gift items. ~ 500 Duval Street; 305-294-2007.

If you don't plan to go deep-sea treasure hunting yourself, you can arrange to buy an authentic piece of booty at **Mel Fisher's Treasure Exhibit and Sales**. ~ 200 Greene Street; 305-296-9936, 800-434-1399; www.melfisher.com.

For exotic kites, colorful nylon windsocks and just about any toy that flies, visit the **Key West Kite Company,** the first kite store in Florida. They also carry a wide variety of flags and banners. ~ 408 Greene Street; 305-296-2535; www.keywestkites.com.

The **K-W Light Gallery** is the project of photographer-painter Sharon Wells, whose work the gallery features. Also on display is a collection of historic archival images of the Keys and, during the winter and spring months, the works of local guest artists. ~ 534 Fleming Street; 305-294-0566, 305-923-5133; www.kw lightgallery.com.

It's impossible to miss the **Environmental Circus**, parked as it is on the middle of Key West's main drag, sending billows of in-cense smoke into the street, beckoning with windows full of wa-ter pipes and counterculture patches. Inside this vintage estab-lishment, one of Florida's biggest and oldest head shops, are postcards albums and books on growing pot. ~ 518 Duval Street; 305-294-6055; www.e-circuskeywest.com.

Tikal Trading Co. carries women's and girls' clothing made from handwoven knits and featuring local artist Leigh Hooten's original tropical prints. This is your place for sundresses, sports-wear, party skirts and a complementary line of jewelry. ~ Two lo-cations: 129 Duval Street, 305-296-4463; 910 Duval Street, 305-293-0033.

Despite the tourist crowds, make a special stop at **Wild Side Gallery**, whose unusual, nature-inspired art comes in many mediums, from ceramics and wood and glass to jewelry and oils, and by many artists across the country. There are wall masks of raku and gourd, burnished earthenware jars, copper and wire sculpture—all brilliant, delicate, exceptional. ~ 1108 Duval Street; 305-296-7800.

Haitian Art Co. imports metal and wood sculptures, carvings, papier-mâché and brilliantly colored paintings in handcrafted frames by Haitian artists. ~ 600 Frances Street; 305-296-8932; www.haitian-art-co.com.

Key West Island Books carries a large collection of natural history books, books about Key West and books by authors who have lived here. They have new, used and rare volumes, and have book signings and readings throughout the year. ~ 513 Fleming Street; 305-294-2904.

Harrison's Gallery features the work of sculptor Helen Harrison, who carves, shapes and assembles wood into graceful forms and figures. Using mahogany, coconut, sea hibiscus and even palm husks, Harrison reveals the shape within—anything from a male form to a woman's sexy shoe. The gallery showcases other artists as well. ~ 825 White Street; 305-294-0609; www.harrison-gallery.com.

For fun and functional artwork, including sculptural jewelry, check out the **Wave Gallery**. Anything from original paintings to garden ornaments to kitchen magnets might catch your eye. The collection features local and national artists working in oils, acrylics and other mediums. Closed Sunday during the off season. ~ 1100 White Street; 305-293-9428; www.thewavegallery.com.

RELIEF FOR REEFS

Before you visit the coral reef, stop by the **Reef Relief Environmental Center and Store**. The tiny place is packed with exhibits and information on the fragile coral reef ecosystem—the reef, mangrove forests and seagrass beds—and how to protect it. It's run by the nonprofit Reef Relief, one of Florida's most powerful environmental organizations. Closed Sunday. ~ 201 William Street; 305-294-3100, fax 305-293-9515; www.reefrelief.org, e-mail reef@bellsouth.net.

Lucky Street Gallery is a marvelous cache of paintings, glass-works, pottery, jewelry, metal sculptures and other zany pieces for the avant garde. Closed Sunday. ~ 1120 White Street; 305-294-3973.

HIDDEN ► Even for Key West, the **Lazy Way Shops** are strange. Tucked inside a makeshift building is a helter-skelter maze of crystals, wood pelicans and other tourist items, including "Conch Republic" silver coins. Closed Sunday. ~ In the alley just east of the intersection of Elizabeth and Greene streets; 305-292-5058.

Located in Bahama Village, **Besame Mucho** carries a small but diverse selection of great gifts from around the world: hand-cut soaps from Europe, hand painted boxes and ornaments from Mexico, silk purses, nouveau art-print coasters and other little treasures. ~ 315 Petronia Street; 305-294-1928.

HIDDEN ► It's hard to know whether **Five Brothers Grocery** should be classified as a shop or a restaurant, but I'll choose the former be-cause there are no chairs or tables, just some cramped shelves of basic groceries and some favorite items for local Spanish cooking. The main reason for stopping here, though, is the counter food; locals maintain the Cuban sandwiches and *bollitos* are the best any-where. You can also take out espresso, *café con leche*, *papa rellena* and a can of papaya for dessert. This is not a tourist place but a tiny neighborhood grocery. In fact, a sign warns, "This isn't Burger King. You do it My Way!" Closed Sunday. ~ 930 Southard Street; 305-296-5205.

AUTHOR FAVORITE

The hands-down perennial greatest place for fresh gourmet and organic food shopping is the **Waterfront Market**. Crafted upon an original produce stand, the market sells culinary specialties, from the best local seafood (such as hog snapper and stone crab claws) to secret-recipe deli salads (try Linda's basmati rice and shiitake mushroom concoction), sushi and freshly juiced veggies and herbs. This is a great place to pick up a made-to-order deli sandwich on artisan bread, just out-of-the-oven sticky buns or a good bottle of wine to go—and you'll also find edible gifts to take home. It's an artsy place, too. Check out Wyland's marine-life mural, known locally as the Wyland Wall, outside the building, and Key West artist David Laughlin's unique abstract and surreal landscapes in-side. ~ 201 William Street; 305-296-0778.

If you wondered where the nighttime action was as you traveled down the Keys, you'll discover it's almost all here in Key West. Entertainment begins long before sunset and goes on far into the early morning hours. A number of nightclubs seem to spill right out through their open windows and doors onto the street.

You should at least stick your head into **Sloppy Joe's** because it has hooked onto the Papa Hemingway legend in as many ways as it can. Papa and Sloppy Joe were drinking buddies, apparently, and it's said that some of the tales that showed up in literature were founded on stories they shared in the backroom here. Just follow your ears and you should find it most anytime of the day or night. There's live rock: softer music in the afternoon, rhythm-and-blues and a rockin' band until 4 a.m. ~ 201 Duval Street; 305-294-5717, fax 305-294-4085; www.sloppyjoes.com.

Capt. Tony's Saloon, "where everybody is a star," is the location of the *real* Sloppy Joe's, where Ernest Hemingway wrote *To Have and Have Not*, among other titles. Anyway, the real star here is Cap'n Tony, a wiry white-haired codger who has polished his role as local character until it shines. Rowdy and fun, with all sorts of live musicians from country to blues, it's a Key West institution dating back to 1851—the oldest bar in all of Florida. Come and see memorabilia of all the famous people who have had a drink here, or play pool. ~ 428 Greene Street; 305-294-1838; www.capttonyssaloon.com.

On the sunset deck of second-story **Havana Docks Bar** you can get an eyeful of the Gulf and an earful of live tropical island music entertaining the crowd. ~ Pier House Resort, 1 Duval Street; 305-296-4600.

For those who must have predictable surroundings, the **Hard Rock Cafe** awaits on Duval Street. In 1996 Hard Rock moved into the elaborate old Queen Anne building occupied by the Elks Club most of this century. ~ 313 Duval Street; 305-293-0230; www.hardrock.com.

The Top has the best view of any night spot in Key West, from the top of the 1925 La Concha hotel. Listen to relaxing music while you sip your drink and watch the sunset. ~ 430 Duval Street; 305-296-2991.

You'll find a bar, live rock-and-roll and blues every night and, of course, plenty of Jimmy Buffett music at the **Margaritaville**

Café, where Jimmy, no longer "wastin' away," makes occasional impromptu appearances. You can enjoy the music and American-Caribbean food until closing time. ~ 500 Duval Street; 305-292-1435, 800-262-6835; www.margaritaville.com.

While not a club proper, **Mangoes** attracts an eclectic late-night mix of locals, visitors and bar-hoppers. People-watchers love the view from the open patio bar/restaurant. Located on a busy downtown block, Mangoes' patrons are practically guaranteed a cultural "show" as the post-midnight parade rambles along Duval Street. Enjoy the impromptu scene over a mango colada or another exotic drink. ~ 700 Duval Street; 305-292-4606.

Drop in at **Flagler's Lounge**, where you can enjoy jazz or contemporary music in a glamorous, brass-and-glass, 150-seat nightclub surrounded by history. ~ Wyndham Casa Marina, 1500 Reynolds Street on the ocean; 305-292-6215.

Should the mood strike for a really good glass (or three) of wine, drop by **Grand Vin**. The wine bar in this old white, Bahamian-style house offers numerous possibilities by the glass, including "flights" of three half-glass tastings. Sit out on the porch and people-watch, or inside at the bar, where the owner will keep opening bottle after bottle after bottle. . . . ~ 1107 Duval Street; 305-296-1020, fax 305-292-2220.

Two Friends Patio Restaurant features karaoke nightly in its big, popular open-air lounge. The festivities sometimes spill out onto the street. There is a patio restaurant attached and a raw bar for late-night eating. ~ 512 Front Street; 305-296-9212.

Once a turtle cannery, the **Turtle Kraals Bar** is now an old-style Key West eating and drinking spot. You can see turtles and

POOL AT THE PARROT

Some would say you haven't really done Key West until you've played pool at the Parrot, and that would be the **Green Parrot**. The bar seems ancient, and it is in fact a long-time haunt of the island's more peculiar and dubious characters, who hold forth at the bar beneath a parachute and old ceiling fans set at top speed, and who take turns at the pool tables and juke-box. The floors are coming up and the walls are covered with strange signage (including a cockeyed sign that simply says, "Balance"). Stop in for a nice cold draught. ~ 601 Whitehead Street; 305-294-6133.

other sea creatures here while you relax and have a drink. ~ 2
Land's End Village, end of Margaret Street; 305-294-2640;
www.turtlekraals.com.

   Schooner Wharf Bar, once strictly local, has been "found" by
at least part of the masses, though it's still big fun. Pick a plastic
chair in the pearock or beneath a wood shake awning, with painted
buoys and fishnets everywhere, dogs roaming (lots and lots of
dogs!), the Key West Bight swollen with boats. Bands play most
of the time, and when they're not, the "bar magician" will show
you his tricks. ~ 202 William Street; 305-292-9520, fax 305-292-
9520; e-mail schoonerwb@aol.com.

   The best place to see Key West's power elite isn't a posh hotel
bar by the sea but an inland street corner filled with flotsam.
B.O.'s Fish Wagon, camped out on the corner parking lot at   ◄ HIDDEN
Caroline and William streets, is where old-monied families come
to drink long-neck beer, catch up on island gossip, and listen to
live jazz and blues on Friday. ~ 801 Caroline Street; 305-294-
9272.

   For those occasions when only a dive will do, head to **Don's
Place Bar**, the sit-down part of a combination lounge, drive-
through liquor store and delivery business. Mingle with the locals
inside or at the tiki bar. ~ 1000 Truman Avenue; 305-296-5271.

THEATER, SYMPHONY AND DANCE   The arts are alive in Key
West, too. A variety of popular and classical concerts, plays and
dance programs are presented at the **Tennessee Williams
Theatre**. 5901 College Road; 305-296-1520; www.tennesseewil
liamstheatre.com.

   The **Waterfront Playhouse**, operated by the Key West Players,
Inc., presents an assortment of plays, reviews and musical come-
dies throughout the year. ~ Mallory Square; 305-294-5015 box
office; www.waterfrontplayhouse.com. The **Red Barn Theatre** is
a professional company presenting several productions from
December through June. ~ 319 Duval Street; 305-296-9911,
866-870-9911; www.redbarntheatre.org.

   And, yes, it's true. There actually is a **Key West Symphony**, a
true orchestra that draws its talent from all over the country.
Over 70 musicians, most of whom perform with professional or-
chestras, fly to Key West for rehearsals one week before their island performances. Generally, they are on vacation or a leave of

absence from other symphonies. Performances occur at the Tennessee Williams Theatre one week in December, February and April, with two children's programs on Wednesday and main performances on Friday and Saturday nights. ~ 1025 White Street; 305-292-1774, 305-296-1520 (box office); www.keywestsym phony.com, e-mail info@keywestsymphony.com.

Not in the mood for classical music? Then try the island's other musical phenomenon, the **Key West Pops Orchestra**. This group consists of 45 to 50 local and visiting professional musicians under the direction of Vincent Zito. Performances range from Broadway to light classical and feature local singers, guest conductors and guest artists, who have included Lee Roy Reams and Metropolitan Opera singer Barbara Conrad. Three performances each season are held at the Tennessee Williams Theatre. ~ 305-296-8288, 305-296-1520 (box office), fax 305-296-6219; www.keywestpops.com.

A current listing of arts and cultural events in Key West (and throughout the Keys) can be found on the Florida Keys Council of the Arts website. ~ www.keysarts.com.

Home of the Key West Film Society, the **Tropic Cinema** presents world-class cinema in its 8000-square-foot public theater and media center. Two nice cool screening rooms offer independent, domestic and foreign films, as well as noteworthy mainstream flicks. A community non-profit arts organization, the Tropic Cinema also presents exhibits, performances, seminars and classes through the Key West Film Institute. This is one of the island's creative jewels. ~ 416 Eaton Street; 305-294-5857, fax 305-768-0465; www.tropiccinema.com, e-mail info@keywestfilm.org.

BEACHES & PARKS

It's a surprise to many visitors that Key West has very few beaches, and those it does have are far from sensational. On the south side of the island, along the Atlantic Ocean, you can dip into the water or lie in the sun at one of several narrow public beaches that tend to get very crowded.

SMATHERS BEACH This city-owned beach is where locals lie in the sun in the daytime and take walks at night. There's nice water for swimming but a rocky bottom. Facilities include restrooms, picnic areas, bathhouses, watersport rentals and concession stands. ~ Off South Roosevelt Boulevard west of the airport.

HIGGS BEACH This beach area is popular with families, as swimming is possible and there are a number of recreational facilities nearby. Facilities include picnic areas, restrooms, a bath-house, a playground, tennis courts, watersport rentals and conces-sion stands. ~ Located along Atlantic Boulevard between White and Reynolds streets.

FORT ZACHARY TAYLOR STATE HISTORIC SITE

Though the chief attraction at this state historic site is the ex-cavated and restored fort, the park also contains one of the nicest little beaches, especially for sunset-viewing and boat-watching, in the area. A grove of trees provides some rare seaside shade. You can fish in the shipping channel. Swimming is good, but watch for drop-offs. There's excellent off-shore snorkeling. Facilities here include picnic areas, restrooms, kayak rentals, nature trails and concession stands. Day-use fee, $1.50 per person (walk- or bike-in) and minimum $4 per car. ~ Located off the western end of Southard Street; 305-292-6713, fax 305-292-6881.

Key West Gay Scene

With so much to do concentrated on such an attractive little island, it's no surprise that Key West has become a popular destination. From its snorkeling trips and sunset cruises to its kitschy conch houses and trolley rides, Key West draws gay travelers from around the world. Even though it now appears that gay visitors are outnum-bered by straights most times of the year, the gay community con-tinues to have a strong presence in Key West. Gay visitors are welcomed everywhere and Key West's elected officials and business community continue to reach out to gay travelers.

The casual island atmosphere that prevails in Key West com-pels everyone who sets foot on its soil to let his or her hair down. Its gay guesthouses set the standard for elegance, amenities and decor, while most innkeepers provide the kind of personal service that is unmatched by any hotel staff. Whether you are sampling its many superb restaurants, browsing its shops or cruising its night-spots, you will find people in Key West extraordinarily sociable.

The Key West Business Guild operates the **Gay & Lesbian Visitor Info Center,** where you can pick up its informative *Key West Map and Directory.* The guide is also available at gay guesthouses or by contacting the guild, which is the island's gay business asso-ciation. ~ 513 Truman Avenue; 305-294-4603, 800-535-7797, fax 305-294-3273; www.gaykeywestfl.com, e-mail keywestgay@aol.com. The monthly publication, *Southern Exposure,* also offers information for gay travelers as well as timely listings of events and performances. But if you can't wait to find out the happenings in Key West before you arrive, tap into *Southern Exposure's* website, which is updated every month with the same timely details as the magazine. ~ 305-294-6303; www.gaykeywest.net, e-mail feedback@gaykeywest.net.

Dedicated to Key West's homosexual population and culture, the **Gay and Lesbian Community Center** is open to anyone who supports its goals. This is a great, non-commercial place to become acquainted with the island's gay scene. The Hal Walsh Archives, created to document and preserve the island's gay heritage, contains photos, published materials, video interviews and profiles of early gay businesses. The center also coordinates the annual Pridefest and there's a library and internet café on-site. ~ 532 Truman Avenue; 305-292-3223, fax 305-292-3237; www.glcckeywest.org.

LODGING   Gay visitors will find numerous guesthouses—many of which are exclusively for gay men and women. Several clothing-optional inns cater to young, single, party-minded males, while other, more intimate houses appeal to professional couples.

The famous purple-and-yellow-painted **Atlantic Shores Resort** is a gay party compound on the sea, complete with clothing-optional pool and pier, and motel rooms with lilac-washed walls, wall unit ACs humming all night, and faux Deco headboards and nightstands. All in all, a little battered but generally clean, and not badly priced. Though rates begin in the moderate range, budget prices are sometimes offered to walk-ins. ~ 510 South Street; 305-

WALK ON THE ARTY SIDE

The art galleries in the White Street Art District keep their doors open late the third Thursday of every month for the **Night on White Gallery Walk**. Fun and free, these mini-events are built around opening receptions for new exhibits at galleries located in the 900 to 1200 blocks of White street, including Lucky Street, The Wave, Harrison's Gallery and Kimberly Narenkivicius's photo studio. The relaxed, no-pressure atmosphere borders on jovial as browsers and buyers sip wine and stroll the area from 6 p.m. to 9 p.m. This cultural mixer is attended by locals and visitors alike. ~ The 900 to 1200 blocks of White Street.

296-2491, 888-324-2996, fax 305-294-2753; www.atlanticshores resort.com, e-mail atlshores@aol.com. DELUXE.

Papa's Hideaway is indeed hidden, its tin-roofed bungalows shrouded in dense garden down an Old Town sidestreet just two blocks from Duval. It's a popular destination for those looking for relaxation and quietude instead of a party scene. Check into the comfortable studios furnished with king-sized beds and complete kitchenettes; the conch-style cottage has two bedrooms, two baths, a full kitchen, sundeck and wraparound porch. Every room has a private porch, and there's a heated pool and jacuzzi set amid palms and orchids. Continental breakfast. ~ 309 Louisa Street, off Whitehead Street; 305-294-7709, 800-714-7709, fax 305-296-1354; www.papashideaway.com, e-mail papashideaway@juno.com. DELUXE.

◄ HIDDEN

A 19th-century Victorian conch house, **Marrero's Guest Mansion** has 14-foot-high ceilings, hardwood floors and beautiful antiques. Bedrooms feature brass and wicker furniture, ceiling fans and, in some cases, balcony views of Old Town. A large clothing-optional pool is also popular at this 12-unit establishment. Continental breakfast and happy hour included. No children. ~ 410 Fleming Street; 305-294-6977, 800-459-6212, fax 305-292-9030; www.marreros.com, e-mail info@marreros.com. DELUXE TO ULTRA-DELUXE.

Two life-size bronze herons stand sentinel outside the high walls, and once inside the heavy wooden gates, frazzled travelers can see that **Heron House** is the haven of calm and relaxation they were looking for. The small courtyard is dominated by an attractive pool with a tiled heron at its bottom, and all is shaded and beautified by tall palms and fuchsia bougainvillea that runs riot to the second-story sundeck. Everywhere, orchids peep shyly or boldly from the foliage. The rooms are accessed through French doors topped by stained-glass transoms; inside are comfortable Caribbean-style furnishings, ceiling fans, mirrored walls and gray granite baths. Continental breakfast is spread by the pool each morning. Heron House is gay-owned and operated, but its guests are mainly straight; all are welcome. ~ 512 Simonton Street; 305-294-9227, 800-294-1644, fax 305-294-5692; www.heronhouse.com, e-mail heronkyw@aol.com. ULTRA-DELUXE.

Part of the neighboring Cypress House complex, **Cypress House Studios** is really two houses—a four-suite, circa-1895 structure now gleaming with pale blue clapboard, violet shutters, and lots of white gingerbread and picket fence; plus a conch-style cottage out back with two rooms. All rooms are nonsmoking, air conditioned and attractively furnished with colorful, comfortable furniture and lace curtains at the windows. All open onto an attractively landscaped courtyard that surrounds a deck. An upper-level sundeck ties the two buildings together. The nearby Cypress House boasts a 40-foot lap pool and bike rentals. Continental breakfast is served each morning, and evening cocktails are offered by the pool. ~ 601 Caroline Street; 305-294-2887, 800-525-2488, fax 305-296-1174; www.cypresshousekw.com, e-mail cypresskw@aol.com. ULTRA-DELUXE.

If you are looking for a relaxing house featuring a peaceful pool and patio area, check into the **Curry House**. This 1890 Victorian home offers nine rooms, all furnished with antiques, and all with French doors that open onto a long veranda or a private deck. In the heart of Old Town, this three-story, yellow-and-green shuttered guesthouse welcomes all. Rates include a full breakfast and poolside cocktails. ~ 806 Fleming Street; 305-294-6777, 800-633-7439, fax 305-294-5322. DELUXE.

At the **Oasis** you'll find an early 1900s mansion, three restored conch houses and a young, swinging, all-male crowd. All 47 rooms are spacious and comfortable; some have two-person jacuzzis. There are three swimming pools, three hot tubs and a spacious nude sunbathing deck. ~ 823 Fleming Street; 305-296-2131, 800-362-7477, fax 305-296-9171; www.keywest-allmale.com, e-mail oasisct@aol.com. DELUXE TO ULTRA-DELUXE.

The elegant **Coral Tree Inn**, located across the street, has lush, palmy grounds; art deco sconces give off a special glow in the halls. The turn-of-the-20th-century building has been

OUTSHINING THE COMPETITION

Key West's tropical maritime climate is the best year-round option among the gay resort towns. Its warm, sunny winters outshine Provincetown's unseasonably cold ones, and during the summer, when everyone in Palm Springs bakes in temperatures soaring above 100°, cool ocean breezes keep Key West's temperatures bearable. In fact, its average summer and winter temperatures generally vary only 10°; Key West has never recorded temperatures colder than 41° nor hotter than 97°.

painstakingly restored, and all 11 guest rooms are sumptuously furnished with gleaming pine and oak furniture. There is a large pool and four-man jacuzzi. Guests of both the Oasis and Coral Tree Inn have full use of both hotels' facilities. This inn is also exclusively for men. ~ 822 Fleming Street; 305-296-2131, 800-362-7477, fax 305-296-9171; www.keywest-allmale.com, e-mail oasisct@aol.com. DELUXE TO ULTRA-DELUXE.

With its old-fashioned pine floors and ceilings and contemporary furnishings, **Alexander's** blends old with new and gives the feeling of a very comfortable home. In the landscaped courtyard, flaming bougainvillea dangle above a cobalt blue pool, and 17 rooms and suites are spread among three houses; a jacuzzi rounds out the amenities. Each room is decorated individually, though particularly appealing are the second- and third-floor treehouse rooms with their stained-glass windows and skylights. There's a primarily gay and lesbian clientele, but straight visitors are welcome. Extended continental breakfast and daily open bar are included. ~ 1118 Fleming Street; 305-294-9919, 800-654-9919, fax 305-295-0357; www.alexghouse.com, e-mail alexghouse@aol.com. DELUXE TO ULTRA-DELUXE.

The hubbub of Duval wafts upward to **New Orleans House,** a second-floor gay guesthouse that sits atop the Bourbon Street Pub. For those who want to be in the center of the action and the sonic chaos, this small lodging offers a garden area with a pool, a hot tub, a sun deck and lots of insider tips about the happening gay spots in town. ~ 724 Duval Street; 305-293-9800, 888-293-9893, fax 305-293-9870; www.neworleanshousekw.com, e-mail getaroomkw@aol.com. MODERATE TO DELUXE.

Catering to gays and lesbians, the **Fleur de Key** is a beautiful two-story, plantation-style house surrounded by verandas and tropical gardens. A lovely pool and a spiral staircase leading up to the sundeck make this bed and breakfast particularly inviting. Sixteen rooms are furnished with English antiques, ceiling fans and all amenities. Complimentary poolside drinks in the afternoon. ~ 412 Frances Street; 305-296-4719, 800-932-9119, fax 305-296-1994; www.fleurdekey.com. DELUXE TO ULTRA-DELUXE.

Open to women only, **Pearl's Rainbow** offers six suites and 29 rooms, all with private bath, some with private or shared kitchens. This Old Town inn features two pools, two jacuzzis and a poolside bar. Lush landscaping and tropical decor add to the charm of this historic guesthouse. An expanded continental breakfast is included in the rate. ~ 525 United Street; 305-292-1450, 800-749-6696, fax 305-292-8511; www.pearlsrainbow.com, e-mail info@pearlsrainbow.com. DELUXE.

Big Ruby's Guesthouse is a small successful international chain of gay lodgings. Here in Key West it is a popular favorite, and it's easy to see why. The 22 rooms, spread between four buildings, are tastefully decorated and have TVs, VCRs (with free movies), all-cotton bedding and extra-thick bath towels. The grounds are lushly landscaped and the pool is clothing-optional, open 24 hours and heated in the winter. Every morning a substantial breakfast of eggs Benedict, breakfast burritos, french toast and the like is served poolside; the pool is also the place where guests gather in the evening for wine. Guests are mainly men, but women are always welcome. The staff will be happy to assist you in deciding on the island's various tours and activities. ~ 409 Appelrouth Lane; 305-296-2323, 800-477-7829, fax 305-296-0281; www.bigrubys.com, e-mail keywest@bigrubys.com. DELUXE.

DINING

By day, **Diner Shores** attracts the vast spectrum of Key West visitors and inhabitants for their breakfasts of eggs and hash and pancakes. The brie, tomato and spinach omelette is a favorite. But at night, especially late at night, the '50s-style diner is where gays and lesbians meet for after-club cocktails and cigarettes. There's a popular streetside terrace, and tables inside on the terrazzo. Open until 2 a.m. ~ 510 South Street, at Atlantic Shores; 305-296-2491. BUDGET.

The owners of Virgilio's bar can do no wrong with **La Trattoria**. Expect savory Italian fare dished out in a charming rustic setting decorated with statues and plants; its windows look out

AUTHOR FAVORITE

Like sipping a cup of coffee in a neighbor's house, **The Coffee & Tea House of Key West** is cozy and welcoming. Couches, comfy chairs and local artwork decorate the rooms. Wind chimes clink on the front porch. And inside is a smorgasbord of international coffees, teas and an array of bagels and sweets for morning noshes. ~ 1218 Duval Street; 305-295-0788. BUDGET.

onto bustling Duval Street. Start with baked eggplant stuffed with ricotta and roasted red pepper. Then move on to the tortellini with cream sauce or penne with blue crabmeat, mushrooms and sun-dried tomatoes. Also on the menu are veal, seafood, lamb and chicken dishes. Dinner only. ~ 524 Duval Street; 305-296-1075, fax 305-293-8169; www.latrattoria.us, e-mail info@latrattoria.us. DELUXE.

For intimate, elegant dining New York style, saunter over to the **Square One,** which is popular with gays and straights alike. The atmosphere is enhanced by soft piano music and, if you're seated outside, the courtyard garden. Try one of the salmon or snapper dishes, or perhaps the blackberry tea–smoked duck with creamy semolina and wilted spinach. You'll also find steak, rack of lamb and a variety of seafood prepared New American style. ~ 1075 Duval Street; 305-296-4300, fax 305-292-5039; www. squareonerestaurant.com, e-mail squareonerestaurant@yahoo. com. MODERATE TO DELUXE.

The flamboyant if not notorious guesthouse La Te Da is a fun backdrop for the **Ocean Grill Restaurant**. The menu reflects Italian, Greek, Caribbean and American Southwest cuisines. There's plenty of seafood, from the seared ahi tuna with red pepper pesto and peppercorns, to the signature lobster stuffed with crabmeat in an apple brandy sauce. Or order from their Caribbean grill selection. Breakfast, lunch and dinner served daily. ~ 1125 Duval Street; 305-296-6706 ext. 39. MODERATE TO DELUXE.

Key West offers a wide variety of shopping opportunities; you'll find many wonderful items tucked away in its boutiques and shops. As you would expect, all the stores in Key West welcome gay shoppers, but there are also establishments that cater specifically to the island's many gay visitors.

SHOPPING

The best starting point for your shopping tour—and a recommended place to start any visit to Key West—is **Flaming Maggie's.** Key West's alternative bookstore stocks mainly gay and lesbian literature. And if you can't wait to get home to begin your book, there's a friendly coffee bar and art gallery located in the store where regulars meet to chat. Closed Sunday. ~ 830 Fleming Street; 305-294-3931.

◄ HIDDEN

Chapel By the Sea of Key West, Inc., a commitment and wedding service, offers "stress-free" wedding packages in a variety of settings for same-sex couples and can handle any details you can't attend to. ~ 205 Elizabeth Street; 305-292-5177, 800-603-2088; e-mail sunlion@sunlion.com.

Slip on a handful of handcrafted rainbow rings and other gay pride jewelry for sale at **Sunlion Jewelry**. Owner Neal Goldberg will custom-make commitment rings for you and your significant other. ~ 513 Duval Street; 305-296-8457, 800-226-8457; e-mail sunlion@sunlion.com.

The island of Cuba is a close neighbor of Key West and has influenced the culture here. For a retail sampling of all things Cuban, the store for more is **Cuba Cuba**. Paintings by island and exile artists, cigars, books, maps and music are all here. ~ 814 Duval Street; 305-295-9442; www.cubacubastore.com.

NIGHTLIFE   Generally speaking, the island's drag scene has reached an all-time high in both quantity and quality. Ranging from bawdy gigs to fine-art forms, the island's drag offerings dot **Duval Street**.

A fun dance spot that attracts a mix of both men and women, **Aqua** has a little bit of everything: a small dancefloor for those who want to groove, two main bars sheltered under tiki huts, a waterfall, a cozy outdoor bar and patio for those who need a breather and a stage for those who want to be a star. This late-night danceteria hosts a variety of nightly specials and raucous drag shows. Occasional cover. ~ 711 Duval Street; 305-294-0555; www.aquakeywest.com.

On Thursday nights, the Atlantic Shores Resort shows a movie under the stars: a wall in the parking lot becomes the screen and everyone gathers on lawn chairs.

The nightly drag shows upstairs are guaranteed to keep you amused at the neighborhood **801 Bourbon Bar**. If you prefer to create your own amusement, mosey on downstairs and hang out with the local crowd of gays and lesbians who frequent this place. ~ 801 Duval Street; 305-294-4737; www.801bourbon.com.

At **La Te Da**, things heat up poolside with a bar and a two-story restaurant. For other entertainment at this laidback and sophisticated spot, try the "Best in Drag" show six nights a week and nightly shows at the Crystal Room Cabaret. ~ 1125 Duval Street; 305-296-6706.

Near dusk, the party continues at the **Atlantic Shores Resort**, which has a bar and a clothing-optional pool side by side, and "Tea by the Sea" on the pier. Admission. ~ 510 South Street; 305-296-2491; www.atlanticshoresresort.com.

Bobbie's Monkey Bar is your basic neighborhood gay bar. Located off the main strip, it caters to both locals and visitors who like to play pool and listen to jukebox music. Check out Sunday afternoon football; Sunday and Friday has karaoke; Monday nights it's pizza (and football). ~ 900 Simonton Street; 305-294-2655.

Wax is frequented by both gays and straights, and rightly so. Everybody wants to get in on the action at this hip nightclub, really a posh martini bar with a deejay spinning house and trance music. ~ 422 Applerouth Lane; 305-296-6667.

ATLANTIC SHORES Neither beach nor park but a motel pool and dock on the Atlantic, it's absolutely the daytime destination of gays and lesbians looking for socializing and a suntan. The scene is a tawdry, gossipy one, with bodies all oiled up and close together on their beach loungers, lots of bloodshot eyes and talk of the night before. Some sunbathers wear swimsuits, but plenty prefer to bake in the buff. Techno music throbs from speakers. A blender grinds out piña coladas. Burgers hiss from the barbecue grill. The chair boy's well-honed muscles glint in tropical heat (everyone must have a chair, for which there is a charge). ~ 510 South Street.

HIGGS BEACH DOCK Located along Key West's southern stretch of shoreline, Higg's Beach is popular with travelers for its fine beach and extensive park facilities (see the "Key West Beaches & Parks" section above). The dock, which juts out into the western end of the park, is active throughout the day with gay visitors enjoying the tropical atmosphere by swimming, sunbathing and socializing here. ~ Atlantic Boulevard and Reynolds Street.

BEACHES & PARKS

Outdoor Adventures

SPORTFISHING

From Key West you can fish in the Atlantic or on the Tortuga Banks. From November through April, **Yankee Fleet** has a two- or three-day trip on a headboat (complete with sleeping quarters, galley and onboard cook) for bottomfishing along the Tortugas. They also provide ferry trips to the Day Tortugas. ~ Oceanside Marina, Stock Island; 800-942-5464; www.yankeefleet.com. MV **Florida Fish Finders** also fishes out of Key West and the Dry Tortuga Islands and spends two to three days out on the water.

~ 5555 College Road, Key West; 305-296-0111, 800-878-3474; www.floridafishfinder.com.

Owner/captain Karen Luknis' friendly **Venus Charters** specializes in non-invasive, eco-friendly adventures inside the reef, including light-tackle fishing, backcountry tours, dolphin watching, snorkeling, and personalized excursions. These are fun, educational full- or half-day trips, emphasizing a no- or low-impact nature appreciation. The 25-foot Proline open fishing boat accommodates four to six passengers; children are welcome. ~ Garrison Bight Marina, Palm Avenue and Eisenhower Drive; 305-292-9403; www.venuscharters.com.

Chartering Captain Craig Eubank's 46-foot sportfishing yacht is an exercise in style. **Mr. Z** is air-conditioned and boasts a stereo, TV, VCR and fully equipped wet bar and galley. Oh, and if you decide to get around to fishing, all licenses, ice, bait and tackle are provided on any of the half- to full-day trips. ~ 700 Front Street, Key West; 305-296-0910; www.keywestfish tales.com.

DIVING   From Key West, call **Dive Key West Inc.** In addition to morning and afternoon dives, they also go at night, which is prime viewing time for crabs, lobsters and dozens of varieties of night-blooming corals. ~ 3128 North Roosevelt Boulevard; 305-296-3823, 800-426-0707; www.divekeywest.com.

A PADI five-star facility, **Southpoint Divers** satisfies the diving needs of first-timers and experienced divers, and offers three-day PADI open-water certification. Daily trips are conducted aboard state-of-the-art dive boats to deep wrecks and the reef. Snorkelers are welcome on dive trips. ~ 500 Truman Avenue #9; 800-891-3483, 305-292-9778, fax 305-296-6888; www.south pointdivers.com, e-mail southpoint@aol.com.

AUTHOR FAVORITE

The **Captain's Corner Dive Center** offers a first-hand look at what happens below Key West's azure waters. Two daily three-and-a-half-hour snorkeling trips, take you aboard a 60-foot dive boat to a beautiful coral reef teeming with marine life. ~ 631 Greene Street; 305-296-8865; www.captainscorner.com, e-mail info@captainscorner.com.

If you don't know where to start in renting a boat, hie yourself to **BOATING**
Charter Boat Row at Garrison Bight. Inspect the boats and chat
up the captains before making a decision. Will it be the *Grand
Slam*, the *Cha Cha II*, the *Relentless* or the *Can't Miss*? These and
many other beauties are available most days. ~ Roosevelt Street
and Palm Avenue.

Nature lovers and folks who desire a gentle, even romantic,
adventure in the sanctuary and refuge waters will find it aboard
the 1930s-style, 30-foot, wooden river cruiser **Mangrove Mis-
tress**. Sunrise and sunset trips, led by environmentally savvy Capt.
Lynda Shuh, focus on sea life, native birds, and sensitive reef and
mangrove habitats. The leisurely charters are customized and include "no seasickness" eco-tours, visits to secluded spots, coral-
reef snorkeling and diving on shallow wrecks, all at a slow pace.
Taking up to six passengers, all trips include chilled fruit and
other snacks, and a cooler for your use. Life vests and quality
snorkel gear are provided. ~ Murray Marine, Route 1, MM 5;
305-745-8886, fax 305-745-1482; www.floridakeys.net/man
grovemistress, e-mail captainlynda@aol.com.

The Flagship of the Conch Republic, the **Wolf**, a classic 74-foot
topsail schooner, is Key West's own tall ship. Holding 44 passengers, she's available for day sails, sunset or starlight cruises, or
custom charters. ~ Stock Island; 305-296-9694, fax 305-294-
8388; www.schoonerwolf.com.

For catamaran cruises out of Key West, call **Sebago**. They also
offer snorkeling and parasailing. ~ 211 William Street; 305-292-
4768, fax 305-292-7788; www.keywestsebago.com, e-mail
info@keywestsebago.com.

You and five of your mates can spend several days aboard the
60-foot *Playmate*, enjoying day and night dives along the Florida
Keys or the Dry Tortugas, snorkeling, fishing, birdwatching and
the fine cuisine provided by **Sea-Clusive Charters**. One-day charters are also available. ~ Key West; 305-872-3940.

Key West Boat Rentals rent 17- to 26-foot motorboats and
offer jetski rentals and jetski tours around the area. ~ 617 Front
Street; 305-294-2628; www.keywestboatrentals.com.

Kayaking is terrific in the back country just north of Key West, **CANOEING**
and several outfitters will take you there from the island. The **& KAYAKING**
best kayaking trips in town are organized by **Mosquito Coast**.

Wildlife experts lead small group tours into the hidden water-ways of the Keys. ~ 310 Duval Street; 305-294-7178; www.mos quitocoast.net.

Adventure Charters & Tours advertises trips for "anyone seeking an alternative to the party boat/booze cruise atmosphere." Half-day trips go to Great White Heron National Wildlife Refuge, with kayaking through a maze of tidal streams and basins where one can look at sponges, starfish, sea cucumbers and sometimes conch. But best is the full-day adventure using the 42-foot *Island Fantasea* catamaran as a base—kayaks are launched upstream and met downstream by the *Fantasea*. ~ 6810 Front Street; 305-296-0362, 888-817-0841, fax 305-294-3340; www.keywestadventures.com, e-mail capt.tom@keywest-fl.com.

SAILING   For luxurious catamaran cruises, call **Sebago**. Try parasailing or relax on their sunset cruises. ~ 328 Simonton Street (main office), booking at the end of Williams Street at the Old Historic Seaport, Key West; 305-294-5687; www.keywestsebago.com.

You and ten of your friends can spend several days aboard the 60-foot air conditioned *Playmate*, enjoying day and night dives along the Florida Keys or the Dry Tortugas, diving, snorkeling, fishing, kayaking, birdwatching and the home cooking provided by **Sea-Clusive Charters**. One-day charters are also available. ~ Key West; 305-744-9928; www.seaclusive.com.

AUTHOR FAVORITE

Key West and the Lower Keys offer some of the world's best birding habitat, and you don't need to be experienced to enjoy it. **Bone Island Bird Expeditions** leads both beginning and expert birders on light treks to hardwood hammocks, shorelines, salt ponds and other environments in search of anything from a tiny ruby-throated hummingbird to the magnificent frigatebird. Owner/guide Mark Hedden is a certified Florida Master Naturalist and has been birding this region for more than a decade. Resident and migrational species number about 200, including the white-crowned pigeon, mangrove cuckoo and great white heron. The three-hour early-morning or late-afternoon small-group trips are by appointment only, and each is tailored to suit your interests. Custom all-day or targeted trips are also available. ~ 305-587-6059; e-mail mark@boneisland.com.

You can rent windsurfing equipment and Hobie Cats from several companies who set up shop at Key West's Smathers Beach on South Roosevelt Boulevard and Higgs Beach on Atlantic Boulevard. Located at both beaches, **Tropical Sailboards** rents windsurfers, Hobie Cats, kayaks and snorkeling gear. ~ 305-294-2696. At Smathers Beach, **Sunset Watersports** offers windsurfers, parasailing equipment, Hobie Cats and kayaks. ~ 305-296-2554.

WIND-SURFING

On Stock Island, **Key West Golf Club** has an 18-hole course spotted with lakes, palm trees and mangroves over rolling fairways with public tee times. ~ 6450 College Road, Key West; 305-294-5232.

GOLF

In Key West you can play for no charge at **Bayview Park** on one of their five outdoor lit courts. There's also a pro shop and instruction available. ~ 1310 Truman Avenue; 305-294-1346. There are also public courts at **Higgs County Beach**. ~ Atlantic Boulevard between White and Reynolds streets.

TENNIS

Bicycling is a good way to explore Key West. Residents and visitors alike can be seen pedaling around on "conch cruisers," which seem to be any old bikes whose handlebars have been replaced with high-handled affairs that look just right in Key West.

BIKING

Bike Rentals   The Bicycle Center carries everything you might need and includes helmets with rentals. ~ 523 Truman Avenue, Key West; 305-294-4556. **Adventure Scooter and Bicycle Rental** has several locations to rent from in Key West: Key Plaza, North Roosevelt Avenue, 305-293-9933; Hyatt parking lot at Simonton and Front streets, 305-293-9944; and Pier House, Duval Street, 305-293-0441. **Conch Bike Express** rents bikes by the day or week, including light, lock and basket. They'll deliver the bike to you at no extra charge. ~ 930-B Eaton Street; 305-294-4318.

Route 1, the Overseas Highway, leads directly over the bridge from neighboring Stock Island into Key West. You can reach Old Town by following Roosevelt Boulevard either to the right or left, along the Gulf of Mexico or the Atlantic Ocean. Once in Old Town, auto driving is difficult. Island traffic and parking run from frustrating to downright impossible, and city meters have insatiable appetites for quarters.

Transportation

CAR

It's clearly best to travel long distances via city bus, shuttle, taxi, or bicycle. Sightseeing is best done on foot or bicycle or via tour train or trolley (see "Key West Sights" in this chapter).

Visitors with vehicles should consider the city's **Park & Ride** garage, located near Land's End Marina. The covered garage is open 24 hours; the all-day $13 fee includes a shuttle ride downtown. ~ Caroline and Grinnell streets; 305-293-6426.

AIR

Many visitors to Key West choose to fly to Miami International Airport (see Chapter Two for information). You can also fly into the small **Key West International Airport,** which is serviced by American Eagle, Continental Connection, Delta Air Lines and US Airways. However, a look at the map of Florida shows that by far the shortest distance as the crow flies from a major city on the mainland to Key West is from Naples. **Cape Air** has several regularly scheduled flights daily from Naples, Fort Myers and Fort Lauderdale. ~ 800-352-0714; www.flycapeair.com.

BUS

Greyhound Bus Lines services Key West. ~ Key West Airport, 3535 South Roosevelt Boulevard; 800-231-2222; www.greyhound.com.

CAR RENTALS

Rental agencies at Key West International Airport include **Avis Rent A Car** (800-331-1212) and **Dollar Rent A Car** (800-800-4000). Pick up at the airport can be arranged through, **Budget Rent A Car** (800-527-0700), **Enterprise Rent A Car** (800-325-8007) and **Hertz Rent A Car** (800-654-3131).

While potentially mistaken as giant Easter eggs, **Key West Cruisers** are brightly painted electric rental vehicles that require no gas. Shaped like eggs, the two- and four-seaters reach speeds of 25 mph. They offer a safe, comfortable and fume-free alternative to scooters or regular cars. ~ 500 Truman Avenue; 305-294-4724, 888-800-8802.

PUBLIC TRANSIT

The **City of Key West Port and Transit Authority** operates color-coded buses (that stop at same-colored bus stops) that run the entire length and partial width of the island. ~ 627 Palm Avenue; 305-292-8165, fax 305-292-8285; e-mail kwcdot@aol.com.

Four Bone Island Shuttle buses circle the island from 9 a.m. to 11 p.m. daily. Spaced 30 minutes apart, two of the buses run clockwise and two run counter-clockwise. Each bus stops at four key locations: Key West Bight, Bahama Market, Mallory Square and Casa Marina among them. This is a good way to move between Old Town and New Town. An all-day ticket for the privately owned ride is $8. ~ 305-293-8710.

Florida Keys Taxi Cab (305-296-7777) and **Friendly Cab Co.** (305-295-5555) serve Key West International Airport. The **Five Sixes Maxie Taxi** operates in Key West. ~ 305-296-6666.

TAXIS

Index

Lodging Index

Dining Index

HIDDEN GUIDES

Adventure travel or a relaxing vacation?—"Hidden" guidebooks are the only travel books in the business to provide detailed information on both. Aimed at environmentally aware travelers, our motto is "Where Vacations Meet Adventures." These books combine details on unique hotels, restaurants and sightseeing with information on camping, sports and hiking for the outdoor enthusiast.

PARADISE FAMILY GUIDES

Ideal for families traveling with kids of any age—toddlers to teenagers— Paradise Family Guides offer a blend of travel information unlike any other guides to the Hawaiian islands. With vacation ideas and tropical adventures that are sure to satisfy both action-hungry youngsters and relaxation-seeking parents, these guides meet the specific needs of each and every family member.

Ulysses Press books are available at bookstores everywhere. If any of the following titles are unavailable at your local bookstore, ask the bookseller to order them.

You can also order books directly from Ulysses Press
P.O. Box 3440, Berkeley, CA 94703
800-377-2542 or 510-601-8301
fax: 510-601-8307
www.ulyssespress.com
e-mail: ulysses@ulyssespress.com

HIDDEN GUIDEBOOKS

____ Hidden Arizona, $16.95
____ Hidden Bahamas, $14.95
____ Hidden Baja, $14.95
____ Hidden Belize, $15.95
____ Hidden Big Island of Hawaii, $13.95
____ Hidden Boston & Cape Cod, $14.95
____ Hidden British Columbia, $18.95
____ Hidden Cancún & the Yucatán, $16.95
____ Hidden Carolinas, $17.95
____ Hidden Coast of California, $18.95
____ Hidden Colorado, $15.95
____ Hidden Disneyland, $13.95
____ Hidden Florida, $19.95
____ Hidden Florida Keys & Everglades, $13.95
____ Hidden Georgia, $16.95
____ Hidden Guatemala, $16.95
____ Hidden Hawaii, $19.95
____ Hidden Idaho, $14.95
____ Hidden Kauai, $13.95
____ Hidden Los Angeles, $14.95
____ Hidden Maine, $15.95

____ Hidden Maui, $14.95
____ Hidden Miami, $14.95
____ Hidden Montana, $15.95
____ Hidden New England, $18.95
____ Hidden New Mexico, $15.95
____ Hidden New Orleans, $14.95
____ Hidden Oahu, $13.95
____ Hidden Oregon, $15.95
____ Hidden Pacific Northwest, $18.95
____ Hidden San Diego, $14.95
____ Hidden Salt Lake City, $14.95
____ Hidden San Francisco & Northern California, $19.95
____ Hidden Seattle, $13.95
____ Hidden Southern California, $18.95
____ Hidden Southwest, $19.95
____ Hidden Tahiti, $18.95
____ Hidden Tennessee, $16.95
____ Hidden Utah, $16.95
____ Hidden Walt Disney World, $13.95
____ Hidden Washington, $15.95
____ Hidden Wine Country, $13.95
____ Hidden Wyoming, $15.95

PARADISE FAMILY GUIDES

____ Paradise Family Guides: Kaua'i, $17.95
____ Paradise Family Guides: Maui, $17.95
____ Paradise Family Guides: Big Island of Hawai'i, $17.95

Mark the book(s) you're ordering and enter the total cost here ⇨ [   ]

California residents add 8.75% sales tax here ⇨ [   ]

Shipping, check box for your preferred method and enter cost here ⇨ [   ]

❏ BOOK RATE   **FREE! FREE! FREE!**

❏ PRIORITY MAIL/UPS GROUND   cost of postage

❏ UPS OVERNIGHT OR 2-DAY AIR   cost of postage

Billing, enter total amount due here and check method of payment ⇨ [   ]

❏ CHECK   ❏ MONEY ORDER

❏ VISA/MASTERCARD _____EXP. DATE_____

NAME _____PHONE_____

ADDRESS _____

CITY_____ STATE _____ ZIP_____

MONEY-BACK GUARANTEE ON DIRECT ORDERS PLACED THROUGH ULYSSES PRESS.

ABOUT THE AUTHORS

ANN BOESE has written for *Newsweek*, the *Miami Herald*, *ArtNews*, *Raw Vision* and other periodicals and websites. Her book credits include contributions to *Hidden Florida*, *Key West: A Collection* and others. Formerly editor/co-publisher of the literary journal *Bone Island Sun*, her recent projects focus on Key West art, history and Cuban émigré culture. A Key West resident since 1986, she is currently writing a book about the Keys. Ann is a member of the Society of American Travel Writers.

CANDACE LESLIE is a co-author of Ulysses Press' *Hidden Florida* and contributor to the *Texas Monthly Guidebook to Texas* (Gulf Publishing). Her work has appeared in *Reader's Digest*, *Coast to Coast*, *Chevron Odyssey*, the *Houston Chronicle*, *Texas Highways* and other publications. A member of the Society of American Travel Writers, Candace is also travel columnist for *Insite Magazine* and the *Bryan/College Station (TX) Eagle*. She was raised in Florida, a state she has "rediscovered" and writes about often.

ABOUT THE ILLUSTRATOR

NORMAN NICHOLSON, a graduate of the Art Center College of Design in Los Angeles, has successfully combined a career in illustration and painting. His artwork has appeared in national ads, book and magazine illustrations and posters. His paintings have hung in important government collections as well as private and corporate collections throughout the United States. He currently teaches painting at the Academy of Art in San Francisco.